Hegel's First American Followers

Ohio University Press
Athens, Ohio

HEGEL'S FIRST AMERICAN FOLLOWERS

The Ohio Hegelians: John B. Stallo, Peter Kaufmann, Moncure Conway, and August Willich,

with Key Writings

LOYD D. EASTON

Ohio University Press

1966

Library of Congress Catalog card number 66–22062
Manufactured in the United States of America
by American Book–Stratford Press, Inc., New York

CONTENTS

PREFACE

WITH A LONG-STANDING interest in the history of philosophical ideas as related to the American scene, I was attracted in my reading by references to "colonizations" of the St. Louis Hegelian Society in Chicago, Milwaukee, and Cincinnati after the Civil War. The reference to Cincinnati seemed to provide a happy opportunity to combine my interest in philosophy, including Hegel's complicated but fertile thought, with an interest in the past of my adopted state. As I pursued this combination of interests, I could find no evidence of an Hegelian "colony" in Ohio stemming from St. Louis. Instead, I found something else, something which was at once more interesting and seemingly more significant.

I found that four Ohioans, linked by ties of friendship and attention to one another's views, had championed and applied Hegel's philosophy over a decade before the St. Louis Society was organized. One of the Ohio men had written an Hegelian book in 1848 which was known and studied in St. Louis sixteen years later. Two of them became "auxiliaries" of the St. Louis Society. As I went deeper into the writings and activities of the Ohio Hegelians, I found that their philosophical views, often perceptive and influential, left wide marks in their colorful public lives.

The result of these findings is the book at hand, an exposition and interpretation of the Hegelian views of J. B. Stallo, Peter Kaufmann, Moncure Conway, and August Willich in their historical setting and with the light they throw, sometimes new light, on Hegel's philosophy. In addition to this exposition and interpretation I have provided an appendix of highly inaccessible and rare "key writings," some translated from German, in which the Ohio men speak for themselves about the meaning and application of Hegel's thought.

My research in its early stage was made possible by a Grant-in-Aid from the American Council of Learned Societies. A Grant-in-Aid from the American Association for State and Local History and a Faculty Fellowship from Ohio Wesleyan University facilitated further research and writing. For all this aid and the encouragement it implied I am deeply grateful.

Some portions of the following chapters have previously appeared as articles in journals. I am grateful to the editors for permission to use parts of my articles on "Hegelianism in 19th Century Ohio" (*Journal of the History of Ideas*, July, 1962), "German Philosophy in 19th Century Cincinnati," (*Bulletin of the Historical and Philosophical Society of Ohio*, now entitled *Bulletin of the Cincinnati Historical Society*, January, 1962), and "August Willich, Marx, and Left-Hegelian Socialism" (*Études de Marxologie: Cahiers de L'I.S.E.A.*, Août, 1965).

For permission to quote from manuscripts and original documents my thanks go to Miss Eleanor Conway Sawyer, the Committee of the South Place Ethical Society in London, the Ohio Historical Society, the International Institute for Social History in Amsterdam, the Ernst-Mach-Institut in Freiburg/Br., the Dickinson College Library, the Milwaukee Public Library, and Mr. Boris Nicolaevsky. I am indebted to the staffs of the following libraries for facilitating my research: the Ohio Historical Society Library, Slocum Library of Ohio Wesleyan University, Columbia University Library, Meadville Theological School Library, Cincinnati Public Library, and the Midwest Interlibrary Center.

For first arousing my interest in Hegel and helping me to see the fecundity of Hegel's thought, I am especially indebted to the late Edgar S. Brightman of Boston University, a great teacher and friend. From many others I received encouragement and aid in research and writing. I extend a special word of thanks to my faculty colleagues at Ohio Wesleyan University—particularly to Professors Benjamin Spencer and Harry Bahrick—to Mr. James Barnett of Cincinnati, and to my helpful and patient wife.

L.D.E.

Delaware, Ohio
March 1, 1966

Hegel's First American Followers

I

THE INTELLECTUAL AND SOCIAL MILIEU

AROUND THE MIDDLE of the last century, particularly in the dozen years preceding the Civil War, there was a group of Ohioans whose major views were shaped by the ideas of Georg W. F. Hegel, Germany's most comprehensive and influential philosopher of the nineteenth century. The group consisted of J. B. Stallo, Peter Kaufmann, Moncure Conway, and August Willich. While Kaufmann spent most of his adult years in Canton, Ohio, the others were residents of Cincinnati during formative years of their lives. All except Conway, as might be expected, were of German origin. As a group they were not part of an organized philosophical club or association like that of the St. Louis Hegelians after the Civil War. Stallo's thought was well known and highly regarded among the St. Louis Hegelians. Both Stallo and Willich were auxiliary members of the St. Louis Philosophical Society. But there is no evidence that there was an organized branch of the St. Louis movement in Cincinnati.[1]

The relationship among the Ohio men, rather, was one of favorable attention to each other's views, mutual acquaintance, and in some cases warm personal friendship. This book is the story of their philosophical ideas and views as related to major events in their lives and their participation in public affairs.

The Ohio Hegelians

Stallo, Kaufmann, Conway, and Willich were "Hegelians" in the sense that their leading ideas show the impress of Hegel's philosophy either directly or through the views of other thinkers who were themselves distinctively indebted to Hegel. Only Stallo presented an extensive exposition and interpretation of Hegel's main writings in his *General Principles of the Philosophy of Nature* published in 1848. But all of the Ohio group subscribed to major Hegelian ideas and communicated them to their contemporaries in a variety of ways—through books, pamphlets, editorials, and public addresses. They were particularly vocal and active in the period from 1848 to 1860.

Other earlier or contemporary writers, as we shall see presently, were influenced by Hegelian ideas and publicized Hegel's views. But more than this must be said about Stallo, Kaufmann, Conway, and Willich. They were Hegel's followers in the special sense that they agreed with and championed a number of his major views. They embraced major aspects of Hegel's thought as his partisans. They adopted and used some of his major concepts and credited him by name. If "follower" is used to mean such sympathetic, general, and overt endorsement of a preceding thinker's views, the Ohio men must be called Hegel's first American followers.

The Ohio men differed considerably in how they appropriated and applied Hegel's ideas. In Stallo's case, Hegelian principles significantly shaped his philosophy of science and views on government. For Kaufmann, a dialectical view of knowledge and truth was background for a moral perfectionism leading to social reform. Moncure Conway used those aspects of Hegel's philosophy of religion which had been appropriated by David Friedrich Strauss in criticism of supernaturalism and miracles. And August Willich used Hegelian ideas, especially as they had developed in Ludwig Feuerbach and Karl Marx, to advance the cause of "Humanity" and socialism.

Their influence was felt more in the realm of public affairs than in institutions of higher education. While teaching German and mathematics in Cincinnati in the early 1840's, Stallo had little opportunity to utilize the views of Kant, Hegel, Schelling, and Oken to which he had earlier been attracted in Germany. Though Asa Mahan of Oberlin College gave some attention to Hegel's thought in his teaching and writing around 1845, philosophy in Ohio colleges generally reflected national conditions, and Hegel was little known until later in the century when the influence of the St. Louis movement and its *Journal of Speculative Philosophy* began to be felt, the poet Whitman's attachment to Hegel was publicized, and large eastern institutions such as Yale and Harvard began regular instruction in German philosophy. Like men of the later St. Louis group, the Ohioans addressed themselves to the general public and its current concerns rather than to philosophy in the colleges.

Previous Attention to Hegel

Prior to the publication of Stallo's *General Principles* in 1848 a number of writers and scholars referred to Hegel's thought or helped make his views known to the American public.

Usually, however, they had little sympathy with or understanding of Hegel's ideas. A possible exception was F. A. Rauch, who has been called "the first bearer of Hegel's teaching to America." Examination of these uses of Hegel's thought prior to 1848 will provide at once the intellectual background and setting for views of the Ohio Hegelians and also illuminate major facets of Hegel's philosophy for those unfamiliar with its complex features.

George Bancroft, one of the first of a group of Americans to study in Germany, attended Hegel's lectures at the University of Berlin for part of a term. In his journal and a letter of 1820 he gave his impression of Hegel as "sluggish" and stopped attending lectures because he found them to be a "display of unintelligible words." Slightly more than a decade later Francis Lieber's *Encyclopedia Americana* carried a sketch of Hegel which summarized his views, recorded the main facts of his life, indicated his relation to other German philosophers, and listed a number of his writings.[2] This treatment of Hegel at least placed his name before the American public.

Another early but highly unsympathetic and inaccurate presentation of Hegel's views appeared in the *Princeton Review* at the beginning of 1839. Analyzing Cousin's history of philosophy, J. W. Alexander and A. B. Dod characterized Hegel's thought as "the lowest deep in the circling vaults of German wisdom" following Kant, Fichte, and Schelling. Hegel seeks to prove, Alexander and Dod alleged, that "all things are the same," that only "ideas of Reason" exist, and that "God exists only as knowledge." Such a view leads straight to pantheism which denies sin and subverts all morality.[3]

A year later the *Princeton Review* carried an article by C. Hodge on "The School of Hegel." Its tone and attitude were reflected in the heading at the top of each page—

namely, "The Latest Form of Infidelity." The author charged Hegel's followers—Strauss, Tholuck, and Heine—with denying the personality of God, the Incarnation, and the truth of the Gospel. Such views, like Hegel's, lead only to pantheism, rationalism, mysticism, and similar "indecent ravings" which subvert all morality and dignify the worst in man. They are really "atheism in its worst form" which has already, unfortunately, "set its cloven foot in America" among the Unitarians of Boston.[4] Such diatribes as these from Princeton tell less about Hegel than about the fearful reactions of religious orthodoxy. But their very force and length also suggest a swelling wave of interest in Hegelian ideas.

With the writings of Theodore Parker (1810–1860) Hegelian ideas received wider attention partly as a result of Parker's place in the transcendentalist movement and also as a result of his frequent, independent-minded involvements in theological controversy. Emerson referred to Parker as the "Savonarola" of the transcendentalist movement which emerged within Unitarianism in the 1830's under the influence of Emerson's thought and German philosophy transmitted through Coleridge and Cousin. As Emerson explained:

> The Idealism of the present day acquired its name of Transcendental from the use of that term by Immanuel Kant of Königsberg, who replied to the sceptical philosophy of Locke, which insisted that there was nothing in the intellect which was not previously in the experience of the senses, by showing that there was a very important class of ideas or imperative forms, which did not come by experience, but through which experience was acquired; that these were intuitions of the mind itself; and he denominated them Transcendental forms.[5]

Though Emerson's statement may need some qualification as an interpretation of Kant, it clearly indicates a debt to

German philosophy which Parker and other transcendentalists openly shared.

Parker's attention to Hegel was very likely a by-product of his interest in David Friedrich Strauss. At least his interest in Strauss and his study of Strauss's *Leben Jesu* came earlier, beginning in 1836 or 1837 when he borrowed the book from a fellow minister who had purchased it in Germany. The results of this study came to public expression in a lengthy, detailed review appearing in the *Christian Examiner* of April, 1840. After a close analysis of Strauss's argument section by section, Parker's review became critical—vigorously and harshly critical. More than once he noted Strauss's presupposition that "the Idea precedes man" and that "the Idea" expressed in myth is prior to the events reported in the New Testament.[6] Parker thus recognized Strauss's philosophical idealism but did not mark it as derived from Hegel. Following Hegel, Strauss held that all historical and natural events are manifestations, externalized expressions, of an all-embracing Idea, Thought, or Spirit. The Idea manifests itself lawfully and rationally in a process moved by internal opposition toward increasing wholeness, a wholeness which always preserves its constituent elements in a new harmony. On this basis, miracles of the New Testament are to be explained as "myths" expressing the Jews' historical, messianic consciousness, not as natural facts. Strauss's view of myth was directly derived from Hegel's philosophy of religion though Parker made no mention of that debt. In religion, Hegel had maintained, truth takes the form of "imaginative presentation" transmitted by the community.[7]

In spite of his strong criticism of Strauss's book Parker regarded it as having "profound theological significance," noted its great influence, and rejoiced in its publication. He courageously referred to Strauss as "an individual raised by God" to bridge the chasm between "the frozen realm of stiff supernaturalism" and "the fair domain of free religious thought" by a necessarily negative and destructive book—"the most melancholy book we ever read." But neither Strauss's book nor the philosophy of Hegel, Parker concluded, would ever weaken true religion which holds that the New Testament rests on historical grounds though mythical elements have entered it. His attitude toward Strauss and Hegel was thus somewhat ambivalent. Though he could hardly be called a champion of Strauss's views, their impact is apparent in his sermon of 1841 on "The Transient and Permanent in Christianity" whose title was taken from one of Strauss's essays. In that sermon Parker asserted that doctrines of the origin and authority of the Old and New Testament must be classed among the transient elements of Christianity. "On the authority of the written word man was taught," asserted Parker, "to believe impossible legends, conflicting assertions; to take fiction for fact, a dream for a miraculous revelation of God, an Oriental poem for a grave history of miraculous events, a collection of amatory idyls for a serious discourse 'touching the mutual love of Christ and the Church.' "[8] As might be imagined, these views created a furor. Parker was virtually ostracized by the clergy, and there was considerable consternation over "the latest form of infidelity."

Though Parker's relation to Strauss's thought was somewhat ambiguous, he was generally hostile to Hegel. He protested in 1841 against being called a pantheist with Hegel, who taught that there is "no difference between God's *being* and being *not*" and that God comes to consciousness in man and *self*-consciousness in Christ. Further, Parker flatly condemned Hegel's doctrine of the trinity and his notion of "a variable God, who learns by experience, and who grows with the growth and strengthens with the strength and growth of the universe."[9] In *A Discourse of*

Matters Pertaining to Religion (1842) Parker referred to "the pleasant remarks of Hegel" on the charge that philosophy is too pantheistic, has "too much" of God, and directed his readers to *The Encyclopedia of the Philosophical Sciences* containing the broad outline of Hegel's whole system. But a careful student of the *Encyclopedia* would have difficulty finding in it the view of God Parker attributed to Hegel. To be specific, Hegel was very careful to show how his Absolute Spirit is not a form of pantheism and in itself is eternal, beyond the vicissitudes of temporal change.

As an omnivorous reader and indefatigible student who read German easily, Parker did much to interest his contemporaries in the views of Hegel and particularly Strauss who carried Hegel's ideas into Biblical criticism. But he was too much of an independent thinker to become the champion of any single philosophical system or even major ideas in that system. Certainly his views were too inconsistent with those of Hegel and Strauss, and possibly even some others of his own, for him to be called an Hegelian in any firm sense of the word.

Previous Use of Hegel by Rauch

During the years Parker was giving closest attention to Strauss and Hegel, Frederick Augustus Rauch (1806–1841) was engaged in presenting major Hegelian ideas in his teaching and writing at the Mercersberg Seminary of the German Reformed Church and as president of Marshall College in Pennsylvania. Rauch has been called an "enthusiastic Hegelian," "probably the first bearer of Hegel's teaching to America." Prior to his emigration from Germany in 1831 he had become well equipped to understand and interpret Hegel. He had studied theology and philosophy at the universities of Marburg, Giessen, and Heidelberg. While at

Heidelberg he became a student and personal friend of Carl Daub to whom Hegel had entrusted the revision of his *Encyclopedia.* Thus Rauch's Hegelianism was only narrowly removed from its source and was acquired at a time when Hegel's influence was at its height in Germany.[10]

Rauch's views came to fullest and most systematic expression in his book on *Psychology, A View of the Human Soul Including Anthropology* published in 1840, a year before his death. It received wide circulation, with two editions and four reprintings by 1850. In spite of Rauch's reputation as an "ardent Hegelian," however, his book was not overtly an exposition or defense of Hegel's views. Hegel was mentioned by name only once, along with seventeen other writers to whom Rauch declared his indebtedness including Locke, Reid, Rosenkranz, Daub, Kant, Herbart, and Hartmann. Nor was the structure of the book as a whole Hegelian in its pattern or sequence of ideas, though Rauch included under anthropology some of the same topics as Hegel in considering the dependence of mind on body and natural processes. But frequently in its contents Rauch's *Psychology* endorsed and defended major Hegelian ideas. Some instances and examples will help to delineate Rauch's position and at the same time introduce the reader to major Hegelian themes in anticipation of later chapters.

After confessing his aim "to unite German and American mental philosophy" in a principled whole, Rauch hoped that the contents of his book would "bear witness of one and the same *objective* spirit, which formed all the parts into *one* life, as the specific life of a tree changes all the particles into one juice."[11] Here, at the very outset, Rauch revealed his commitment to Hegel's objective idealism in which Idea, Mind, or Spirit is seen not as a subjective faculty of an individual person but as a movement toward organized wholeness in nature, history, the growth of nations, various human capacities, various forms of religion, and all such areas as Rauch considers from time to time in various parts of his *Psychology*.

Rauch's debt to Hegel is apparent in his view of the ground and substance of the natural world:

> Nature does not think, is not conscious of itself, *has* not reason, as man has it; but its productions are full of reason and thoughts that are corporealized; the mechanical systems of the starry heavens; the productions of the earth; the minerals and their qualities, the vegetables in their more or less regular formations; the animals with their more or less perfect organizations; all give witness of reason, and show the union of *thought* and of *being*, even in nature.[12]

Similarly for Hegel the entire realm of nature was "the Idea in the form of otherness" or externality. It was the all-embracing concept or Idea of the universe expressing itself in the pattern of objects in space and time, from the mechanical relations of matter through physical things to the most fully formed unity of living organisms.

In the area of moral consciousness Rauch closely distinguished between acts of will or choice informed by knowledge and acts resulting from mere desire. The former are the core of morality, the latter are morally irrelevant. "Acts of the will," he concluded, "always have reference to rights; I may demand what I will; acts of desire do not regard them, but we frequently desire what we have no right to long for. Our natural desires, are therefore indifferent to right and duty, and consequently have in themselves no elements of moral goodness."[13] This is essentially Hegel's view. Reflection working with impulses and inclinations, Hegel insisted, moves them "beyond their particularity and their natural immediacy, and gives their contents a rationality and objectivity in which they exist as necessary ties of social relation, as rights and duties."

Rauch's Hegelianism is even more apparent in the important area of philosophy of history. "History, in what it records," Rauch held, "is the development of mind." He further asserted:

> The truth of history consists in the spirit that produces the action, in the development of national intellect, prosperity, intercourse, etc. so that one action is interwoven with another by one and the same national spirit. This *spirit*, this national exertion to preserve, to improve, to advance itself, is the truth of history.[14]

Here a number of Hegel's main ideas about history are apparent. The fundamental fact about history, said Hegel, is that "its development has been a rational process." "It is the exhibition of Spirit in the process of working out the knowledge of that which it is potentially." Since reason or spirit is self-contained existence in contrast to matter, history may also be thought of as "the progress of the consciousness of freedom." The primary unit of the historical process is "the spirit of the nation" which is expressed in every aspect of its social life—its religion, politics, ethics, science, art, and mechanical skill. Thus Rauch unmistakably followed Hegel concerning the substance of history, history as entailing progress, and the "national spirit" as being a cultural whole of interacting and interrelated elements.

At some points, however, Rauch clearly departed from Hegel. In the field of his own special interest, religion, Rauch did not follow Hegel on the difference between truth in religion and philosophy—namely, that in the former truth takes the form of "imaginative presentation," a position Strauss developed into his "myth" theory, and in the latter truth is conceptual and systematic. Rauch did consider true religion as "*a peculiar activity of God*, which, announcing itself to the *heart* of man charges it, converts it, and restores man to peace with himself, with the world, and with God."[15] But this position was never specifically related to a view of revelation, redemption, or the trinity following Hegel's line of thought. Again, with Rauch there was no overt discussion or fully clear illustration of dialectic as the pattern wherein reason moves through opposition and conflict from an incomplete position toward greater unity and wholeness. Hegel regarded dialectic as the method of genuine knowledge and the point of his particular advance beyond Kant. In view of these significant departures from Hegel and Rauch's failure to attribute some of his key ideas to their source, one must conclude that he did not think of himself as Hegel's champion or an "enthusiastic Hegelian." His loose relation to Hegel was well formulated by one of his closest associates at Mercersburg:

> He felt himself impelled to attempt the work of transferring in some measure into the literature of this country, not Hegel's philosophy as such, nor the metaphysics of Germany as a distinct and separate interest, but the life and power of German thinking generally, under its more recent forms, in all that relates to the phenomenology of the soul.[16]

The wide circulation of Rauch's *Psychology* in German Reformed circles, among transcendentalists like Brownson, and among Unitarians at Harvard did, however, insert some major Hegelian ideas into the moving pattern of American thought.

Prior to 1848 there were at least three other instances of attention to Hegel's thought which deserve notice. In his *Sketches of Modern Philosophy Among the Germans* (1842) James Murdock devoted a chapter to "Pantheistic Idealism: Hegel's Absolute Idealism." He confessed, however, that after a fortnight of study he was almost as ignorant of the whole movement of Hegel's thought as when he began.

"Hegel," he said, "is the most unintelligible writer I have ever read."[17] There was some comfort in the fact that even the Germans complained of his obscurity. The last part of Murdock's chapter on Hegel was largely a series of quotations from secondary sources on the relation of "Being" and "Nothing" to "Becoming," Hegel's emphasis on the world's unity, and the denial of free will implied in Hegel's view that the rational is the actual.[18] The weakest part of Hegel's system, Murdock loosely concluded, was his philosophy of religion where God was identified with "psychological and historical apparition." But Murdock's book, in spite of its inaccuracies and misrepresentations, was of some importance in establishing affinities between Hegel's thought and transcendentalism. Its concluding chapter, moreover, brought Rauch and his *Psychology* to a wider public.

A few years later President Asa Mahan of Oberlin College devoted a few pages of his *System of Intellectual Philosophy* (1845) to Hegel's thought and its difficulties along with Kant, Fichte, and Schelling. Though he acknowledged intellectual indebtedness to Coleridge, Cousin, and Kant and recognized the independence and rigor of German philosophical thought, his most sympathetic lines were devoted to "common sense" as a corrective to philosophical speculation. In his discussion of the "System of Hegel" Mahan inaccurately accused Hegel of resolving "all realities into pure thought, without a subject."[19] The natural outcome of such a view, Mahan alleged, is pantheism, and Hegel "was no thinker at all, if his own system be true." Hegel's difficulties were clinched by a diatribe quoted from Murdock on "a God without holiness," theology without revelation, and "a Religion without religion." Like Murdock, Mahan linked Hegel's views with "modern transcendentalism" and proceeded to damn it as "pantheism" and other self-evidently bad errors. Mahan's attitude toward Hegel was typical of many conservative religious minds. What is noteworthy is that he did take account of Hegel and transcendentalism and apparently felt that they were important enough to deserve vigorous attack.

F. H. Hedge's treatment of Hegel in his *Prose Writers of Germany* (1847) was of an entirely different order from that found in the writings of Murdock and Mahan. For one thing, Hedge's book was essentially an anthology of translated essays, stories, and selections from books. It included writings of literary figures and intellectual leaders as well as philosophers in the specialized sense. The authors ranged from Luther and Boehme through Kant, Lessing, and Goethe to end with Tieck and Adalbert von Chamisso. Thus the contents of the book reflected the inclination of Hedge's interest—as much toward literature of the Romantic era as toward philosophy.

Being essentially an anthology, *Prose Writers of Germany* allowed Hegel to speak for himself through a straightforward, well-organized translation of main portions of the "Introduction to the Philosophy of History" and an essay on "Who Thinks Abstractly?" Hedge's "Preface" attributed the translation and introduction to "an anonymous friend possessing peculiar qualifications for that difficult task." The anonymous friend was Henry Boynton Smith, who had studied at Halle and Berlin from 1837 to 1840, established a friendship with Hegel's widow, taught briefly at Bowdoin College, and was pastor of a Congregational Church in West Amesbury, Massachusetts, when *Prose Writers of Germany* first appeared.[20] H. C. Brokmeyer, the mentor of the St. Louis Philosophical Society whom we shall meet presently, was first led to Hegel by Hedge's book.

But neither Hedge nor Smith were followers of Hegel. In fact they were unsympathetic with Hegel's views to the point of hostility. In philosophy Hedge allied himself with idealists and intuitionists against sensationist or Spencerian views. He greatly admired Kant but thought that Schopenhauer was a better continuer of Kant's teaching than Hegel "who seemed to him something of a charlatan." Smith's reservations about Hegel were not, apparently, so strong, though his wife said he regarded German philosophy in general as a "*monstrum horrendum*." His introduction to the translations he made for Hedge's *Prose Writers,* though accurate for the main outlines of Hegel's thought, repeated a number of invidious charges similar to those made by Mahan and other religious conservatives. "Its present position," Smith charged, "is that of hostility to Christianity." "It is reputed to be the most comprehensive and analytic of pantheistic schemes."[21] Apparently Smith, in contrast to Theodore Parker, was "thoroughly scared" by developments among some of Hegel's followers, particularly Strauss. Though Hedge and Smith wanted their contemporaries to become knowledgeable about Hegel, they certainly did not want them to adopt his views.

The Later St. Louis Hegelians

Except for the Ohio Hegelians—Stallo, Kaufmann, Conway, and Willich—Americans concerned with philosophical issues had to wait until after the Civil War for followers of Hegel, for writers and speakers who sympathetically presented and applied Hegel's main ideas. They came with the St. Louis Philosophical Society or "St. Louis movement," as it is sometimes called, led by H. C. Brokmeyer, W. T. Harris, and Denton Snider. Of these three Harris was pre-eminent in terms of quantity of publication, prominence in public affairs, activity as prime mover of the Philosophical Society, and editor of *The Journal of Speculative Philosophy,* the Society's main achievement. Some details on Harris's thought will provide additional perspective on the intellectual setting, in which the Ohio Hegelians made their influence felt.

William Torrey Harris (1835–1909) attended preparatory schools in his native Connecticut and thence entered Yale College. He left Yale for "the West," specifically St. Louis, in the middle of his junior year, dissatisfied with the lack of modern science and literature in the curriculum. Shortly before leaving Yale he was led to philosophy by Bronson Alcott's "Conversations" on Platonism which persuaded him of "the ideality of the material world" through "insight and reliance on reason."

After a year in St. Louis, where he was to remain as a public school teacher for eight years and an administrator for twelve, Harris met Henry C. Brokmeyer, a Prussian immigrant who had become enthusiastic about Hegel from Hedge's *Prose Writers of Germany* (1847) during some disputatious months at Brown University. In 1858 Harris, Brokmeyer, and a few friends began meeting informally as a Kant Club to find the grounds of Hegel's thought. Harris imported a copy of Hegel's larger *Logic* and particularly encouraged Brokmeyer to undertake a translation which was never satisfactorily finished but did circulate in manuscript. Following the Civil War, adherents of the Kant Club went into the St. Louis Philosophical Society, organized in 1866 with Brokmeyer as president, Harris as secretary, and Denton Snider, G. H. Howison, A. E. Kroeger, and Thomas Davidson among its leading members.

When the editor of the *North American Review* rejected an article by Harris as vague and dogmatic, "the mere dry husk of Hegelianism," the St. Louis Society, at Harris's initiative, started *The Journal of Speculative Philosophy*. Edited by Harris for its entire life from 1867 to 1893, *The Journal* printed numerous translations of German philosophy, particularly Hegel, and published original essays by Emerson, J. H. Stirling, James Ward, William James, John Dewey, and C. S. Peirce. In defending and interpreting Hegel's views in America, Harris and Brokmeyer were preceded by the Ohio group including Stallo and Willich, who became "auxiliaries" of the St. Louis Society along with Emerson, Henry James, Karl Rosenkranz, and Ludwig Feuerbach. But Harris was outstanding as an active public lecturer, leader in the St. Louis movement and Concord School of Philosophy (1879–1887), U.S. Commissioner of Education (1889–1906), editor of America's first regular journal devoted primarily to philosophy and author of some 500 articles and several books, one interpreting Hegel's *Phenomenology* and *Logic.*[22]

Like Hegel, Harris saw philosophy as a science concerned with necessary factors in experience related systematically to a first principle. Reflection on sensible objects and their changes, Harris believed, immediately reveals two necessary factors with which philosophy is concerned—space and time. Both are "infinites" as conditions of all experience. From a parallel analysis of experience Harris concluded that there are three grades or stages of knowing. The first concentrates on the object and shallowly confines itself to the surface of things as isolated and independent. The second sees how things exist only in relation to other things and thus concentrates on their dependence, on what they are not by themselves as separate and isolated. The third "discovers the independence and self-relation underlying all dependence and relativity"; in discovering what is self-related it discovers "the infinite."[23] The content of these three, mutually related stages is to be found in every aspect of experience, and since there are no "things in themselves" behind experience, these three movements characterize all aspects of our internal and external environment. Harris thus attempted to put into American English the main features of Hegel's "dialectic." Through Brokmeyer, Harris came to believe that such a dialectic illuminated the Civil War (legal right to be unified with moral right), American politics, and even problems of school administration—a use of philosophy which pleased the practical, institution-minded lawyers, politicians, judges, teachers, and physicians of the St. Louis movement.

Proceeding dialectically from "seeming" to "truth," Harris analyzed "causality" to conclude that it incorporates space and time in a higher unity but also implies a "self-separation" of energy whereby a cause sends a stream of influence to other things. Without such self-separation a cause could not act upon an effect. So conceived, causality must be grounded in "self-activity" which is necessarily self-related and thus independent, free, and creative. Ultimately, in Harris's view, the only authentic "self-activity" is God, conceived with Aristotle and Hegel as the unmoved motion and self-contained existence of Reason which, as Reason, is also personal. Like Hegel, Harris believed that philosophy approaches Absolute Reason through conceptual analysis to first principles while religion receives the absolute "into the heart" through symbols.[24]

As a corollary of his key notion of "self-activity," which also presupposes relatedness and context, Harris saw education as the self-development of the individual mediated through the salient traditions of civilization which the student must come to share on his own. With the self-development of the individual in mind, he linked public schools with democracy as self-government involving women's suffrage and separation of religion from government. With the traditions of civilization in mind, he criticized excessive vocationalism. Along similar lines, his social philosophy saw true freedom, the freedom of civilization rather than savagery, as the will of the individual working through such institutions as family, civil society, state, and especially the Invisible Church, the "absolute institution" uniting all men of all time.[25] In spite of his stress on institutions, Harris apparently gave some kind of precedence to "self-activity" *simpliciter* as he admired the ruthless economic individualism of "the Gilded Age" and condemned socialism in all its aspects and forms.

The Social Setting

The two previous sections focused on the intellectual setting of the views of Stallo, Kaufmann, Conway, and Willich. The main theme was the interrelationship of ideas viewed primarily in terms of logical similiarities, affinities, and differences. But such an emphasis provides only a one-sided and partial picture of the setting in which the ideas under consideration emerged. Hegel's philosophy, particularly his thought on the "spirit of a nation," warns against just such one-sidedness and partiality. Any philosophy, according to Hegel, is a special conformation of ideas and doctrines of a given time and place. "Just as every individual is a child of his time, so also is philosophy an expression of its time in thought." But to understand it one must consider more than ideas, doctrines, and their logical relationships. To stop there would yield only what Hegel called an "abstract" view—a view which has removed the object in question from its full and effective context, its active relationships, and its dynamic connection with what is different from and opposed to it. To understand a set of ideas one must view them "concretely" in relation to the whole social milieu in which they appear. One must see them as aspects of a cultural whole, as conditioned by and reflecting changes in geography, immigration, economic activities, political developments, artistic achievements, and the religious concerns of groups of men at a given time and place. Such an approach to understanding ideas and theories now seems commonplace, but it was first clearly emphasized by Hegel and introduced by him into modern western thought. Following Hegel, then, we turn to the wider social and cultural setting of the views of Stallo, Kaufmann, and their associates.

An obvious and important factor in the intellectual direction of the Ohio thinkers was their status as immigrants. Three of them emigrated, as their names suggest, from Germany. Moncure Conway was also an immigrant to Ohio, in that he was born in one of America's seaboard states and educated or first employed in others. But all the Ohio thinkers brought with them a firm pride in the locale where they had spent their early years. It was natural, then, that Stallo and Willich should want to perpetuate in their new home one of Germany's recognized glories, its classical philosophy beginning with Kant and culminating, they were aware, in Hegel whose own theories or those of his followers were dominant in Germany's intellectual life until after midcentury. Kaufmann brought from his native land a religious concern which predisposed him toward Hegel's philosophy, and Conway was proud of his association in Boston with such "left-wing" Unitarians as Parker and W. H. Channing who had, in some measure, come to terms with German idealism. Further, as immigrants to Ohio, Stallo and his Hegelian associates showed something about their personalities and temperament—namely, that they were energetic, enterprising, and ready to try something different. "The West" to which they came was then very little removed in space and time from the frontier.

Another factor in the espousal of Hegelian ideas in Ohio from 1848 to 1860 was the favorable cultural atmosphere of

Cincinnati and Canton. Both were highly literate cities, particularly Cincinnati. In the 1850's almost one third of the population of Cincinnati was of German origin, a sufficient number to support a half a dozen daily newspapers or weekly magazines printed in German in addition to several newspapers in English, while Canton was the center of a county with some 3,000 German-speaking residents and one, sometimes two, German papers. The German papers were more than purveyors of the latest local and overseas events. They published novels in serial form, book reviews, editorials which expanded on philosophical themes, and advertisements for the classics of German literature by Schiller, Goethe, and Heine. In Cincinnati, moreover, there were more than a score of publishing houses and several libraries, one of which had been established as early as 1814. Only New York and Philadelphia surpassed Cincinnati in the number of bookstores which regularly imported German writings for public sale.

Numerous literary clubs and *Vereine* stimulated the intellectual life of Cincinnati by lectures and discussions, sometimes on philosophical themes. *The Western Messenger,* a Unitarian monthly with high literary standards and strong transcendentalist sympathies, was edited from Cincinnati and Louisville from 1835 to 1841. It first published some of the poems of Emerson and Keats. Though it never touched on Hegel or his followers, it cautiously publicized some trends in German religious thought after Kant. Prominent visitors from the East—Emerson, Holmes, Agassiz, Theodore Parker, and Bronson Alcott—addressed large audiences on themes which frequently overlapped points in Hegelian philosophy. The Queen City was also outstanding in music, thanks in large part to its German element, with a Haydn Society and yearly *Sängerfeste.* The arts of the theater were well represented in both German and English. In short, as

Conway put it, "Cincinnati was the most cultivated of the western cities."[26] Its literary and artistic culture favored public attention to a group of men, a small group to be sure, who would expound and defend Hegelian philosophy.

Still another factor in the adoption of Hegel's ideas was the appearance and growing importance of several forms of social conflict in the 1850's alongside a strong concern for national unity. Both Cincinnati and Canton, particularly the former, were industrial centers. Cincinnati was the great mart of ready-made clothing for the Western and Southern states with approximately 10,000 workers, most of them German, employed in this activity. Canton also had its industries, particularly woolen mills and iron foundries. The late 1850's saw a growing labor movement in both cities in response to poverty and misery among the workers, accentuated by the depression of 1857. A visible proletariat was emerging, and conflicts between employers and employees became apparent in strikes.[27] Under Willich's editorship the *Cincinnati Republikaner* closely reported these conflicts. In 1859, for example, Willich devoted three long columns to the details of a cabinetmakers' strike and called for the establishment of shop committees in each factory to unify action and coordinate demands on wage-rates. The *Republikaner* repeatedly condemned the evils of growing monopoly and on one occasion publicized a play entitled *The Proletarian* which depicted the grinding hardships of working-class life.

Other forms of social conflict developed in the 1850's. There were "nativist" and "Know-Nothing" movements which sometimes erupted in violence against the foreign-born Germans and Irishmen. The first all-German military organization in Cincinnati was formed for defense against quarrelsome Know-Nothings. In 1854 there was a knife and gun battle between members of the *Turnverein* and Know-

Nothings in which one person was killed and many were wounded. Another German organization clashed with Cincinnati police over the visit of a Papal Nuncio. One of the most serious of these conflicts was the election riot of 1855 in which the Germans barricaded bridges "over the Rhine" and Cincinnati took on the appearance of a European capital in the throes of revolution. Well-trained German militia units repulsed a mob of nativists who tried to storm the barricades, and only after three days of violence was civil order restored.[28]

So far as the unity and identity of the nation as a whole is concerned, the most serious conflict emerging in the 1850's was that concerning slavery. "It keeps up," a sensitive German-American historian wrote in 1854, "a constant agitation; throws the apple of discord, year after year, into Congress and even into whole churches; and in 1850 brought us to the brink of a formal division of the republic." A compromise on the issue saved the union, but the agitation continued. In the historian's words:

> That there are in the United States over three million of negro slaves, who may be bought and sold as common merchandise, is certainly the most palpable contradiction to the first principle of that government that all men are born free and equal; or, as it should be more properly expressed, are born destined for freedom.[29]

By virtue of its geographical position Ohio was particularly exposed to this issue. Separated from Kentucky only by the breadth of the Ohio River, Cincinnatians were disturbed by the Fugitive Slave Law and Dred Scott decision. They were alarmed over the struggle in bloody Kansas since all sides of the slavery issue were represented in southern Ohio. The execution of John Brown produced a tense demonstration of protest led by August Willich through the streets of Cincinnati. Abolitionists, widely supported by Germans and refugees from the German Revolution of 1848, were uncompromisingly and unalterably opposed both to Southern secessionists and more moderate unionists.

Some of Hegel's major ideas were particularly relevant to these conflicts and their outcome. Hegel saw all thinking and all events, we noted earlier, as characterized by opposition, conflict, and reconciliation which he called "dialectic." History is the theater of conflict, frequently punctuated by violence. At times, Hegel noted, history is a veritable "slaughter-bench." Some of the Ohio thinkers saw this aspect of Hegel as particularly relevant to their experience. August Willich, for example, was well aware that Marx had developed his doctrine of class struggle, the dialectic of social classes, out of Hegel's analysis of "civil society" as including an opposition between rich and poor, the few and the masses. As Hegel put it:

> If unimpeded, civil society *expands* internally in *population* and *industry*. Accumulation of wealth is increased by *generalizing* people's interdependence through their needs and by *generalizing* methods of providing means to satisfy those needs—for from this double generalization the greatest profits are derived. On the other hand, the *atomization* and *restriction* of particular forms of labor, and hence the *dependency* and *misery* of the class bound to such labor, entail the inability to feel and enjoy the larger possibilities, particularly the spiritual advantages, of civil society. A great mass of people sinks below a certain automatically necessary level of subsistence and thereby loses the sense of justice, integrity, and the honor to exist by one's own activity and labor. This produces the proletariat [*Pöbel*], which in turn facilitates concentration of excessive wealth in a few hands.[30]

But Hegel also maintained that every clash, every dialectical conflict, necessarily and essentially contains the promise of its resolution in a higher unity. His philosophy thus provided an optimistic doctrine of progress and pointed toward social and national unity manifest in a higher, all-embracing community. "Germany is no longer a state," Hegel lamented in 1802. It was an internally divided and torn collection of principalities and duchies. So Hegel sought to develop a political philosophy, as Stallo and Willich were aware, which would reveal at once the conditions of unity and freedom in dialectically harmonized institutions. Such ideas as these readily lent themselves to use in Ohio of the 1850's. Hegel's dialectic could help his followers assimilate the struggles and conflicts taking place around them. But in addition he directly and indirectly provided clues for a higher and truer community more fully conscious of its self-identity. As immigrants from Germany and naturalized Americans, Stallo, Kaufmann, and Willich were particularly sensitive to the problem of national self-identity, and sometimes they were passionate about America's promise and destiny as a nation.

A final factor explaining the appeal and relevance of Hegel's thought in Ohio of the 1850's was the growth and increasing influence of religious institutions. Protestant sects of all kinds were mushrooming, erecting new buildings, and promoting colleges throughout the state. The Roman Catholic Church was growing in wealth and membership, heavily supported by working-class immigrants. Like the readers of Edward Mühl's free-thinking, Strauss-colored *Lichtfreund* published earlier in Cincinnati, the Ohio Hegelians were skeptical about this institutional growth. Willich was firmly and overtly hostile to it. Others noticed an increasing emphasis on externals, forms, and the trappings of religion while its substantive message—the element which Emerson, Parker, and other radical transcendentalists viewed as the permanent truth of Christianity—was being slighted. The outward forms of Protestant Christianity such as Bible-reading and prayers were being required in public schools operated by local government. Sabbath-legislation was encouraged by many churches and some were crusading for a Maine law to prohibit the sale of alcoholic drinks. Further, the widely-accepted supernaturalism seemed to threaten genuine, scientific learning and put a premium on superstitious ignorance by emphasizing miracles and mysteries. Too often, in the views of Willich and Kaufmann, organized Christianity stood on the side of special privilege and accentuated the social problem instead of resolving it.

For such concerns several aspects of Hegel's philosophy were attractive. Its argument for a firm, clear-cut separation of church and state could comfort those concerned with Bible-reading in schools and Sabbatarian legislation. Hegel's avowed Protestantism and defense of it as more favorable in principle to freedom than Roman Catholicism, which he frequently and invidiously criticized, appealed to others. Three of the Ohio men with whom we are concerned were particularly partial to Hegel's view that God is immanent in nature, history, and the movements of social life. This emphasis undercut all dualistic separations of the divine and human, sacred and secular, supernatural and natural, science and miracle, revelation and experience. Stallo and Conway in particular found such a view of divinity congenial to their thought, and Conway merged it with an evolutionary naturalism. Thus in a number of respects Hegel's thought lent itself to criticism of various manifestations of organized religion in the 1850's.

In his own writings Hegel saw America as the land of the future where the next major movements of world history were to take place. He saw the possibility of a struggle and clash between North and South America and felt that only America with its great size and movement could provide the proper subject matter for a future epic. There was thus a peculiarly fitting turn of history in the fact that some of Hegel's major views on society, history, and religion were championed by a group of thinkers and writers who were chronologically and geographically at the center of nineteenth-century America.

II

EVOLUTIONARY IDEALISM OF THE YOUNG STALLO

Of all Ohio's philosophically-minded thinkers in the dozen years preceding the Civil War, John Bernard Stallo (1823–1900) was outstanding in mastery of philosophy and public influence. Though he regarded his *General Principles of the Philosophy of Nature* published in 1848 as a failure, it was actually a landmark in publicizing Hegelian and evolutionary ideas. It had an important influence among scientists, philosophers, and men of literature. As a successful lawyer and judge in Cincinnati, Stallo was a leading figure in the community and became known for his ideas both in the application of the law and in his addresses on important public occasions.

Education and First Writing

Stallo was born at Sierhausen in the southern part of Oldenburg, Germany, on March 16, 1823.[1] Though his family name might seem to be Italian, it was actually an old Friesian name meaning "forester." His ancestors on both his father's and mother's side were country school teachers and hence people of modest means and circumstances. From them he inherited a thirst for learning, respect for knowledge, and an inclination from his father's side of the family toward scientific studies. His education, like John Stuart Mill's, began very early, thanks to the vocational interests of his father and grandfather. At the age of four he was reading and doing arithmetic problems. His father concentrated on his instruction in mathematics. His grandfather taught him Greek, Latin, and English, but he had to study French secretly with his father because his grandfather intensely hated *Franzentum.* Knowledge of English, French, and Dutch was important in the region of Stallo's boyhood due to the extensive foreign trade there and the practical needs of commerce.

At the age of fifteen Stallo went to the free, Catholic normal school at Vechta where he also had the advantage of instruction from professors in the local *Gymnasium*, an institution of high repute. In his course of study he attended lectures in psychology which included, as was customary at the time, a number of topics in philosophy, particularly theory of knowledge. Thus in addition to learning about such psychological matters as temperament, feelings, and capacities of the human soul, the young Stallo was exposed to philosophy as he studied the nature of concepts, classes of judgment, rules of inference, sources of error, and the relation of knowledge to perception.[2] What he learned about the relation of concepts to sense-impressions and about the *a priori* character of space and time largely followed Kant's position in *The Critique of Pure Reason.* Thus Stallo's first formal exposure to philosophy brought him into contact with some main themes of German idealism.

Stallo's education at Vechta adequately prepared him to enter a university, but his father lacked the means to send him. The alternative, then, was to continue the family's line of school teachers or to emigrate to America. Stallo chose America and was influenced in this direction by the example of his uncle, Franz Joseph Stallo, who had been a prosperous printer in a nearby village, an active physical scientist, a discoverer of new agricultural methods, and a man of radical ideas which brought him into conflict with the local authorities. In 1831 Franz Stallo, followed by a number of his countrymen, emigrated to America and founded a socialistic community in Auglaize County, Ohio. The community failed after a few years but to this day Stallotown, now Minster, remains an almost solidly German settlement.

In the spring of 1839 young Stallo arrived in Cincinnati bearing letters of introduction from the rector of the Vechta *Gymnasium* and the priest of his native village. He thought of seeking employment in a publishing firm but through the pastor of Cincinnati's Trinity Church became a teacher in a parochial school. Finding a great need in his classes for a good German spelling book and reader, Stallo wrote one, *A B C, Buchstabir und Lesebuch, für die deutschen in Amerika.* It appeared without the author's name in 1840 and was popular enough to be reprinted in many editions.

In addition to his teaching duties and the writing of a spelling book, the young Stallo tried his hand at poetry. He had acquired an interest in poetry from the enthusiasms of his professors at Vechta where he was particularly fond of classical philosophy, Plato and Aristotle, and the natural sciences. He also studied Oken, Kant, Schiller, and Goethe's scientific writings before leaving Germany. While at Vechta he wrote a poem on "The Expectation of the Prophets" which was first published in Cincinnati by the *Wahrheitsfreund* in 1839. It was consistently and conventionally Biblical in its themes and references, thanks in part to the omission of two verses expressing the Kantian philosophy of nature. Those verses were omitted at the wish of the editor, Father Henni, as being out of harmony with policy of the *Wahrheitsfreund.*

Two years later Stallo published other poems in the *Wahrheitsfreund.* One was an elegy occasioned by the death of his father, and the other was an ode to "God in Nature." The latter particularly reflected Stallo's absorption of Goethe's philosophy of nature and also foreshadowed some themes he was to develop conceptually in *The General Principles of the Philosophy of Nature.* In one verse Stallo poetically declared the unity of God and nature as follows:

> He who guides the Whole is all-prevailing,
> In each special thing is all-entailing;
> And His harmony is omnipresence!
> When the planets circle in their orbits,
> Trailing fire in their brightest limits,
> God imparts them glory in His presence.[3]

A few months after the publication of "God in Nature" Stallo began teaching German at St. Xavier's College, newly founded by French and Belgian Jesuits. Along with his duties as teacher of German he was given the opportunity to continue his own studies in mathematics and Greek, and during his last two years at St. Xavier's in 1843 and 1844, he was teaching more mathematics than German. The college had an extensive library in physics and chemistry and also laboratory facilities which were outstanding for the time. Stallo devoted his spare hours to the study of physics and chemistry under the direction of a Jesuit professor and finally achieved such competence that in the autumn of 1844 he was called to St. John's College at Fordham, New York, as professor of physics, chemistry, and higher mathematics.

In respect to the direction of his thought and choice of a vocation Stallo's four years at Fordham were among the most eventful of his life. But some of the important happenings in that period remain hidden. He never told his biographers that he was a Catholic priest, apparently wishing to suppress that part of his life-story. Though the date of his ordination has not been determined, the St. John's College catalog listed him as "Rev. J. B. Stallo, A.M." He did, however, reveal something of his studies at Fordham. In addition to the philosophers with whom he had become familiar in Germany—Leibniz, Kant, Herbart, Fichte and particularly Oken—he turned to those which had been forbidden in his home. He read Descartes, Spinoza, Newton, and Hume. He studied Humboldt's *Cosmos* in its first edition and read in Schelling and Hegel "with great enthusiasm." As a result of these studies he wrote, while at Fordham, *The General Principles of the Philosophy of Nature, With An Outline of Some of Its Recent Developments Among the Germans; Embracing the Philosophical Systems of Schelling and Hegel and Oken's System of Nature.* By the time the book was published in Boston in 1848, however, and perhaps even as a let-down from writing it, Stallo had decided on a legal career and enrolled in a law school in New York. He returned to Cincinnati to study law in the office of an older attorney. Toward the end of 1849 he passed his bar examination, was admitted to the bar, and thereafter came rapidly into a large practice.

Self-Evolutions of Spirit

The first part of Stallo's *General Principles*, one-third of its total of 520 pages, was "programmatic." It consisted of Stallo's development of general points of view for the philosophical study of the natural sciences under section-headings entitled "Views and Prospects," "Grounds and Positions," and "Evolutions." The last of these sections was the longest. Its 130 pages dealt with space and time, the solar system, physical processes, chemistry and electricity, organic life, the human mind, and the organization of society. The second part of Stallo's *General Principles* was a summary of the philosophical systems of Fichte, Schelling, Oken, and Hegel, particularly as they related to the philosophy of nature. The summary of Fichte's system was preceded by an analysis of Kant's *Critique of Pure Reason* with special attention to its concepts of "intuition," "understanding," and "reason." The direction of Stallo's intellectual sympathy is suggested in the fact that almost two-thirds of the pages summarizing philosophical systems were devoted to Hegel. Stallo recognized this emphasis in his preface: "I cheerfully acknowledge, that for many of my views I am indebted to the study of Hegel's philosophy, although, generally, these views are as independent of Hegel as Hegel is (if it be permitted *magnis componere parva*) of Schelling." Stallo's qualification does not retract his debt to Hegel since Hegel was, for a time, a follower of Schelling, edited a philosophical journal with him, and sought to put some of Schelling's main conclusions on different grounds.

The major assumption of Stallo's whole book, including his own views in the first main section, was that mind or thought is fundamentally identical with the forces which activate the whole natural world. In Stallo's words:

> The fundamental principle upon which, according to my conviction, all true philosophy of nature rests, is, that the different manifestations of the vitality which bursts forth in nature's phenomena are comprehensively united, centered in the mind; that the implacable rigor of cosmic laws, which sways *extensive matter*, is identical with the eternal freedom of *mind in its infinite intensity*.[4]

Such a principle, Stallo recognized, was opposed to the dominant materialism and "misconceived Baconism" of the day as well as to the old dualism perpetuated in Kant's philosophy between matter and spirit, the objective and subjective. It was, however, the core of "German idealism" since Kant. It asserted, in contrast to English philosophy, the "reality of the Ideal." Stallo hoped to make that idealism better known. Anticipating his own conclusions in "Grounds and Positions," Stallo further noted that the German language, in contrast to English, was especially well fitted to deal with process, development, and evolution. As in the case of "*werden*," the German can use verbs substantively and make pure actions the subjects of sentences. There are, accordingly, special difficulties in putting a thing's process of origination and the "process of its evolution" into English.

In opposition to those who saw nature as completely determined matter, the spontaneous act of God, or the expression of specific implicit goals, Stallo found the unity of man and nature, of subjectivity and objectivity, in a unitary evolutionary idealism. The true position, he held, is that "the phenomenal world is but self-revelation of Deity," and "Deity" is to be conceived as the vital "innervation" of the totality of nature. "All manifestations of life—change, motion, progressive development—are but a process verifying the vital innervations of the Whole."[5] Without "union with the vivifying Whole" there would be no revolutions in the solar system, no circulation of waters, no attraction or repulsion of molecules, no growth of living things. On this basis Stallo concluded with Goethe that the life of the Whole is reflected in every part, that the development of each organic form is a miniature reproduction of entire nature, and that the gradation of natural forms depends on the degree of "universality" in them, *i.e.*, on their representation of nature in its totality. Since the terminus of any evolution will never coincide with its beginning, "the development of all individual forms," Stallo inferred, "will be spiral."[6] Though Stallo did not overtly mention it, his emphasis on the unity of things as including their particularity and on the spiral character of evolution could easily be traced to Hegel, as his subsequent summary of Hegel's philosophical system was to suggest.

In presenting his own "Grounds and Positions" Stallo drew out the consequences of the universality of process or evolution in relation to material substance, the nature of Spirit, and the relation of Spirit to nature. Those who believe that somewhere in the ceaseless movements and processes of nature there must be an absolute rest as bearer and source of motion have made, in Stallo's view, a false assumption. They have assumed the logical priority of rest to motion. Such an assumption, Stallo argued, is not justified. "It is impossible to conceive rest without the concomitant idea of equilibrium, and therefore of motion. It is impossible to construe motion out of rest; rest is an incident to motion, and consequently to be explained from the nature of the latter." "There is," Stallo concluded, "nowhere absolute rest, but motion everywhere."[7]

On this basis he insisted that the search for an ultimate substance as some kind of rigid, fixed substratum behind the changing phenomena is a foolish quest from the outset. The unity of the changing phenomena cannot be found in matter which exists not by itself but only in extension or exclusion as related to other matter. If one takes away from a material substance its gravity, heat, color, and other qualities, there is nothing left. Furthermore, it is a mystery to say that these qualities are present *throughout* the substance and contrary to common sense to say that they do not interfere with each other as in Dalton's law asserting that gases, no matter how compressed, act as vacua in regard to each other.[8] No, the ultimate unity of changing phenomena can lie only in what is self-mediated and exists by itself—namely, Mind or Spirit. In Stallo's words:

> Mind is the absolutely Restless in itself, the absolutely Creative, the absolutely Free. Mind is not the blank of abstraction, not the *caput mortuum* of the External. The Deity, the absolute Mind, is the absolute intrinsic process,—the substance which causes, produces itself,—gazes into its own eye.[9]

Not only did Stallo follow Hegel's view, even his words, in regard to the nature of matter and Spirit but he also adopted Hegel's overall position on the self-evolution of Spirit in three dialectically-related phases as expressed in the major points of *The Encyclopedia of Philosophical Sciences.* The three phases of Spirit, Stallo held, are:

> 1. The Spiritual as the absolute origin of all existences, abstractly taken. 2. The exterioration of the Spiritual, as the manifestation in existence, abstractly taken. 3. The Spiritual as thus sustaining itself, regenerated in its exterioration, or the Spiritual taken in its concrete identity and truth.[10]

Hegel viewed the first of these phases as logic, the reality of all things viewed as implicit, as Idea. He thought of the second as nature, the Idea outside itself in space and time. The third, in Hegel's view, was the realm of Spirit—man's mind, morality, society, and history—as emergent from nature and expressing the reality of the universe concretely, fully, and in all-sided wholeness.

On the basis of this conception of Spirit, matter, and their relationship, Stallo attempted under "Evolutions" in the *General Principles* to trace out the various specific modes of the "self-unfolding development of the Spiritual" as "a unital infinite, internal Substantial movement." He sought to show how "Every individual existence is but a living history, and its truth, its real being, is its entire development through all its phases *taken as a unity.*"[11] The solar system is thus to be viewed as a process, an evolution. It shows no resting original matter on which motion was conferred. Similarly, the vibratory nature of heat shows that there is no such thing as "caloric matter." In the evolutions of nature, chemical elements of a general nature give rise to individualized substances, and organic phenomena manifest individual acts as related to the whole serial activity of the world. Stallo allowed that these evolutionary processes, though spiral and progressive, are also marked by strife and struggle because endless activity, endless life, is the very essence of Spirit or Deity which is "Absolute intrinsic process."[12] As Stallo traced out the various evolutions of nature, utilizing his considerable knowledge of the natural sciences, he occasionally referred to and corrected Hegel's writings which were related to his argument, particularly Hegel's "*Naturphilosophie.*"

Knowledge, Society, and Hegel

Two further "Evolutions" in the first part of *The General Principles,* where Stallo was developing his own view, indicate that he took the word "nature" in a very broad and capacious sense. After his discussion of the solar system, physical world, chemistry, and the biological order he turned to evolutions of "The Mind" and "Organization of Society." Apparently, like Kant and Hegel, he understood nature as the totality of phenomena, the totality of objects that can be experienced by external, sensuous observation and introspective observation as well. This broad conception of nature is especially apparent in his discussion of "The Mind" where psychology, as it would be called today, coalesced with theory of knowledge.

After considering the relation of mind in its "potential"

form to man's sensory equipment emerging from the evolutions of organic life, Stallo turned to his stronger interests, "The Conscious Mind" and "The Thinking Mind." His interests in these areas were stronger because, as we shall see, they involved issues in theory of knowledge, particularly knowledge in the natural sciences, his lifelong interest and that aspect of Hegel's philosophy he was careful to include fully in his summaries. Stallo thought of conscious mind as an active interchange with seemingly external objects which at once reveals the ideal or mental character of those objects and at the same time its own reality in and through them. This interchange, Stallo held, involves three progressive phases:

> The conscious mind, in facing an object, first perceives its particularities—of time, place, etc.; it is *perception.* But these particularities . . . are not insular existences, but *relations,* whose "ensemble" expresses the *idea* of the object; in becoming sensible of an object in this light, consciousness appears as *observation.* Finally, then, the unity of this idea and of its relations, the complete object, becomes the property of the mind in *cognition.*[13]

These three phases—perception, observation, cognition—are not only a direct illustration of Hegel's dialectic as applied to conscious reflection, but each phase was substantially similar to Hegel's views on the subject as revealed in Stallo's subsequent detailed summaries from *The Phenomenology of Mind.* For example, in regard to "perception" Stallo argued that external objects are not engraved upon the mind but rather their particularities become general qualities and relations. "Objects are thoroughly relative; their being is a complex of relations."[14] Summarizing the section of *The Phenomenology* on "Certainty of the Senses" Stallo found Hegel showing how any particular perceived "here" or "now" must turn into "a bare generality" related to our knowing of it. In Stallo's summary:

> First the "now" is pointed out and asserted as the truth; but next it is pointed out only as *having been*,—the first truth, its *being*, is revoked; thirdly, what *has been*, is not,—the revocation is revoked, the negation denied, and I return to the original truth as general: the "now" is. This movement exhibits the truth of the "now," namely, a "now" reflected into itself, a *general* "now," a multiplicity of "nows" comprised in a unity.[15]

Again, in regard to the second phase of conscious mind, a phase of special interest to the philosopher of science, Stallo concluded that "observation" determines an object's "*general*, but distinct *predicates*, which are finally resumed in the ideal unity of the object (or, speaking with reference to the predicates, the *subject*). Once more: the predicates *are* the subject; they are not glued, plastered upon it, and torn off, when the subject is idealized. Everything exists *in* its properties, not *beside* them."[16] Summarizing the section of *The Phenomenology of Mind* on "Observation," Stallo found Hegel saying, in a very complex dialectical exposition, that the observed object is its qualities. Since these qualities as differing from one another involve relationships, the unity of the object depends on the observer and "the individual object is nothing more than the relation to other objects."[17] Other key ideas in Stallo's theory of mind such as "understanding," "judgment," and "reason" can be similarly traced to Hegel or shown to be substantially in agreement with Hegel's views as found in his *Encyclopedia of Philosophical Sciences* or *Phenomenology of Mind.* Major portions and divisions of both books were summarized in the 190 pages Stallo devoted to Hegel in the second main part of *The General Principles.*

In "Evolutions" as instanced in the "Organization of Society" Stallo set forth his social and political philosophy, which is of special interest in view of his practical effort on behalf of freedom of mind and his participation in the partisan politics involved in a democratic form of government. With an obvious debt to Hegel's "Philosophy of Mind" as summarized in the second part of *The General Principles,* Stallo saw three phases in the progress of man's socialization, an evolution which itself is "embodied reason." In the first phase, "Person," the individual is related to others in property and labor. In the "Family," the second phase, there arises on an organic, sexual basis a spiritual unity of man and woman which socialists aiming at brotherhood mistakenly reject and which the "emancipation of women" would wrongly render contractual. Here property and inheritance make possible the family's special function, education.

In the "State," the third phase, universal reason is manifest as law reproducing itself in and from the individual. "The incorporated authority of the law, the state," held Stallo, "is nothing else than society organizing itself; it is not a machine, of which the individuals are the material." Since society as a "brute mass" is the bearer of universal spiritual life, the law is to be viewed as the expressed consciousness of society and the movement of society, thus the progression of Spirit. Stallo further held that

> It is the destiny of the individual to identify his private reason and will with universal reason and will; and, obviously, this can take place only if the latter, in the form of law, be in the consciousness of the individual, and reproduce themselves *in* and *from* him. The organization of society is, therefore, *essentially democratic.*[18]

Government cannot possibly embody the life of society in proceeding from only a few individuals or in being superimposed from without. A government which does not represent the people's reason and will, Stallo held, is an "abomination," "a stronghold for the imprisonment of the divinity in man." From these premises Stallo condemned socialism as failing to see that individuality expressed in property and the family must be preserved "in their full validity" with reference to the state. In seeking the brotherhood of man by annulling "the immediate reality of the relations of brother and sister" in the family, socialists offer "ends without means." The truth, however, in the appearance of socialism, Stallo went on to note, is "that society is to be indeed a community, and that all are responsible for the sustenance of each one."[19]

In holding that the state must be "essentially democratic," Stallo departed, of course, from Hegel, who endorsed constitutional monarchy as the true embodiment of spirit in providing a unity for the state rooted in nature. This departure is particularly interesting because on other points Stallo was in wide agreement with Hegel. Stallo's conclusions about democracy were a result of an internal criticism of Hegel. He showed that Hegel's premises about the nature of the state and its relation to law and reason led not to constitutional monarchy but rather to democracy. In summarizing Hegel's "social morality (politics)," Stallo directly quoted Hegel as saying:

> In the perfect form of the state, in which all the moments of the idea have their free existence, this subjectivity is not a so-called moral person, or a resolution of the majority,—forms in which the unity of the resolving will has no real existence,—but a real individuality, the will of one resolving individual,—monarchy.[20]

After this quotation Stallo put three exclamation points and a footnote stating: "As if the true subjectivity of a state, or of any thing organic, could be something extraneous,—which the power of the prince always is,—something else than a *reflex objectivity!* But Hegel wrote in Prussia." Thus Stallo argued that if the state is to be truly an organism, if it is to be a real whole of subjectivity and objectivity or an organic unity of particularity and generality as Hegel himself had held it must be, it cannot be a monarchy but rather must be a democracy.

With Hegel, Stallo saw history as the manifestation of Spirit in distinct and recognizable stages. History, wrote Stallo, is "the life of the absolute Spiritual and its events are the manifestations in which the Spiritual comes to the knowledge, the identification, the absolute possession of itself, in its eternal self-evolution or origination."[21] Echoing Hegel's philosophy of history, Stallo saw an evolution of cultures from the "immediate union of man with nature" in Greece, through the formulae of nationality in Rome and the formalization of Christianity in the Middle Ages, toward the reconciliation in our own time of matter and spirit, faith and understanding, laboring and intellectual classes, Christianity and actuality.

Thus Stallo's key concepts in *The General Principles*—"process," "relations," "Spirit," and "evolutions"—enabled him to provide a sweeping perspective on man's total environment and place in it. He was able to show how the same principles which operate in a grain of sand or one man's reflections are also manifest in the solar system and the sweep of history. All these phenomena are essentially self-revelations of Mind or Spirit. Thus his philosophy as expressed in *The General Principles* was essentially an evolutionary idealism substantially based on Hegel. The attractive thing in Hegel was that he overcame the dualisms between reality and idea, matter and spirit, left by Kant through a "process philosophy" which could see the particular things of the world as they truly are, as complexly related to one another and not deduced from some abstraction. In Stallo's own words:

> Hegel does not attempt to evolve concrete forms from an abstraction; his "Absolute" is essentially concrete.—The reason for so many anomalies (as they are termed) in the philosophy of Hegel will now be apparent. Since truth is apprehended, not as something reposing in the bosom of its own being, but as the "Whole in its development," as the Absolute, not abstractly taken, but also in its phenomenal existence, in its individual exterioration, the system of metaphysics, which formerly consisted of nothing but formalities, must encroach upon the domain of all science. Instead of an establishment of certain forms, merely for construing the various material, form and material now stand in necessary relation; the material—nature, &c.,—enter as essentially into metaphysical reasoning as the old formulas. It cannot, therefore, be startling, to see that the natural sciences, history, &c., are an integral part of metaphysics. "The true form in which truth exists," says Hegel, "is its scientific system alone." Formerly, all the realities of life were excluded from philosophical speculation; they were beneath the level of thought; in the logic, &c., of Hegel, the idealities are exhibited as producing themselves in and through these realities.[22]

Influence on Emerson

In Stallo's eyes his first book was a failure. For religious believers it was too "godless" and for materialists it did not go far enough. One of Stallo's relatives reported that he tried to suppress *The General Principles* and Stallo himself later declared, "I sincerely regret its publication." There were, he allowed, aspects of the book of which he was not ashamed, but it "was written while I was under the spell of Hegel's ontological reveries—at a time when I was barely of age and still seriously affected with the metaphysical malady which seems to be one of the unavoidable disorders of intellectual infancy." Thus in the preface to his *Concepts and Theories of Modern Physics* published in 1881 Stallo not only repudiated *The General Principles* but also sought to cut his ties with Hegel. His biographer, H. A. Rattermann, once asked him whether the failure of his *General Principles* had been the reason for his leaving the teaching profession for law. Stallo replied:

> See here, my friend, I had rather not discuss that. I found out that the American spirit was not yet ready for philosophy. Only its superficial growths flourish here. I desired primarily to make sure of a secure living for the future so I came to Cincinnati. I wanted to become practical, as Americans are.[23]

But in the years immediately following its publication and often unknown to its author *The General Principles* had an influence and effect which suggest that it was far from the failure Stallo believed it to be. At least one Ohioan was enthusiastic about the book. Friedrich Grimke, Chief Justice of the Ohio Supreme Court, travelled from Chillicothe to Cincinnati to meet and congratulate the author of *The General Principles*. Further, the book had a noteworthy influence among scientists. One scientific writer credited it with having marked an epoch in the education of American thinkers. Not only did it present a new conception of the organic unity and evolution of nature which had scarcely entered the minds of English-speaking students of science, but it also introduced a more complete analysis of Hegel's philosophy than had yet appeared in English. In addition, it summarized the organismic philosophy of Lorenz Oken whose views were already influencing the teaching of Richard Owen, eminent master of natural history in London. The impact of *The General Principles* on scientific literature was especially apparent in the writings of T. Sterry Hunt whose papers after 1842 reflected Stallo's influence and whose books on physiology and chemistry in the 1880's confess their debt to him. Hunt dedicated his book on *A New Basis for Chemistry* to J. B. Stallo, "citizen, jurist, and philosopher" and noted in its preface that *The General Principles* had early been a source of inspiration.[24]

Stallo's *General Principles* was known and used among writers and students of philosophy in the specialized sense. Two years before William Torrey Harris took the lead in organizing the St. Louis Philosophical Society he compiled in his "commonplace book" a rudimentary dictionary of Hegelian terms as translated by Brokmeyer, Stallo, Hedge and others. Harris used the results of his study of Hegelian terminology in his widely circulated "Outlines of Hegel's Logic." Mr. C. H. Goddard of Marietta, Ohio, who was a friend of Stallo and familiar with *The General Principles*, later became active in the society of St. Louis Hegelians as an "auxiliary" or out-of-town member along with Stallo, Willich, R. W. Emerson, Karl Rosenkranz, J. H. Stirling, and Ludwig Feuerbach.[25]

Stallo's *General Principles* also had an impact on American literature. Though George Ripley, leader of Brook Farm "communism" and assistant editor of *The Harbinger*, felt that *The General Principles* offered "no points of contact with the American mind" since the views of Hegel were only "intellectual gymnastics" lacking in "scientific analysis of facts," J. Eliot Cabot praised the book in the *Massachusetts Quarterly Review* as "the best thing on its subject that has yet appeared." "Its analysis of the German systems from Kant to Oken," wrote Cabot, himself an assiduous and competent student of those systems, "is just, clear, and comprehensive—just the thing for our meridian." Cabot's enthusiastic review may have led Emerson and A. Bronson Alcott to read *The General Principles.*[26] A. Bronson Alcott had a copy of the book on his shelves at Orchard House in Concord. Its frequent marginal markings and underlinings suggest that Alcott studied it carefully. Ralph Waldo Emerson not only studied *The General Principles* but also made extensive use of its ideas in his journals and essays, as H. A. Pochmann has amply shown in *German Culture In America.* "All in all," according to Pochmann, "Stallo's *General Principles of the Philosophy of Nature* was the most persistent influence to keep Emerson's mind occupied with German thought."[27] It not only kept Emerson's mind occupied with German thought but changed it about Hegel. The philosophy dominant in the fourth and last period of Emerson's intellectual life was a synthesis of Hegelian idealism and Darwinian evolution.

Prior to reading Stallo's *General Principles* Emerson had little knowledge of or sympathy with Hegel's views. Rather, he was absorbed in the "grandeur" of the efforts of Schelling and Oken to unite natural and moral philosophy. Beginning in November, 1849, Emerson copied extracts from *The General Principles* into his journals as follows:

> The configurations of Nature are more than a symbol, they are the gesticular expression of Nature's inner life. . . . Whatever exists, exists only in virtue of the life of which it is an expression. . . . Every individual existence is but a living history. . . . The development of all forms will be spiral. . . . Matter is only by its relativity. The quantitative qualitative existence of matter is an uninterrupted flight from itself, a never terminating whirl of evanescence. . . . Animals are but foetal forms of man.[28]

These extracts indicate that Emerson was particularly attracted to several leading ideas in *The General Principles* which were noted earlier in this chapter, namely, Stallo's view of nature as manifesting evolutionary process, his doctrine of relativity, and his affirmation of idealism in denying the independent reality of matter.

Further, the alerted reader can detect reflections of Stallo's idealism, and thus indirectly Hegel's, in the following passages from Emerson's essay on "Fate," written in 1852 with overt references to Schelling and Hegel by name and use of Oken's ideas on cell structure:

> Man is not order of nature, sack and sack, belly and members, link in a chain, nor any ignominious baggage; but a stupendous antagonism, a dragging together of the poles of the universe. . . . Relation and connection are not somewhere and sometimes, but everywhere and always. . . . Let us build altars to the Beautiful Necessity, which secures that all is made of one piece; that plaintiff and defendant, friend and enemy, animal and planet, food and eater are of one kind. . . . Why should we be afraid of Nature, which is no other than "philosophy and theology embodied"?[29]

Again, Emerson used some of Stallo's main ideas in his essay on "Poetry and Imagination," particularly its introductory section which was presented in a lecture in 1854. Emerson endorsed Stallo's doctrine of nature as perpetual process in the following passage:

> This magnificent hotel and conveniency we call Nature is not final. First innuendoes, then broad hints, then smart taps are given suggesting that nothing stands still in Nature but death; that the creation is on wheels, in transit, always passing into something else, streaming into something higher; that matter is not what it appears:—that chemistry can blow it all into gas.[30]

Emerson followed Stallo's idealism in asserting that "Identity of law, perfect order in physics, perfect parallelism between the laws of Nature and the laws of thought exist." Again, Emerson used Stallo's doctrine of relativity as well as his idealism in asserting that

> Science was false by being unpoetical. It assumed to explain a reptile or mollusk, and isolated it,—which is hunting for life in graveyards. Reptile or mollusk or man or angel only exist in system, in relation. The metaphysician, the poet, only sees each animal form as an inevitable step in the path of the creating mind.

Stallo's *General Principles* had two important bearings on the direction of Emerson's thought after 1850. First, it led him to adopt some of Hegel's views as his own. With Hegel, and aided by the explanations of Emmanuel Scherb, a German exile living in Concord in 1849, Emerson came to hold the principle, also found in Schelling, that "The Absolute is the union of the Ideal and the Real." Further, Emerson came to firm agreement with Hegel that "Liberty is the spirit's realization of itself." Both of these Hegelian positions were related to what Emerson prized as the "doctrine of immanence" by which "everything is the cause of itself, or stands there for its own, and repeats in its own all other" and also "everything is organic, freedom also, not to add but to grow and unfold." The Young Hegelians in particular, Emerson believed, dared to consummate this doctrine in natural science, politics, ethics, law, and art so that "all the old tottering, shadowy forms" were undercut.[31] A second bearing of Stallo's *General Principles* on the direction of Emerson's thought lay in its doctrine of evolutionary development. This provided Emerson the principles sufficient for his interest in the subject. In 1873 Emerson observed that while Darwin's *Origin of Species* appeared in 1859, a decade earlier Stallo had written that "animals are but foetal forms of man." "The lines of our ancestry," Emerson continued from Stallo, "run into all the phenomena of the material world."[32]

From Stallo's *General Principles* and its Hegelian themes Emerson developed his mature and final view of nature, though he confessed that Hegel's own writings were so hard to read, such "dry bones of thought," that they gave him a headache. Abandoning his earlier dualistic view of nature as reflecting transcendent mind, he adopted a doctrine of immanence. Mind or spirit was seen to be the inner life, the inner principle, of all phenomena. On this basis Hegel, mediated through Stallo, had a particular appeal for Emerson in providing for the "unfolding" of nature from mind through a progressive, evolutionary process. This appeal was reinforced by Emerson's later contacts with W. T. Harris and the St. Louis Philosophical Society.

Champion of Denkfreiheit

In his early years as a practicing lawyer in Cincinnati Stallo soon became a prominent public figure. When Friedrich Hecker, one of the heroes of Germany's unsuccessful republican revolution, visited Cincinnati with his family in 1849, he was greeted at a large mass meeting at which Stallo gave the address of welcome "in warm words and beautiful form."[33] In 1853 the governor of Ohio appointed Stallo to fill a vacancy in the Court of Common Pleas of Hamilton County. Shortly after his appointment the voters elected him to that post, which he held until 1855. Even after he had retired from the bench, he was generally referred to as "Judge Stallo." In the year he became judge of the Court of Common Pleas his special abilities as a lawyer came to public prominence in his defense of a German physician, Dr. Bartholomew Weber, who was accused of poisoning a sick child. Stallo diligently studied medical writings in English, German, French, Italian, and Dutch to show that Weber's prescription agreed with the latest scientific research and was in no way responsible for the child's death. Dr. Weber was completely vindicated and Stallo scored a triumph in court which was for many years a subject of conversation in Cincinnati.

Despite professional demands on his time and energy, Stallo continued his studies in those areas on which he had concentrated in his *General Principles,* namely, political philosophy and philosophy of science. In an address on "Thomas Jefferson" delivered at the Cincinnati *Turnhalle* in 1855, Stallo specifically applied some of the principles of democratic freedom he had first espoused in *The General Principles.* In a closely-reasoned essay against "Materialism" published in the *Atlantis* magazine of 1855, Stallo explored the foundations of scientific knowledge in relation to views of leading European philosophers, including Hegel.

Thomas Jefferson, in Stallo's view, was pre-eminently the philosopher of American freedom. Whereas the American Revolution had been primarily a movement for independence grounded in particular historical events, Jefferson moved the issue from a national question to one of principle. Thus Jefferson put into play "the higher spiritual interests of all peoples." He was the first to put the doctrine of liberalism on general and philosophical grounds so that even today we speak of "Jeffersonian principles" as the foundation of freedom. Though Jefferson, like Franklin and Paine, was called an "unbeliever" and "infidel" he was never, insisted Stallo, a Danton among Jacobins or a Vergniaud among Girondists. Rather, he led the people to build a great republican party.[34]

At a number of points, Stallo observed, Jefferson saw freedom not as a feudal privilege but equally "the heritage of all reason-dedicated men, without distinction of nation or race." Thus Jefferson vigorously opposed the alien and sedition laws of his time. He was unalterably committed to separation of church and state. He was always an exponent of unlimited religious freedom. Hence Germans, Stallo insisted, are especially sympathetic to Jefferson's principles. They have always given first place to *Denkfreiheit,* whereas the English have done little to defend freedom of conscience since Milton, and Rousseau among the French openly espoused a state religion.[35]

Stallo saw little evidence in 1855 that Jefferson's ideas had entered the blood of the American people. On the contrary, the Bill of Rights, he felt, had largely become a dead letter, the republic had in many respects become a police-state, and Maine laws against alcoholic beverages had deprived the individual of freedom in his home and even in his own skin. "Hypocritical fanaticism," said Stallo, is in the saddle. This state of affairs shows that republican government is no instinct but must be learned. Further, it needs grounding in philosophical principles at which Germans are particularly adept. German inquiry and German deeds, said Stallo in a ringing conclusion, can yet spangle the American banner with other stars.[36]

Events in Stallo's life in the years immediately following his address on Jefferson reflected, directly and indirectly, his commitment to the principles of freedom. When a clash occurred on a Sunday in 1856 between beer-drinking Turners on one side and their Know-Nothing, Sabbatarian opponents on the other, Stallo helped restore the peace. Those arrested were acquitted largely through his efforts. In the same year, he shifted his political allegiance. Up to this time he had been a loyal adherent of the party of Jefferson, the Democrats. But in view of the strangle-hold of the "slave-holding aristocracy" on the Democratic party under President Pierce, Stallo called a "halt" and became one of the founders of the Republican party, believing that once the issue of slavery was settled, the rank and file of the party could deal with its nativist and conservative elements. He was a presidential elector in the Fremont campaign, the only political office he was to hold for the next thirty years.

A year or two later Stallo was proposed by some interested fellow-citizens for a place on the bench of the newly created Superior Court of Cincinnati. He was attacked by nativist and puritanical Cincinnati newspapers as a Catholic, a pupil of Jesuits, a former teacher in a Jesuit college, and a servant of the Pope. Instead of ignoring the attack, Stallo answered it and in the process alienated the greatest possible number of voters. He announced that he was no longer a Catholic, had been married as a Protestant, and had his children baptized as Protestants. This was indeed an important shift for a man who a decade earlier had been a Catholic priest teaching in a Catholic college. It paralleled his commitment to Jeffersonian principles of freedom regardless of whether it was their effect.

In 1855 Stallo had married Helene Zimmerman of Cincinnati, who survived him with two of their seven children, Hulda and Edmund. According to one of Stallo's relatives, his home was typical of upper-middle-class European families, a bit of transplanted Europe. The father was dominant and the mother was not permitted to learn English so that the children might be exposed to the German language only in its purest form. If this report is true, Stallo did not practice "freedom for all" within the home and adhered to his earlier views, reinforced by Hegel, on the emancipation of women. But in accordance with Hegel's admonitions on family responsibility, he did pay close attention to his children's education, which was completed in Europe. Though Stallo had many friends in the Cincinnati literary club to which he belonged and in the circle which met every afternoon in Wielert's tavern for beer and conversation—among them were Moncure Conway, August Willich, Pastor Kroll, Dr. Max Lilienthal, Dr. Karl Schneider, and August Recher—his home was open to very few.

Critique of Materialism

Stallo's essay on "Materialism," published the year of his marriage in 1855, was one of the most important of all his writings. Not only was it outstanding for its vivid style and careful argument, but it also marked the transition in his thinking from a speculative philosophy of nature overtly based on Hegel to a critical philosophy of science extensively grounded in reports of laboratory research.

The all-saving doctrine being preached from "the pinnacles of modern scientificality," Stallo wryly observed, is that "There is no mind; only matter and its motion is actual." This cardinal doctrine of materialism involves the central issue of all knowledge, namely, the nature of matter and its relation to mind. While the Christian supernatural God as a metaphysical, incorporeal entity, Stallo allowed, belongs to the past of our knowledge, it is doubtful that we can be satisfied with the current formulas of materialism as found, for example, in Karl Vogt's notion that the brain secretes thought as the liver secretes bile.[37]

The materialist, according to Stallo, rests his case on the Lockean principle that "only what is sensuously perceptible is actual." On this basis it would follow that only what exists in space is actual, and the materialist concludes that where there is no object outside the mind, there can be no representations to copy them and no ideas to summarize sense impressions. For the materialist, objects are independent of mental representations, and everything actual, including the mind, is composed of atoms and molecules in differing groups and motions. But if we ask the materialist what he means by temperature or color he tells us that these are impressions of the object. How does he know that? Through being conscious of it. But his sensuous awareness, Stallo rejoined, goes no farther than a series of particular states of his consciousness, and the object lies entirely in his self, his "I."

If the materialist insists that his experiences are effects of external causes, he must be reminded that he does not know this from sense-experience since all efforts to deduce causality from sense-experience are logically circular. Sense-experience presupposes causality, and to try to find the causal principle by observation, Stallo noted, is like the Bavarian cuirassier who, wanting to fix his plume to his helmet which he could not reach, stood up on a stool. These criticisms of materialism, Stallo allowed, are hardly new. Since Kant, if not Berkeley, it has been widely held that "the world is only our representation and all external things exist only in so far as they are perceived or thought." Hence the actuality of external things and even the materialist's distinction between "inner" and "outer" presuppose a truth independent of and transcending sense experience.[38]

Stallo pressed his case further, noting that the materialist treats matter as though it were a thing in itself in which properties inhere like raisins in a cake. But if we take away specific weight, color, and temperature, absolutely nothing remains of the object. These properties, furthermore, have no inherent condition. Reviving an idea from Hegel which he had used in *General Principles,* Stallo noted that the properties of objects exist only through contrast and relation to others. Without green there is no red. Without resistance there is no power. Without alkali there is no acid. Hence "every so-called material thing is only a complex of relations to other things."[39] Strictly on the basis of observation the materialist has no right to speak of ultimate, irreducible particles such as atoms or molecules. Chemical combinations will not make his case because his atomic theory cannot be squared with recent experimental work on atomic valence.

To prove this point Stallo analyzed the experimental results of Köpp, Laurent, Hunt, and Dana for eight pages, with frequent quotations from scientific journals.

In concluding his case against materialism Stallo further revealed his sympathies with an experience-based idealism. The hunger for truth, he noted, is essential to the progress of scientific inquiry, and in any case problems of the nature of man and man's relation to nature cannot be answered by the materialist since the "world of thought" cannot be determined by Wheatstone's light meter. Hence, Stallo urged,

> One can always read with profit the "Critique of Pure Reason" of old Kant or Hegel's "Phenomenology" if one is bent on getting to substances and forces; in both books there are many things close to our materialists. Their authors were not only metaphysicians but had learned something sound and "positive" as well. At least one should take into account people like Beneke, in their way empiricists, who admittedly do not seek the foundation of things with a telescope or microscope.[40]

A critical look at current materialism and empiricism reveals, Stallo held, that three-fourths of the elements with which they operate are "metaphysical fictions," various "powers" and the like which stand on the same ground as the medieval scholasticism which Lord Bacon once exposed as a galaxy of "Idols." Whereas the medieval scholastic put God and mind on one side and the physical world as a mere aggregate of mechanical powers on the other, contemporary materialists have merely crossed out the first side. "But crossing out," Stallo concluded, "is no very great art."[41]

At several important points in "Materialism" Stallo still held the Hegelian positions he had maintained in *General Principles.* Like Hegel, he remained an idealist in his interpretation of the physical world though he referred this position to Berkeley and Kant. Furthermore, he retained the Hegelian view, developed in the *General Principles,* that the properties of objects are relational, even dialectical, as involving the contrast (*Gegensatz*) of one to another. Again, shortly after alluding to the positivism of Hegel's *Phenomenology,* he attacked metaphysics—the search for an ultimate, fixed substratum behind phenomena—in exactly the same terms as he had in the *General Principles* where he summarized in detail those portions of Hegel's *Phenomenology* which had inspired him.[42] Thus heavily indebted to Hegel, Stallo was groping for a philosophy of science which would faithfully reflect the results of experimental research and at the same time avoid the "metaphysical" errors of materialism. That groping was to lead to his *Concepts and Theories of Modern Physics* twenty-six years later.

Two other events in Stallo's public life prior to the outbreak of the Civil War reveal the direction of his intellectual interests and concerns. At a large memorial service in Cincinnati after the death of Alexander Humboldt in 1859 Stallo gave the main address and revealed his increasing interest in natural science. He compared Humboldt's *Cosmos* to the writings of Kepler, Newton, and Laplace and saw it as outlining man's future world-view. Further, he particularly praised Humboldt for seeing the many-sided relations of things and for grasping phenomena in their historical development, their "becoming."[43] Thus what Stallo had earlier found in Hegel he now preferred to attribute to a hero of natural science, Humboldt. But there was a connection in "the German spirit," Stallo believed, between his earlier and later mentors. Only the people for whom Kant and Hegel philosophized and for whom Schiller and Goethe poetized could produce an Humboldt and recognize the form of its own spirit in his insights.

Stallo's part in his city's tribute to Humboldt was carefully reported by the *Cincinnati Republikaner* whose "responsible editor" was August Willich. It was largely through Stallo's initiative and persuasion that Willich came to Cincinnati to become editor of the *Republikaner* in 1858. Fully aware of Willich's revolutionary past and his "reddest of red" socialist convictions, Stallo apparently was ready to forget his previous criticisms of socialism in the interest of the *Denkfreiheit* he later championed as indispensable to the dialectical growth of society. Thanks to Stallo, Willich's pen and leadership in the labor movement accentuated that dialectic in Ohio as the clouds of the Civil War drew near.

III

PRINCIPLES OF FREEDOM AND PHENOMENALISM IN STALLO'S MATURE YEARS

Stallo's thought in his mature years from the outbreak of the Civil War until his death in 1900 focused on two broad sectors of philosophy with which he had been concerned in his first book on *The General Principles of the Philosophy of Nature*. He remained interested in the problems of political philosophy, particularly the nature of the state and the relation of law to individual freedom in a democracy. In this area his views were sharpened and refined by a number of striking experiences in practical politics and the courts.

At the same time he continued to study and write in his major field of interest, philosophy of nature, which increasingly became what is now called philosophy of science. In this area his thought became less speculative in the grand manner of Hegel and more devoted to analytical interpretation of the findings and the logic of the practicing physicist, chemist, and geometer. Yet his major writing in philosophy of science extended and refined basic ideas he had derived from Hegel and had used in his *General Principles* and essay on "Materialism." Under the impression that he had decisively broken with Hegel, Stallo labeled his mature philosophy "phenomenalism."

Freedom and School Bible-Reading

A number of events in Stallo's life in the 1860's and 1870's provided him opportunities to apply and refine his political views.[1] With the outbreak of the Civil War and the encouragement of his law partner, Robert S. McCook, Stallo led in the call for an all-German regiment from Cincinnati to support the Union. Following his public address at the Turner Hall, enlistments in the regiment were filled within twenty-four hours. Four of the companies were organized by August Willich at the Workingmen's Hall. Others were added, commanded by officers who, like Willich, had had military training in Germany. With the election of McCook as Colonel and Willich as Adjutant, the Ninth Ohio Volunteers—also known as "Dutch Devils" and "Stallo's Turner Regiment"—began training under Willich's command, entirely in the German language. In his address at the Turner Hall Stallo depicted the Civil War as a fight against despotism, a fight of particular interest to "freedom-loving Germans." He was proud that the Ninth Ohio could be a model for many other German troops in "the victory of freedom."[2]

A year later Stallo had a dramatic opportunity to show his stand on freedom of speech. Wendell Phillips had been invited to speak in Cincinnati. A bitter prejudice raged against him for his views on the Union and slavery. When Stallo learned that several others invited to introduce Phillips had withdrawn for fear of mob-violence, he said, "That is enough, gentlemen—I will be there." After the introduction Phillips was assailed with various disagreeable missiles, one of which struck Stallo. Mrs. Stallo happened to be sitting behind a man who had risen to aim a stone at the speaker. She reached over and struck his wrist so hard that he dropped the stone with a cry of pain. Like her husband she was instantly ready to take a firm stand in an hour of crisis.

In 1865, with the question of Negroes' right to vote a burning issue, Stallo came out against their immediate voting as being impractical. It would be impractical, he believed, insofar as it was a right without power, and he held with Hobbes that a right without power could only be an ideal and never a real factor in history. On the other hand, a right enforced by military occupation violated the basic principles of the republic. Our government, Stallo insisted, is not a centrally operated machine but rather an organism whose health depends on its constituent cells. On this basis a vote for all is required, but it must be an inner-based vote not an outer-based order of military authority.[3] Here Stallo was trying to temper his idealistic allegiance to freedom with a sense of the realities of political power to which his work as a lawyer was making him increasingly sensitive. During the impeachment trial of President Johnson, he kept his views to himself except to remark that it was power, not right, which was being sought.

Stallo's most eminent and widely known action on behalf of freedom, particularly *Denkfreiheit*, came when he was attorney for the Cincinnati School Board in the court proceedings of 1869 on Bible-reading in the public schools. Over and beyond the issue of intellectual freedom Stallo had a long-standing, active interest in education itself, in its strength as a public enterprise and in the competence of its staff. For seventeen years he was an examiner of teachers for the public schools and part of that time served on the Board of the University of Cincinnati.

From its establishment in 1829 the Cincinnati public school system had included the Bible in its curriculum as "a means of securing good behavior" and after 1839 had provided that each teacher should begin the day's classes with a reading from the King James Bible, without interpretation or comment. In practice there was also usually the singing of a hymn. Though this procedure had been made optional for students in 1842 at the insistence of the Catholic archbishop, the relation of public to parochial schools had become a burning issue in 1869. Many Catholic parents wanted their children to be educated in public schools. Archbishop Purcell demanded public funds for parochial schools as in England, France, and Canada and publicly denounced a Catholic layman who sought repeal of the regulation requiring that the public schools begin each day with a reading from the Bible.

In these confused circumstances the Cincinnati Board of Education passed a resolution by a vote of 22 to 16 to end daily Bible-reading in the schools under its jurisdiction. The resolution brought forth strong protests from "defenders of the faith." Clergymen encouraged their parishioners in public meetings to protest the offensive resolution. One Protestant minister asked, "Shall the Star Spangled Banner be entwined with the black flag of atheism?" As a result, the "defenders of the faith" took the matter to the Cincinnati Superior Court, seeking a writ of mandamus to reverse the resolution of the Board of Education. Stallo and two other eminent attorneys, one of whom later became governor of the state and the other a member of the United States Supreme Court, defended the Board's resolution in court. Their eminence as lawyers did not, however, prevent their being denounced as consorts of the "irreligious, profane, licentious, drunken, disorderly and criminal elements of our population."[4]

In the proceedings of the Cincinnati Superior Court Stallo used all the arguments at his command to defend the Board's resolution. Going far beyond the precedents of common law, he argued that the United States was in no sense specifically Christian, that church and state were firmly separated in American history, that the Constitution of the United States was based on "skeptical" philosophy derived from French rationalists, that both Jefferson and Franklin were openly pagans, and that major achievements of our civilization in science had to overcome the opposition of religious authorities.[5] Stallo's argument showed his unqualified liberalism, versatility, and great fluency based on omnivorous reading. Sometimes, in fact, he was so fluent as to make the judges impatient as he read to the court passage after passage from Lecky's *History of Rationalism in Europe.* But in spite of Stallo's efforts the court decided, 2 to 1, that the Board's resolution was void because depriving the schools of the Bible would leave them without God. Judge Alphonso Taft was the single dissenter supporting the Board's resolution.

As the Board of Education took its case to the Ohio Supreme Court, Stallo publicly defended its resolution in the interest of electing a favorable majority to the Board. At the Workingmen's Hall of Cincinnati in the spring of 1870 Stallo supplemented the arguments he had presented before the Superior Court. The basic American principle of unlimited freedom of conscience, he observed, was being challenged. If Jews are being compelled to read the New Testament, Catholics to support schools in which a Protestant Bible is read, and free-thinkers to pay for the teaching of stories they regard as nonsense, Americans are in the same position as the Dutch were under Phillip II. "The modern champions of Protestant *Glaubenspolizei,*" said Stallo, "thus lend themselves to plundering and robbing Jews, Catholics, and so-called unbelievers with the help of the state—a republican state in the 19th century!—for the purposes of their Biblical orthodoxy."[6]

Behind the drive for Bible-reading, Stallo believed, was a puritanical fanaticism which would strait-jacket all social life, dictating what language men should speak, what they should drink, and how they should be happy—eliminating anything that might be called "rational human freedom." If it were right for the Protestant Bible to be read in public schools, what answer could there be to the Catholic taxpayer who wanted to introduce the rosary and crucifix? If Catholics or Jews as well as Protestants were to have their way, there would be a full establishment of religion by the state. In this matter the unlimited right of every citizen to freedom of conscience was at stake, and it was the particular duty of Germans, Stallo concluded, to defend this right for all:

> When the German people appear before the judgment seat of history, it will have to answer for many sins against freedom; but all these faults can be proudly expiated by the fact that there is one freedom whose banner the Germans have always held high—*freedom of thought.*[7]

Stallo missed few opportunities to identify the spirit of his native land with the spirit of freedom. Sometimes this required considerable explanation and even complex arguments, as when he gave the main address in Cincinnati's Music Hall celebrating the victory of German arms over France in 1870. Stallo saw the victory as a triumph of freedom over despotism. Though the war may have seemed like a struggle between monarchy and a nation traditionally republican, France was no longer a republic. For Germans, however, freedom as bound with order was an innate tendency, not merely something on paper. For them self-determination was an instinct. Stallo concluded with the ringing words: "*Es lebe Deutschland! Es lebe Freiheit!*"[8]

Two years later the Supreme Court of Ohio vindicated

Stallo's stand for freedom of conscience in regard to required Bible-reading in the public schools. In an historic decision subsequently quoted by the majority of the U.S. Supreme Court in 1963, the Ohio Supreme Court reversed the decision of the lower court and upheld the authority of the Board of Education to eliminate daily Bible-reading. Though the Ohio Supreme Court did not hold that Bible-reading *must* be excluded from public schools as unconstitutional, the language of its decision suggested that required reading was inconsistent with the principle of separation of church and state. In words that Stallo himself might have used, the Ohio Supreme Court said that "legal Christianity is a solecism." United with government, religion is merest superstition; and united with religion, government becomes despotic. The only fair method, the court argued, is for each sect to give its own instruction outside public schools. Such a separation of government and religion, the court observed, is rooted in the principles of James Madison who had more to do with the framing of the Constitution than any other man and firmly held that a union of religion and government "is injurious to both."[9]

Shortly before the Ohio Supreme Court's decision on Bible-reading and during the last years of President Grant's first term in office Stallo broke with the Republican party, which he had helped to establish. He could no longer tolerate the open, flaunting corruption of the Grant administration and identified himself with the reform movement. He would not permit himself to be elected a delegate to the "Liberal Republican" convention which met at Cincinnati in 1872 because he no longer regarded himself a Republican, liberal or otherwise. He did, however, attend and address the "Reform Convention" which gathered in the Cincinnati Workingmen's Hall at the same time the Liberal Republicans were meeting. In spite of his detachment from the

Liberal Republicans he had the chairman of their convention, Karl Schurz, and a delegate from Cleveland as guests in his home.

Stallo and members of the Reform Convention hoped to influence the Liberal Republicans to adopt a platform of fundamental reform and nominate Charles Francis Adams as their candidate for president. With Adams lacking the nomination by 2½ votes, Schurz allowed the Liberal Republican convention to adjourn. The next day, apparently after some political trading in night caucuses, Horace Greeley was nominated instead of Adams and the Missouri platform of fundamental reform was scuttled. Greeley and his supporters were distrusted and disliked by those meeting at the Workingmen's Hall. With news of Greeley's nomination the Reform Convention adjourned *sine die*. In the next election Schurz went to the U.S. Senate.

The Liberal Republican convention marked the beginning of a deep estrangement between Stallo and Schurz. Though Stallo made a move to heal the breach, the estrangement became complete in 1876 when Schurz, who had declared himself against the nomination of Hayes, met with Hayes in an obscure hotel in Ohio's capital and shortly thereafter went "on the stump" in his support. Thence for Stallo Schurz was "erased from the book of the living." In all things, even in politics, according to his friend and biographer, Stallo was a "strict, uncompromising moralist."

Stallo actively campaigned in 1876 for Tilden as "the representative of reform" and condemned the Republican party for wasting the nation's resources, robbing the laboring man, and running the country for the benefit of a few "private individuals and corporations."[10] His political activity led one biographer to conclude that he was always and everywhere the tribune of the people: "He was the champion of the people against those who would plunder them through greedy monopolies, the champion of right against power, the champion of truth against hypocritical deception and lies."

Government and Political Dialectic

The fullest and most connected expression of Stallo's political philosophy in his mature years appeared with his booklet on *State Creeds and Their Modern Apostles,* the greater part of which was a lecture he had delivered in 1870 at the Rev. Mr. Vicker's Church in Cincinnati in answer to many sermons advocating the reading of the Bible and the singing of hymns in public schools. The principles at stake in this issue were again brought into prominence in 1872 by a convention of the Christian Associationist party in Cincinnati. The Christian Associationists aimed to secure an amendment to the federal constitution acknowledging "God as the author of our nation's existence and the source of its authority, Jesus Christ as its ruler, and the Bible as the fountain of its laws and supreme rule of its conduct."[11] Stallo devoted the first third of *State Creeds* to answering the Christian Associationists.

In the foreground of Stallo's views in *State Creeds* were the experiences he had had in public life since 1860 with the Ninth Ohio Volunteers, the issue of Negro suffrage, the Bible-reading case in the Superior Court of Cincinnati, and the appearance of gross corruption in the Grant administration. In the background of his views, as we shall see, was a philosophy of history, government, and freedom derived from Hegel and essentially the same as he had espoused in *The General Principles of the Philosophy of Nature* of 1848.

As one might expect, Stallo saw the Christian Associationist movement as threatening "to subvert the most precious of our liberties, the liberty of conscience." Hence it was a movement which could not be ignored or passed off lightly. The difficulties in its plan to Christianize America seemed obvious. "What God, or whose God, is to be acknowledged? What Jesus is to be 'ruler'? The man Jesus or the stern Christ-God? What part of the Bible is to be enforced? The teaching of the patriarchs on polygamy or the apostles on monogamy?"[12] The proposed constitutional amendment, moreover, would put the actual citizenship of every Jew and non-Christian in jeopardy. The Christian Associationists would have America revert to that stage of civilization where "rule of law is not yet discriminated from a rule of religion" and their willingness to use the "sword of the state" to "pull down walls of sin and Satan" would lead to the practices of the Spanish Inquisition.

Those who most ardently defended Bible-reading in public schools and state-enforced observance of the Sabbath saw foreigners and skeptics, usually Germans, as threatening the Christian foundations of the republic. They wanted "an American Sabbath for American people, and a free passport out of the country for all who will not abide by it." "A set of reckless men, native and foreign, chiefly of skeptical or atheistic views," one ardent Sabbatarian charged, "are trying to abolish the American Sunday and make the first day of the week a great, noisy, European holiday." In answer to such views Stallo reminded his audience that the Reverend Peter Muhlenberg and his three hundred German parishioners concluded their worship one Sunday in 1776 by marching off to join General Washington. Stallo also noted that the cemeteries of the Civil War were full of Sabbath-breakers, including "the braves of the Ninth Ohio and Thirty-second Indiana [German] regiments, which, to my certain knowledge, had not a hundred orthodox, Sabbath-observing Protestants in their ranks."[13] By their side the graves of native Americans, Protestants as well as Catholics, testified that freedom of thought and conscience was genuinely American and not a crazy notion of outcast European anarchists.

Further, Stallo reminded those who would unite state and religion to compel observance of the Sabbath and Bible-reading in schools that practically and directly the American government is a government of majorities through the ballot box. Revealing his sense of political realities acquired in practical politics, Stallo said:

> This ballot box stands neither for the absolute truth nor the absolute right; it stands for nothing more and nothing less than the momentary will of those who have the power—of the majority of the people. Ballots are the instruments by which we ascertain, not what is true, nor what is right, but what is the will of those who can, if necessary, enforce that will with the bludgeon and rifle. . . . The ballot is simply a vicarious shillelah.[14]

In a republic men submit to the majority and trust to the future to vindicate right and reason. Rather than fighting battles and breaking heads they resort to counting heads. Hence "voting is a virtual, symbolical row" and "suffrage is a sort of stenographic abbreviation of physical conflict," a trial of strength among conflicting elements of the political community. In view of this characteristic of public power, those who would unite government and religion put religion in a very precarious position. Their theory implies that "there is a religious council or synod held at the polls at every election," but they forget that the Turners' and Workingmen's Halls, not to mention countless lager beer saloons, must furnish their contingent to the "religious council or Synod" on voting days. Further, there are many members of the Roman Catholic Church among the voters, and some day they may get control of the government in a perfectly natural way. Would those ardent Protestants who would unite government and religion want religious observances enforced by Roman Catholics? Could they expect Jews elected to public office to favor laws enforcing "the pure doctrine and divine truths of the Gospel of Jesus Christ"? These possible consequences, in Stallo's view, were enough to show the undesirability of a state religion in terms of the intentions of its most vocal defenders.

Though Stallo could affirm that immediately and practically the state "is as godless as a steam engine" and "there is nothing peculiarly divine in the materials and methods out of which and by which the agencies we call civil government are created," he would not be understood as advocating the doctrine that might is right. He noted that in spite of accusations to the contrary he was no materialist:

> I am not of those who represent the universe as a fraction with a material, mechanical numerator and a spiritual denominator, and then cancel the latter. I believe there is something more than mechanics in the structure and life of this world. I have never believed and do not now believe that the course of history can be accounted for on the principles of hydraulics, or that the operations even of the clerical mind can be made plain and intelligible by a reference to the lever and screw. I have no hope that the real nature of things will ever be discovered by the aid of a microscope, or that a chemist will succeed in distilling their true essence from a retort.[15]

Further, Stallo allowed that there was a sense in which it would be true to say that there is "a divinity that shapes the ends" of civil government as well as all other things. The mastery of force is indirectly a conquest of reason in the fact that there is a law of compensation in the order of the universe whereby partial and momentary wrongs are integrated into a total right and fractional errors are integrated into grand truths. This is illustrated in the constancy of death rates and in the way in which each vote of an Irishman, German, native American, laborer, or capitalist taken singly stands for prejudice, selfish interest, or wrong.

> But take the whole result, and it looks very much like the regular outcome of a dialectical process—like the deliberate result of a process of reasoning. Partial wrongs and obliquities square themselves into universal right, special evils coalesce into general good, particular errors are integrated into collective truth. And the successive generations are nothing but terms in a series before which Eternal Reason places its integral sign.[16]

Hence Stallo could further say that "the very language we inherit and speak on unwitting compulsion, the institutions and other surroundings under which we are born and live, are so many coercives into truth and right." In this sense there is reason in human law, and there is right in the practical administration of government.

In thus rejecting materialism and affirming Eternal Reason in the dialectic process of history and social life, Stallo retained his commitment to central tenets of Hegel's philosophy which he had espoused more than two decades earlier in *The General Principles of the Philosophy of Nature.* He remained an Hegelian idealist and went to Hegel's views for his underlying perspective and interpretation of political life, relating that interpretation to what he had learned about the practical realities of political power and conflict.

On this basis and as a corollary of it he saw intellectual freedom not as a result of some transcendent, immutable "natural law" which he could only treat with skepticism,[17] but as a requirement for the dialectical growth and development of society. Just as Hegel had called for the separation of church and state, so did Stallo on the similar ground that truth and right are dialectically developing wholes whose parts must maintain their particularity and uniqueness if there is to be movement through tension. Applying this view to the relation of church and state, Stallo wrote:

> Government can protect and help to maintain religion, as well as everything else which constitutes the life of the soul, only in one way—by guarding the freedom of its development. Whoever asks it to do more is seeking to convert it into an abominable engine of tyranny and oppression.[18]

Stallo was particularly pleased when he found additional support for his views on the relation of religion to government in an important precedent in constitutional history of which he had not known when he defended the Board of Education in the Superior Court of Cincinnati. He was able to answer from a strong precedent in American history those who asserted that government in the United States should enforce religion because "we are, by all our early history, the customs of our people and their laws, a Christian, as distinguished from Jewish, Mohammedan, or Romish people." In Stallo's words:

> On the 4th of November, 1796, when George Washington was in the presidential chair, and the other fathers of the Republic were in the Senate, the United States of America concluded a treaty of peace and friendship with the Bey and subjects of Tripoli, of Barbary. In this treaty there is a remarkable article, the eleventh. . . . That article reads: "*As the government of the United States is not IN ANY sense founded on the Christian religion*—as it has in itself no character of enmity against the laws, religion, or tranquillity of Mussulmen—and as the said States never have entered into any war or act of hostility against any Mohammedan nation, it is declared by the parties, that no pretext arising from religious opinions shall ever produce an interruption of the harmony existing between the two countries.[19]

Since a treaty is second only to the Constitution itself in legal force, Stallo concluded that the United States is, "or at least ought to be, *not a Christian,* but a *free* people."

Critique of Materialism

While Stallo was active in law and politics in the decade after the Civil War, he was devoting his spare time and energy to refining the philosophy of science he had first set forth in *The General Principles of the Philosophy of Nature* and further developed in the essay of 1855 on "Materialism." His Cincinnati home at 429 Resor Avenue in Clifton was more than the "castle" to which he could retire with his close-knit family and a few select friends for Sunday evening conversation and music. It was also his workshop. His library and study—with busts of Goethe and Humboldt and portraits of Socrates, Aristotle, Shakespeare, Schiller, Newton, Bacon, Darwin, Helmholtz, Mill, Jefferson, and Paine—contained 5,000 volumes in science and philosophy. Stallo was especially proud of his volume of Kepler's astronomical writings from 1609 to 1627. Its margins were filled with notes which Stallo had determined to be Kepler's own handwriting. In this atmosphere of learning and research Stallo occasionally received his visitors and would converse with them in English, German, or French as they might prefer.

The result of his continued study and research was the publication of essays on the mechanical theory and the atomic constitution of matter in the *Popular Science Monthly* of 1873 and 1874. These essays, with revisions, became chapters seven and eleven of *The Concepts and Theories of Modern Physics,* first published as part of the International Scientific Series in 1881 by D. Appleton and Co. in the United States and Kegan Paul in England. The series was an eminent one containing Bagehot's *Physics and*

Politics, Spencer's *Sociology*, Draper's *History of the Conflict Between Religion and Science*, and T. H. Huxley's volume on *The Crayfish*. Soon after the first American edition of *Concepts and Theories* there appeared a French translation which was reprinted three times. A second edition of *Concepts and Theories* in English appeared in 1884 and was reissued in 1888 and 1890. At the instigation of Ernst Mach, *Concepts and Theories* was translated into German by Hans Kleinpeter and published in 1901 with a second edition in 1911. The existence of Italian, Spanish, and Russian translations mentioned by two of Stallo's biographers has not been clearly established.[20] In 1960 the Harvard University Press reissued the 1888 version of *Concepts and Theories* as a "landmark of intellectual history" in its John Harvard Library Series, with an introduction by the late Professor P. W. Bridgman, a Nobel Prize winner.

In an effort to make the scope and purpose of *Concepts and Theories* unmistakable—an effort not always successful with its reviewers—Stallo's first words in the book described it as "a contribution, not to physics, nor, certainly, to metaphysics, but to the theory of cognition." He was concerned with the relation of the physical sciences to the general progress of human knowledge and particularly with reformulating and refining the "problems of cognition" implicit in those sciences.[21] Pursuant to this end, Stallo's chapters fall into two main groups, not designated as such but each having a common aim. The first eight chapters are an internal criticism of the atomo-mechanical view of nature showing how proponents of that view cannot logically square it with widely-accepted conclusions and findings in physics and chemistry. The last nine chapters variously illustrate from the physical sciences and geometry four main "metaphysical errors" derived from Stallo's theory of cognition in the chapter entitled "The Relation of Thoughts to Things."

A clear-cut illustration of Stallo's main theme in his first eight chapters is found in his discussion of the indestructibility and impenetrability of matter in relation to the atomic theory. He saw that theory as a corollary of the mechanical view of nature which had been accepted as axiomatic by almost all physicists since Newton and which asserted that the two ultimates of physical analysis, mass and motion, are disparate, with mass being indifferent to motion and constant. As a corollary, matter is viewed as consisting of elementary units of mass, atoms, which are equal, absolutely hard and inelastic, absolutely inert and purely passive.[22]

Such an "atomo-mechanical view of nature," Stallo observed, had a long history going back to the Greeks, being refined by Newton and Descartes, and finding warm endorsement in his own day by Helmholtz and Clerk-Maxwell. Some of Stallo's contemporaries, moreover, were sure that mechanical principles should be extended into physiology and the organic realm. Stallo wanted to show that the "atomo-mechanical view of nature" did not deserve to be taken as "axiomatic" by most of his contemporaries because it could not be adequately and logically squared with data of observation and experiment. He readily allowed that the atomic theory was useful in chemistry as an expository device and that it had enabled the chemist to trace combinations of elements and anticipate experiment. But those who took this theory and its parent, the mechanical view of nature, as axiomatic went further. They were embracing a metaphysics, a theory of the ultimate stuff and substance of all things whatsoever. Having thought they were beyond the medieval search for "real essences," they were themselves committed to that search. "The general principles of the atomo-mechanical theory, which is said to be the basis of modern physics," said Stallo, "are substantially identical with the cardinal doctrines of ontological metaphysics." Through an internal criticism of the atomo-mechanical theory Stallo wanted "to eliminate from science its latent metaphysical elements," foster experimentation, and support "the great endeavor of scientific research to gain a sure foothold on solid empirical ground, where the real data of experience may be reduced without ontological prepossessions.[23]

Dealing with the indestructibility of matter, Stallo observed that the atomists appeal to experience to show the constancy of mass as in the burning of a pound of carbon. When the pound of carbon is burned, scales show the continued existence of the pound in the products of combustion from which the original weight may be recovered. But what happens, Stallo asked, when the pound of carbon is moved to a mountain top? Relatively its weight is the same in comparison with the scale's balance, but the "absolute weight" has changed as shown if a pendulum is used instead of a pair of scales. The pendulum swings more slowly on the mountain top. This shows that the constancy on which the indestructibility of matter is based is the constancy of a relation and that the weight of a body "is not the equivalent, or rather presentation, of an absolute substantive entity in one of the bodies (the body weighed), but the mere expression of a relation between two bodies mutually attracting each other." Thus masses find their true measure in the persistence of the action of forces, and this persistence is in no sense explained or accounted for, Stallo held, by the atomic theory. The hypothesis of that persistence in the atom throws no light on the conglomerate mass. Breaking a magnet into fragments and showing that each fragment has magnetic polarity, Stallo argues, is no explanation of magnetism. "A phenomenon is not explained by being dwarfed. A fact is not transformed into a theory by being looked at through an inverted telescope." [24]

Similarly, Stallo tried to show that the supposed impenetrability of matter involved in the atomic theory is groundless. The common view that "two bodies cannot occupy the same space," Stallo observed, not only implies that space is an absolute, objective entity but also that there is an absolute limit to the compressibility of all matter whatsoever. Does experience authorize such a limit? Assuredly not, Stallo answered. There may be practical limits to compression by mechanical means, but fluids may be further reduced by mixing as in the case of sulphuric acid and water. Further, the diffusion of gases provides dramatic testimony against the atomists' view of matter's impenetrability:

> Whenever two or more gases which do not act upon each other chemically are introduced into a given space, each gas diffuses itself in this space as though it were alone present there; or, as Dalton, the reputed father of the modern atomic theory, expresses it, "Gases are mutually passive, and pass into each other as into vacua."[25]

On such grounds as these Stallo concluded that the impenetrability of matter as conceived by the atomists is not "a datum of experience." He granted that the atomic theory was an hypothesis. But so were all physical theories, and the acceptance of any hypothesis as true depends on its meeting four criteria: the hypothesis must simplify the data of experience, the explanatory phenomenon must itself be a datum of experience and not some occult quality, the hypothesis must not contradict itself or established laws of nature, and the hypothesis must admit of deductive inferences.[26] In relation to such criteria Stallo found the atomic theory to be grossly defective as science. It was a view of nature to be regarded as "ontological metaphysics."

Physics and Phenomenalism

As suggested in the main aim laid down for *The Concepts and Theories of Modern Physics,* Stallo believed that the mistakes and confusions in the "atomo-mechanical view of nature" might be avoided by an adequate theory of cognition, a proper view of what knowledge amounted to, and an adequate grasp of the vehicles of knowledge, concepts. In broad terms Stallo was willing to define a concept with Sir William Hamilton as "the cognition of the general character, point or points in which a plurality of objects coincide." But such a view required further analysis and refinement which Stallo gave in three points, the core of his theory of cognition which he labeled "irrefragable truths . . . not clearly apprehended until very recent times":

> 1. Thought deals, not with things as they are, or are supposed to be, in themselves, but with our mental representations of them. Its elements are, not pure objects, but their intellectual counterparts. What is present in the mind in the act of thought is never a thing, but always a state of consciousness. However much, and in whatever sense, it may be contended that the intellect and its object are both real and distinct entities, it can not for a moment be denied that the object, of which the intellect has cognizance, is a synthesis of objective and subjective elements, and is thus primarily, in the very act of its apprehension and to the full extent of its cognizable existence, affected by the determinations of the cognizing faculty. Whenever, therefore, we speak of a thing, or a property of a thing, it must be understood that we mean a product of the two factors neither of which is capable of being apprehended by itself. In this sense all knowledge is said to be relative.
>
> 2. Objects are known only through their relations to other objects. They have, and can have, no properties, and their concepts can include no attributes, save these relations, or rather, our mental representations of them. Indeed, an object can not be known or conceived otherwise than as a complex of such relations. In mathematical phrase: things and their properties are known only as functions of other things and prop-

erties. In this sense, also relativity is a necessary predicate of all objects of cognition.

3. A particular operation of thought never involves the entire complement of the known or knowable properties of a given object, but only such of them as belong to a definite class of relations. In mechanics, for instance, a body is considered simply as a mass of determinate weight and volume (and in some cases figure), without reference to its other physical or chemical properties. In like manner each of the several departments of knowledge affects a classification of objects upon its own peculiar principles, thereby giving rise to different series of concepts in which each concept represents that attribute or group of attributes—that aspect of the object—which it is necessary, in view of the question in hand, to bring into view. Our thoughts of things are thus, in the language of Leibnitz, adopted by Sir William Hamilton, and after him by Herbert Spencer, *symbolical,* not (or, at least, not only) because a complete mental representation of the properties of an object is precluded by their number and the incapacity of the mind to hold them in simultaneous grasp, but because many (and in most cases the greater part) of them are irrelevant to the mental operation in progress.[27]

A disregard of some or all of the three "irrefragable truths" in this theory of cognition would lead, Stallo held, directly into "metaphysical or ontological speculation," the attempt to deduce the nature of things from concepts of them. Here thought is misled by language. Through the study of comparative linguistics Stallo had become sensitively aware of the unity of thought and language and also the way metaphors of ordinary speech mislead scientific inference. To be sure, metaphors are inseparable from language, but in science they must be controlled by more precisely observed correspondences, relations of structure, and functional equivalence.[28]

The most common forms of "metaphysical speculation"

which result from disregarding the "irrefragable truths" of cognition are four: the search for things to correspond with concepts; the assumption that the more general concepts and realities pre-exist to the less general; the assumption that the order of the genesis of concepts is identical with the order of things; and the belief that things themselves exist independently of and prior to their relations.[29] Stallo called these forms of speculation the four basic "metaphysical errors" and devoted most of his last nine chapters in *Concepts and Theories* to illustrating them in physical science and geometry.

Stallo found a particularly vivid illustration of the fourth metaphysical error in the classical treatment of space and motion. He quoted the references of Descartes and Leibniz to an "absolutely immovable space" and an "absolutely veritable motion of bodies." He found Newton affirming that "absolute space, in its nature without relation to anything external, always remains similar and immovable; of this (absolute space) relative space is any movable measure or dimension which is sensibly defined by its place in reference to bodies, and is vulgarly taken for immovable space." Further, Stallo found Euler postulating an "absolute immovable space" to explain motion and Neumann arguing that the reality of motion requires a rigid body unchangeable in its position in space.[30]

All such views, Stallo held, involve the "metaphysical error" of believing that things themselves exist independently of and prior to their relations. But the second main principle of his theory of cognition was amply affirmed in Helmholtz's research on vision. "Every property or quality of a thing," said Stallo quoting Helmholtz, "is in reality nothing but its capability of producing certain effects on other things." Thus the solubility of a substance is its behavior toward water; its weight is its attraction to the earth; its color is its action on the eye. A property or quality can never depend on one agent alone. The notion of properties belonging to a thing absolutely is a self-contradiction. On such grounds as these Stallo concluded that the reality of all knowable objects consists in their mutual relations, and the "relativity of all objective reality" is manifest in the law of causality, the conservation of energy, Newton's first and third laws of motion, and many other basic principles of physics. But negatively this meant for Stallo that

> There is no absolute material quality, no absolute material substance, no absolute physical unit, no absolutely simple physical entity, no absolute physical constant, no absolute standard, either of quantity or quality, no absolute motion, no absolute rest, no absolute time, no absolute space.[31]

The "relativity of all objective reality," Stallo was aware, required a redefinition of the relation between what is Real and what is Phenomenal. In the old metaphysical doctrine they were seen as distinct from each other, exact opposites. But in Stallo's view, which he was willing to call "phenomenalism," and in relation to the relativity of all things, the old metaphysical distinction could no longer hold. "There is no physical reality," Stallo held, "which is not phenomenal. The only test of physical reality is sensible experience." The testimony of the senses is conflicting only because the momentary deliverance of each sense is incomplete and requires other deliverances of the same sense or of other senses as when a mirage is found to be a mirage by other observable facts in the refraction of light. Hence Stallo concluded that what is "apparent," in contrast to what is "real," is merely a partial deliverance of sense mistaken for the whole deliverance because the senses are not fully and precisely interrogated and "their whole story is not heard."[32]

Stallo devoted the last chapters of *Concepts and Theories*

to non-Euclidean geometry and cosmological speculations. Utilizing the first of his three principles of cognition he concluded that the propositions of geometry must include both "an element of intuition (as a part of sensation) and an element of arbitrary intellectual determination which is called definition." Because the non-Euclidean geometers who wrote of a fourth dimension of space had neglected the element of intuition, they were as much guilty of the metaphysical error of reifying concepts as were the physicists who used the atomo-mechanical theory. "The hypostasis of space by the mathematicians," Stallo held, "is a strict analogue of the hypostasis of mass and motion by the physicists."[33] In regard to cosmology—conclusions about the universe as a whole—Stallo was especially concerned that the logical implications of the relativity of all physical existences be clearly understood. The second law of thermodynamics, he warned, could not be used to draw conclusions about the beginning or end of the whole universe because that law, like every physical law, is a mode of interaction between particular objects. Since the physical universe as a whole is not a distinct body and there are no bodies outside it with which it could interact, no physical law is applicable to it. On this basis all cosmological speculations about "the origin of the universe as an absolute whole, in the light of physical or dynamical laws, are fundamentally absurd."[34]

In the concluding chapter of *Concepts and Theories* Stallo related his criticisms of the atomo-mechanical theory to his third principle of cognition and to the progress of scientific knowledge as follows:

> All discursive reasoning depends upon the formation of concepts, upon the intellectual segregation and grouping of attributes—in other words, upon the consideration of phenomena under particular aspects. In this sense the steps to scientific as well as other knowledge consists in a series of logical fictions

which are as legitimate as they are indispensable in the operations of thought, but whose relations to the phenomena whereof they are the partial and not infrequently merely symbolical representations must never be lost sight of.[35]

Indebtedness to Hegel

Unlike Stallo's first book, *The General Principles* of 1848, *Concepts and Theories* was a considerable success. It was part of an eminent scientific series, it went through several printings and translations, and it was increasingly recognized in Stallo's lifetime as an important contribution to philosophy of science.

The first reviews of *Concepts and Theories* were mixed and established it as a controversial volume. The editor of *Popular Science Monthly* called it "a profound book, . . . one of the ablest in the series to which it has been contributed." A. W. Reinhold commended it highly in a review in a London journal, *Academy*. On the basis of articles which became two chapters of *Concepts and Theories,* William Torrey Harris of St. Louis named Stallo "the ablest writer of our time" in philosophy of science.[36] On the other side, reviewers of the *Critic* and *Nation* considered the main conclusions of *Concepts and Theories* to be unsound and did not admire its analysis. P. G. Tait in *Nature* found it "a curious work," eminently readable and based on wide study but dangerous to scientific progress because it equally upset "the most irrefragable truth and the most arrant nonsense." Some reviewers so widely misunderstood the book's central purpose and theme that Stallo felt compelled to answer them pointedly in a special introduction to the second edition of 1888 and an article on "Speculative Science" in the *Popular Science Monthly*.[37]

With the passage of time, however, *Concepts and The-*

ories was increasingly appreciated for what it aimed to be, namely, a contribution to "theory of cognition"—philosophy of science as it would be called today—and a trenchant criticism of the unwarranted metaphysical elements in physical science. Shortly after Stallo's death it was called "the profoundest and most original work in philosophy of science that has appeared in this country—a work which is on a par with anything that has been produced in Europe."[38] In Europe, particularly in Germany, its importance was appreciated largely through the attention of Ernst Mach, eminent physicist and father of the recently prominent scientific philosophy called "logical positivism" or "logical empiricism" developed by Otto Neurath, Moritz Schlick, Philip Frank, and others in the Vienna Circle, an outgrowth of the *Machverein*.[39]

Mach's attention was called to *Concepts and Theories* by a reference to it in Bertrand Russell's *Foundations of Geometry* (1897). Mach became very interested in the book and author whose "scientific aims so closely approximated" his own. He began a correspondence with Stallo, took steps to secure a German translation of *Concepts and Theories*, and wrote a special forward to the German edition of 1901. Though Mach could not agree with Stallo's criticism of non-Euclidean geometry, he warmly endorsed the effort "to eliminate from science the latent metaphysical elements" and saw *Concepts and Theories* as a valuable and welcome complement to his own writings. He shared its rejection of the mechanical-atomistic theory "as a world-view," agreed with its understanding of physical concepts as relations, and concurred in its rejection of pronouncements on the "world as a whole." "It would have been encouraging and helpful to me when I began my critical works in the mid-sixties," wrote Mach, "to have known of the kindred efforts of such a colleague as Stallo."[40]

Some subsequent American references to *Concepts and Theories* were similarly favorable though not so penetrating in relation to the details of Stallo's thought. In the course of his "education" Henry Adams received a copy of *Concepts and Theories* from Langley of the Smithsonian Institute shortly before the turn of the century. It "had been treated for a dozen years," Adams observed, "with the conspiracy of silence such as inevitably meets every revolutionary work that upsets the stock and machinery of instruction." Later Adams "would see in such parts of the 'Grammar [of Science' by Karl Pearson] as he could understand, little more than an enlargement of Stallo's book, already twenty years old."[41] In a special introduction written in 1913 for Poincaré's *Foundations of Science,* Josiah Royce of Harvard recalled the shock given to scientific orthodoxy by Stallo's *Concepts and Theories* on its first appearance. It came, however, to be accepted as a valuable contribution to the philosophy of science. Royce observed:

> There can be no doubt that, at the present moment, if his book were to appear for the first time, nobody would attempt to discredit the work merely on account of its disposition to be agnostic regarding the objective reality of the concepts of the kinetic theory of gases, or on account of its call for a logical rearrangement of the fundamental concepts of the theory of energy.[42]

Some interpreters of Stallo's *Concepts and Theories* have suggested its continuity with *The General Principles* of 1848 which overtly followed Hegel in its interpretation of nature. Thus Mach found in *Concepts and Theories* "traces" of Stallo's earlier "Hegelian lines." Others have suggested that Stallo's first book, like David Hume's, would come to be regarded as "the true and original expression of his views."[43] But these suggestions of the Hegelian element in *Concepts and Theories* have not been specifically and pointedly developed. Most discussions of Stallo's thought—including recent ones by Bridgman and Drake[44]—have accepted at face value his claim that the major themes of *Concepts and Theories* break sharply with the Hegelian principles found in his first book. In the "Preface" to *Concepts and Theories* Stallo wrote:

> This treatise is in no sense a further exposition of the doctrines of a book (*The Philosophy of Nature,* Boston, Crosby and Nichols, 1848) which I published more than a third of a century ago. That book was written while I was under the spell of Hegel's ontological reveries—at a time when I was barely of age and still seriously affected with the metaphysical malady which seems to be one of the unavoidable disorders of intellectual infancy. The labor expended in writing it was not, perhaps, wholly wasted, and there are things in it of which I am not ashamed, even at this day; but I sincerely regret its publication, which is in some degree atoned for, I hope, by the contents of the present volume.[45]

Further, in discussing "metaphysical errors" in *Concepts and Theories,* Stallo dismissed Hegel's "pure being" as merely a reified *summum genus,* "the specter of the copula between an extinct subject and a departed predicate. It is a sign of predication which 'lags superfluous on the stage' after both the predicate and that whereof it was predicated have disappeared."[46]

In spite of Stallo's claim to have broken with Hegel's philosophy, the three main points in his theory of cognition in *Concepts and Theories* may readily be identified with Hegelian principles he espoused in *The General Principles.* The theory of cognition, as noted earlier in this chapter, is fundamental in *Concepts and Theories.* It is the basis of the metaphysical errors which Stallo illustrates in detail in the last eight chapters of the book. Stallo called its three points "irrefragable truths . . . not clearly apprehended until very recent times." "Irrefragable" as they may have been to Stallo, they were not universally accepted in his day as shown in his criticism of John Stuart Mill. And in spite of the reference to "very recent times," the true source of Stallo's theory of cognition must be found in Hegel.

The first point in Stallo's theory of cognition asserted that thought deals not with things themselves but "states of consciousness" and every object of cognition is a synthesis of subjective and objective elements so "all knowledge is relative to the cognizing faculty." Stallo had said substantially the same thing in *The General Principles* where, following Hegel's *Phenomenology*, he saw perception and observation as involving an interchange between the conscious mind and seemingly external objects, an interchange which at once reveals the mental character of those objects and the reality of consciousness in and through them. This aspect of Stallo's theory of cognition has been criticized as a form of "psychologism," *i.e.*, the reduction of the objects of physical knowledge to "states of consciousness."[47] But Stallo attempted to avoid this reduction by insisting that objects *of cognition* have both subjective and objective elements. What objects *in themselves* might be he did not know and believed that in principle no one could know. His reference to "objective elements" pointedly suggests that he wanted to avoid a simple psychological or subjective idealism like that of Berkeley. No more than Hegel did he believe that the inescapable relativity of objects to consciousness in knowledge directly makes them states of the knower's consciousness.

The second main point in Stallo's theory of cognition asserted that objects are known through their relations and have no attributes except through their relations. In *Concepts and Theories* Stallo linked this point with Helmholtz's theory of vision, but in 1848 he derived it from Hegel's view that the "sense certainty" of objects perceived as "here" or "now" involves grasping them as relationships. As Stallo put it, "Objects are thoroughly relative; their being is a complex of relations." The third main point in Stallo's theory of cognition held that thought deals only with a selected class of relations, so our thought of things is always "symbolical." *Concepts and Theories* identified this point with views of Leibniz and Sir William Hamilton, but in *The Phenomenology*, which Stallo summarized in 1848, Hegel had maintained that abstractions ("things of the intellect") are indispensable to perception.[48] Thus Stallo's break with Hegel in *Concepts and Theories* was more apparent than real. In the keystone of his mature philosophy of science, his theory of cognition, Stallo remained an Hegelian.

The Hegelian roots of Stallo's philosophy of science suggest an interesting irony in the history of ideas. In condemning metaphysics, *i.e.*, conclusions without specific warrant in observation or experiment, and in viewing scientific concepts as "symbolical," Stallo's phenomenalism anticipated philosophies of experience—forms of empiricism such as experimentalism, logical positivism, and operationalism—which have become increasingly prominent in America since the time of William James. This anticipation is confirmed in the warm endorsement of Stallo's major points in *Concepts and Theories* by Ernst Mach, the spiritual father of recent scientific empiricism. Yet the major and essential elements of Stallo's theory of cognition, as already shown, were rooted in ideas of the one philosopher most empiricists have regarded as their arch-enemy, Hegel.

Last Years and Letters to Mach

While Stallo was first at work on *Concepts and Theories of Modern Physics* he had actively supported the Democratic party, as noted earlier, in the Tilden campaign against

Hayes. During the elections of 1880 and 1884, he confined his political activity to writing open letters to the *New Yorker Staats-Zeitung* on behalf of the Democratic candidate. In 1884 he particularly addressed himself not to personalities in the election but to principles distinguishing the Democratic and Republican parties, particularly the tariff-principle. Stallo had long been a proponent of reduced tariffs and freer trade and had closely studied the economic theory relevant to his stand.

With the election of Grover Cleveland, the first Democratic victory in a quarter of a century, many German supporters were "available"—Carl Schurz not among them—for government posts. Stallo's friends believed that he was the most eminently qualified man for the American embassy in Berlin. Stallo declared that he was not seeking public office but had been intending to go to Europe to continue his studies in science "perhaps for a new, complete volume" to follow *Concepts and Theories*. When the Berlin post was given to George Pendleton of Cincinnati, father of the civil service law, Stallo's friends in journalism and politics secured an offer of the ministry to Rome which Stallo accepted. After four years in Rome, where Stallo's facility in languages and wide culture were greatly admired, he retired to Florence to the Villa Romana which had belonged to the ex-Khedive of Egypt. There, not wishing to start his law-practice anew, he spent the rest of his days on the banks of the Arno.

In the Villa Romana, Stallo was in "the old highlands of thought on the continent of Europe" to which he had long been attracted. He continued his studies in philosophy of science and, at the urging of his friend H. A. Rattermann of Cincinnati, assembled his *Reden, Abhandlungen und Briefe* which began with an address on Jefferson at the Cincinnati *Turnhalle* in 1855, included articles on philosophy of science and such political issues as emancipation of women and Bible-reading in public schools, and ended with an article written in Italy on "Political Conditions in October, 1892." The contents of the volume indicated the scope and focus of Stallo's life-long interests and concerns. Ernst Mach greatly admired the *Reden* for its evidence of Stallo's wide learning, gifted style, sharp historical and psychological observations, subtle humor, and philosophical penetration.[49]

Stallo's last book, the *Reden,* well suggests the basic unity of his entire life. He was preoccupied, on the one hand, with political philosophy, particularly the foundations of democratic freedom. But his interest went beyond reflective analysis of principles to action and practice. In the sphere of politics he was a living example of the unity of theory and practice. Furthermore, there was a unity between his philosophy of science and the principles of freedom in his political philosophy. In his philosophy of science he exemplified freedom of thought in his independence of mind and willingness to take a position virtually alone against the intellectual orthodoxy of his day. In the words of one commentator, Stallo was

> a penetrating and utterly independent thinker, completely unimpressed by the highest authority, impelled by his own intellectual restlessness and prophetic vision to examine the fundamental tenets of the science that was later to become the dominating intellectual characteristic of the era.[50]

Stallo himself saw his most technical work in philosophy of science, *The Concepts and Theories,* primarily as a means of freeing intelligence for growth and openness to experience.

> Its tendency is throughout to eliminate from science its latent metaphysical elements, to foster and not repress the spirit of experimental investigation, and to accredit instead of discrediting the great endeavor of scientific research to gain a sure foot-

hold on solid empirical ground, where the real data of experience may be reduced without ontological prepossessions.[51]

Stallo's interests and temperament in the last years of his life were well reflected in his letters to Ernst Mach. The first letter particularly revealed Stallo's knowledge of Mach's writings but also his independence in arriving at the main principles of his philosophy of science:[52]

Villa Romana, 18 Via Senesa
Florence, 20 October, 1897
Highly Honored Professor,

Your friendly letter of the 24th of the past month and the books and writings which you were kind enough to send me have been in my hands for more than three weeks, and I still have not had an opportunity to write you even a single line. This seemingly irresponsible procrastination was due to my intention of expressing a few thoughts inspired by the study of your writings as evidence of my pronounced interest in your work. Unfortunately, however, I live at the moment in such a state of anxiety and confusion as a result of the serious illness of my wife that it is even today impossible for me to write extensively, and I have to limit myself to expressing my heartfelt thanks to you for your words of recognition and your generous shipment. Perhaps I shall some day be fortunate enough to meet you here or in Vienna and then discuss with you orally some of the matters in relation to which our views (in my opinion, only apparently) diverge.

I have been quite familiar with at least part of your writings for some time. The treatise on the Conservation of Energy, as well as some of your shorter essays which appeared before the middle of the seventies, came to my attention 16 or 17 years ago, and the magnificent book, *Mechanics in its Development,* which came to my possession immediately after its publication, caught my attention the more since, at the time of its publication, I was toying with the idea of attempting a brief exposition of the basic principles of statics and dynamics in the language of the Grassmann's Elasticity-Principle—somewhat in the manner used by Lüroth and Willard Gibbs (in his *Vector Analysis* published only as manuscript), among others. There is no need to tell you what an impression the originality and genius of your intellect, as well as the clarity of your exposition made upon me at the time. You can infer the great interest and real identification I felt for your work from the fact that your "Conservation of Energy" and your "Mechanics" were among the few books I took with me to Italy in 1885. Nothing could have given me a more agreeable surprise than the news of your being called to Vienna as Professor of Philosophy of Natural Sciences" (as it was expressed by the Austrian F. M. L. Hötze, the eldest brother of one of my sons-in-law).

By sending you my *"Reden"* I thoughtlessly caused the misfortune of having you waste your precious time on matters which could obviously have not the slightest interest for you. My only intention was to give you a first token of my appreciation, with the further thought that the remarks on atomism in the article on Materialism, pp. 87–97 from the year 1855, could perhaps give you some satisfaction. I shall try to atone somewhat for the crime of disturbing the peace [*Crimen laesae quietis*] by having sent to you from America a copy of the last edition, or rather the most recent printing (for the book is unfortunately stereoplated) of my "Concepts" in which I corrected some atrocious spelling errors which had remained in the earlier editions. I am mailing you today the translation of a little book, "A New System of Chemistry," by my old friend T. Sterry Hunt who was for many years a chemist and minerologist at the Geognostic Bureau in Canada and who published the volume shortly before his death. I am mailing it under the assumption that you occasionally also take a look at the "evil-smelling part of physics," chemistry. In this volume Hunt pursues the view, in my opinion entirely erroneous, that the so-called elements can be conceived as condensations or specifications of a single basic element. However, his attempt to establish a relation between volumes of solids or liquids and their atomic weights, is certainly not entirely without merit. Prof. A.

W. Hofmann told me a few years ago that Köpp has also often concerned himself with the solution of this problem.

In regard to the last chapter of my "Concepts," in case you have looked at it, I take the liberty of remarking that the works of Willard Gibbs, Massien, Helmholtz, Duhem, and others concerning thermodynamic potential or "free energy" were unknown to me at the time of the writing—which, of course, changes nothing in my demonstration.

Now I have written you a long letter, after all, but my hand is shaking and I must stop.

With most sincere respect and admiration,
J. B. Stallo

Prof. Dr. Ernst Mach,
Vienna

Many thanks for the beautiful photograph which just arrived. Unfortunately I can send you nothing better in return than the moderately true copy of a photograph for which I was forced to pose 14 years ago.

J. B. S.

Stallo's second letter to Mach included an autobiographical sketch which Mach reproduced in his forward to the German edition of *Concepts and Theories*. Then Stallo continued with reference to his writings and studies:

Florence, 11th August, '99.

Most Honored Professor,

Please excuse my delaying the answer to your friendly letter of the 30th of last month until today. I have felt so poorly during the last ten days that I was unable to write. . . .

Of my writings, only the "Concepts" could be considered for Poggendorf Encyclopaedia. To be sure, in the course of the years I wrote a few things particularly about the directional-calculus, as I called it—*i.e.*, complex numbers, quaternions, to which I was inspired by Grassman—and I presented them in our scientific group, but nothing was ever published of these writings. Actually my *opera omnia* (Methods of Judicial Proof and Appraisal) form a considerable group of volumes which stand somewhere on a bookshelf in Cincinnati where they have doubtless had the fate which much higher products of the mind have not escaped—"and busy mice were gnawing on divine poems" [*"et divina opici rodebant carmina mures"*].

I hope your health is improving day by day, and it's a good sign at any rate that you have lost nothing of your perceptiveness and agility.

With best regards, your most devoted,
J. B. Stallo

Dr. Ernst Mach,
Vienna

Stallo's final letter to Mach reflected his humor and sustained intellectual interest in spite of ill health. The next letter to Mach came from Stallo's daughter telling the circumstances of Stallo's death and how much Mach's friendship had meant to him:

Florenz, 30 October, 1899

Most Honored Professor,

For several weeks now I have been so weak and sick that I can hardly hold a pen, and therefore the receipt of the second edition of your Thermodynamics has not even been acknowledged to you, not to mention an expression of appreciation. As soon as I regain my strength, I shall read the book with the greatest care, surely the least thanks I can give you. I am happy to find out indirectly that you are well and are again working hard. Oh, if only I could work once again myself!

With the best and most affectionate wishes for the new year, or (according to the new astronomer, Wilhelm II) for the new century.

Prof. Dr. Mach,
Vienna

Your most devoted,
J. B. Stallo

Florence, 8 Jan., 1900

Much Honored Professor,

Since my dear father is no longer among the living, he can not thank you himself for your gracious lines of the fourth of this month which arrived in Florence twenty-four hours after his death, I feel the need to tell you that he was as pleased as a child with each attention you showed him; your gracious friendship was a great fortune and a great blessing to him during the last years of his life. Papa had been ailing for some time. Several weeks ago his condition became more serious; he had attacks of palpitations and pressures of the heart which worsened continually until last Saturday when paralysis of the heart ended his suffering. It was his wish that his earthly remains be cremated; this afternoon the sad function will take place in the quietude of the Trespiano cemetery.

With greatest respect and esteem,

Yours,

Hulda Stallo

IV

PETER KAUFMANN ON SOCIAL PERFECTION AND DIALECTICS

THROUGHOUT HIS ADULT YEARS Peter Kaufmann's life was marked by a mutual stimulation of opposing factors, a dialectical interplay, between philosophical ideas on the one hand and practical activity for social reform on the other. Just as there were changes in his thinking through his adult years so there were shifts in the focus of his reform activities. Through all these developments he remained an indefatigable student of the powers of the human mind and of religion. He read widely and earnestly if not very wisely and well. Certainly in the penetration of his thought he was not the equal of J. B. Stallo. But his widely circulated pamphlets, almanacs, and books acquainted many of his contemporaries with basic philosophical ideas, including principles of logic and dialectic derived from Kant and Hegel. At the same time his multifarious activities in social reform underlined the dialectical unity of theory and practice which his life exhibited. Kaufmann was pre-eminently a practical philosopher, one who saw every theory as an instrument of human perfection.

Early Christian Perfectionism

The son of a German cavalry officer and a French mother, Peter Kaufmann was born at Münster-Mayfeld in Germany, October 3, 1800.[1] After an ordinary education, apparently not beyond the German secondary level, he emigrated to America around 1820 with the aid and encouragement of Morris Longstreth of Philadelphia who became his lifelong friend. He entered the tobacconist trade, but soon after setting up a business partnership found himself in financial difficulties. Settling in Bucks County, Pennsylvania, he pursued his trade and from 1822 to 1823 studied for the ministry in his spare time but was never ordained.

Kaufmann's theological notebooks of this period contain numerous excerpts from Johannes Tauler's *Imitation of Christ's Life of Poverty.* Tauler was a fourteenth century German mystic, younger than Meister Eckhardt in the same period, who held that God is the true substance of every existing thing, and the union of man's soul with God takes place through love which transcends all concepts and requires "images" for its expression. This emphasis on the unity of man and God and on the unity of all existence anticipated one of the points in Hegel's philosophy which Kaufmann later found attractive. Kaufmann was particularly drawn to Tauler's picture of Jesus as sharing poverty and deprivation with the simple folk of his time. During the last year of his theological studies Kaufmann published his first book. It was written in Latin and entitled *Elogium Petri Magni, Russorum Imperatoris.* No copies of this book are known to exist, but its very title and language, taken along with the contents of his theological notebooks, indicate at once the breadth of Kaufmann's intellectual interests and his facility in languages. Shortly after the publication of *Elogium Petri Magni,* Kaufmann moved to Reading, Pennsylvania.

During the last year of his ministerial studies, 1823, Kaufmann completed his second book. This one was written in German and published in 1825 under the title *Betrachtung über den Menschen.* Using as his motto Pope's dictum that "The proper study of mankind is man," Kaufmann capaciously took the whole of human existence as his province. What he achieved might today be classed as philosophical anthropology, but was markedly short on philosophical argument and long on homiletical exhortation, a reflection of his ministerial ambitions.

Kaufmann explained his purpose in writing *Betrachtung über den Menschen* as an effort to augment the happiness of mankind through knowledge of the foundations of true virtue and genuine religion. His first chapter reflected what he had learned from Tauler. He vividly contrasted the kingdom of Jesus and the kingdom of Mammon which generally prevailed in modern life. But for any real good to be done and for any true virtue to be practiced man must exercise the free will which God implanted in him. In a move toward philosophical argument, Kaufmann held that to deny man's freedom would involve a contradiction because it would limit God's creative power and hence make "the most complete Spirit" incomplete.[2] In the introductory chapter of *Bertrachtung über den Menschen* Kaufmann touched on another of his lifelong concerns, education. He saw the true development of the human spirit in steps toward godliness as being dependent on education which must be spread to the poorer classes of society by all real friends of mankind. Education, in Kaufmann's view, was especially important by virtue of its effects on man's future. As in plants, so in man, the future course of development depends entirely on the early growth.

Kaufmann was also concerned with the more material side of man's existence in addition to his moral freedom and education. In a chapter devoted to "Man in his Physical Aspect" Kaufmann dealt with the nervous system, the various senses and their functions, tastes, and feelings. He saw all man's physical equipment as a necessary instrument of his higher spiritual and intellectual capacities. The nervous system, for example, is primarily a medium of knowledge, man's most important "link to the cosmos [*Weltall*]." The development of his senses, tastes, and feelings has its capstone in the life of thought. Though Kaufmann saw man's "physical aspect" as subordinate to his thought and mind, he nevertheless saw the unity of body and mind, flesh and spirit, in all mankind.

As part of his capacious study of mankind Kaufmann did not neglect social and political life. His chapter on "Man in his Political Aspect" began with the observation that man is by nature a social and political being. Without society man could not achieve his various purposes, satisfy his basic physical needs, or develop guiding concepts of law and virtue. Further, Kaufmann carefully distinguished the main possibilities of political organization as being democratic, aristocratic, and monarchial forms of government. He made his own sympathies and preferences unmistakably clear. Any people is indeed fortunate, he believed, if it can live under a republican constitution, a variant form and adaptation of democracy. Such a constitution is the best of all forms. It is the most direct way to achieve the goal of rational government which is "the welfare and ennoblement of the human spirit."[3] Against this political background Kaufmann viewed the whole of human history as a continuous struggle on the part of free individuals to bring good from evil and to make the better the best.

In the final chapters of *Betrachtung über den Menschen* Kaufmann introduced the main elements of his Christian perfectionism, a position obviously indebted to his study of Tauler and a persistent, major theme of all his subsequent writings. The final purpose of man's existence, the culmination of all his capacities and activities, Kaufmann held, is the development of his essentially permanent and unique aspect, namely, his spiritual existence as the ability to reason and distinguish right from wrong. The development of this aspect of man means continuous progress toward perfection and thus a divinization of the human spirit to become "perfect as our father in heaven is perfect." Progress in perfection, however, is an endless task and movement. There is no peace for the spirit.[4]

Kaufmann saw the road to perfection as a very wide one. He offered no specific, detailed social program but urged on his readers a continuous effort to become one [*Einswerdung*] with God through love. In effect this would mean the continuous growth and spread of Christianity throughout the world, revealing in unmistakable terms that the substance of all existing things and the essence of the cosmos is Spirit, and Spirit in its innermost nature is identical with Love.[5]

In his *Betrachtung über den Menschen* Kaufmann showed himself to be a man of wide-ranging intellectual interests and above all a dedicated Christian perfectionist. His Christianity, like Tauler's, was pantheistic in its main outlines and thrust. Hence Kaufmann had a profound sense of the unity of all life and existence. This outlook predisposed him to accept what he later found in Hegel. He saw the world in monistic terms, as everywhere manifesting one principle and one ultimate fact. Hence he avoided sharp dualisms between mind and body, spirit and matter. Anticipating his later attraction to Hegel's dialectic, he saw human affairs as being in development, in process, ever moving toward a perfection whose nodal point was Spirit, Love, or God—different words for the same reality. Concerning this movement he was irrepressibly optimistic but at the same time called men to act, to exercise their free will, in steps that moved with the realization of the *Weltall*, the development of the cosmos in all its aspects.

Experiment in Christian Community

Like a dynamo Kaufmann's Christian perfectionism drove him into activities for social reform. In the year his *Betrachtung über den Menschen* came off the press he took the lead in establishing America's first Labor-for-Labor store in Philadelphia. In this enterprise he was aided by his good friend Robert Smith, and even after he had left Philadelphia he continued to support the store through regular, detailed correspondence. Though Robert Owen had visited Philadelphia in 1824 and on at least two occasions was a guest in the home of Kaufmann's close friend, Morris Longstreth, the establishment of the Labor-for-Labor store was not likely a result of Owen's influence. Kaufmann, as will be noted later, traced his interest in social reform to other and earlier sources than Robert Owen's socialism. The Labor-for-Labor store, rather, was simply a tradesman's way of implementing Christian perfectionism, a way of meeting the pressing needs of the urban poor as required by the principle of brotherly love.

Shortly after the establishment of the Labor-for-Labor store, Kaufmann became a professor of languages in the Rappite Community near the Ohio River at Economy, Pennsylvania. He was also responsible for giving the "preparatory course" to some two hundred students in the school sponsored by the Community. "The Community of Equality and Society of Harmony" had its origin in a group of German farmers led to America in 1805 by George Rapp, an educated peasant and man of commanding presence who had convinced his followers that he would miraculously take them to Palestine to greet Jesus on his second coming. Members of the Community were dubbed "Economites" by outsiders, and the name has stuck to this settlement.[6]

Life at Economy seemed well suited to Kaufmann's religious and social aspirations. He was particularly pleased to find a band of earnest souls who were actually trying to practice the Christian love they preached. In a letter from Economy, Kaufmann wrote:

> It is the duty and theory of every member of this community to show by practice in reality that he believes. And so the life of virtue of the first Christians is renewed again here, and the image of Christ the Saviour is expressed and painted here in every individual more or less.[7]

The Economites, Kaufmann allowed, were ready to admit degrees in virtue as well as in Christianity, but nevertheless "every member of this community is nobilitated by the exalting feeling for pure and disinterested friendship to wards their fellow members and even towards all mankind." In the pattern of life at Economy Kaufmann felt he had found visible proof that mankind, freed from chains of strife for worldly possessions, turns attention to the pursuit of nobler things. The Economites, like the early Christians, were being persecuted and calumniated for their convictions, but Kaufmann was confident that the time was not far off when all mankind would see the righteousness of their pattern of life.

Kaufmann was so favorably impressed by what he found at Economy that he soon took the lead in establishing a communistic society in Ohio near Petersburg in Columbiana County. The community was to be known as "The Society of

United Germans at Teutonia." Its constitution, drawn up by Kaufmann, Solomon Sala, and Michael Lenz, was signed by nineteen persons who became the nucleus of an experiment in fully Christian living. Kaufmann and his associates called upon all Germans in the United States and North America to join their Society whose capacious aim was "the health and welfare of all mankind."

In its preamble the Society's constitution dedicated all members to "justice, freedom, and equality" in all their activities and pledged them to stand all for one and one for all, permitting no harm to fellow members. The first article of the constitution provided that nothing in the entire document might contradict the Constitution of the United States, the law of the land, or "the teachings of the Gospel." The second article committed the members of the Society to a community of goods. Since the early Christians had lived with such an arrangement and since it would contribute to "the cultivation and perfection of our spiritual and physical powers," each member of the Society, as provided in the next three articles, would pledge his property to communal stores for ten years, share in the community's labor, and agree to devote the community's surplus not to earthly pleasures but to education for homeless children regardless of their race or creed, to the rescue and education of "our black brothers" in slavery, to the winning of all Indians to Christianity, and to spreading "the holy doctrine of the Cross and its eternal truth to the four corners of the earth."[8] The Society also planned to publish a weekly paper, *The Herald of a Better Time,* for the purpose of seeking the source and means of removing human poverty and for considering the highest end of man and ways of realizing it. Since no copies of this paper are known to exist, plans for its publication may have never materialized. The Society itself, however, did materialize and apparently was successful enough to last for about four years, a longer life than that of the Kendal Community of Massillon, Ohio, for which Robert Owen had held high hopes.

In 1831 Peter Kaufmann left the "Society of United Germans at Teutonia" to settle in Canton, Ohio, where he lived the remaining thirty-eight years of his life in the brick house he purchased at 336 Market Avenue, South, the oldest building on Canton's original town site, demolished in 1958 to make way for a parking lot. At first he worked as translator and editor of Soloman Sala's Jacksonian newspaper, *Der Vaterlandsfreund und Geist der Zeit*. Soon Kaufmann became owner as well as editor of the paper and continued its publication for twenty years though the name was changed to *Ohio Staats-Bote* in 1846.

Kaufmann opened the pages of *Der Vaterlandsfreund* to Father Rapp of "The Community of Equality and Society of Harmony" and to Rapp's enemy, Count Leon, in the schismatic dispute which occurred at Economy in the winter of 1831–1832. "Count Leon" was the title one Bernhard Müller of Hessia had given himself as "the Ambassador and Anointed of God, of the stem of Judah, of the Root of David." With views akin to those of Father Rapp, Müller found himself in trouble in Germany and was invited to come to "The Community of Equality and Society of Harmony" with his entourage of some forty people, "Countess Leon" and a daughter. Soon Müller's opposition to celibacy and his charge that Father Rapp was regimenting the Economites led to a split in the Community. The Rappites gave Count Leon and his 176 followers $105,000 to leave at once. They moved ten miles down the Ohio River to Phillipsburg and thence, after an attempt to get more money from Father Rapp and a riot which had to be quelled by the militia, went to Louisiana where the Count soon died of cholera but his followers struggled on for some thirty-five years.[9] As editor of *Der Vaterlandsfreund* Kaufmann publicized the break between Father Rapp and Count Leon. In addition, he devoted his spare hours to a history of Count Leon's establishment at Phillipsburg and completed an account of the German Pietist community at Zoar, Ohio, up to the year 1832.

Reform in Education

Shortly after moving to Canton Kaufmann began a highly successful venture of publishing almanacs, first in German alone and a few years later in both German and English. Though the field was a highly competitive one, Kaufmann's almanacs were an immediate success. By 1839 he was publishing 60,000 copies a year and a decade later more than twice as many, in English as well as German. In addition to their usual purposes of providing calendars, phases of the moon, home remedies, and the like, Kaufmann devoted some of their pages to popular education and philosophical themes. He sought, as one biographer put it, to bring "Hegelian philosophy to the people in popular form."

His interest in popular education also came to expression in his leadership of a General School Committee of Germans in the United States which resulted from conventions held in Pittsburgh, Pennsylvania, in 1837 and 1838 to deal with the problem of school instruction in the German language as well as the English required by Ohio law. This was an important issue because there were, according to one estimate, 400,000 Germans in Ohio in 1837. A tangible result of the Pittsburgh conventions was the establishment of a seminary at Phillipsburg, Pennsylvania—in "the fine building erected by (the so-called) Count Leon"—for training teachers to give instruction in both German and English.[10] Kaufmann's leadership of the General School committee brought him national attention. The subscription list for the new seminary was headed by Martin Van Buren and included many prominent Ohioans. Kaufmann's activity in the School Committee plus the fact that he was an active Democrat—a delegate to national Democratic conventions in 1836, 1840, and 1844—led to his being appointed postmaster of Canton in 1837 by President Van Buren. When Canton was reincorporated the next year, Kaufmann was elected by his fellow citizens to be one of the city's eight trustees.

In the course of his activities for the General School Committee of Germans, Kaufmann publicly delivered an address on popular education, twice in German at the Pittsburgh conventions and once in English before the State Education Convention of Ohio at Columbus in 1838. The address received such a favorable report from the Columbus convention that Kaufmann was induced to give it wide circulation as a booklet entitled *A Treatise on American Popular Education.* His purpose was not only to further the interests of the General School Committee in training teachers who would be competent in both German and English but also, more broadly, to show the immense importance of education so that every citizen would feel "how much it is to his own immediate interest to become and abide a zealous, an efficient and permanent advocate and supporter of a thorough, a national, a republican system of education."[11]

In his *Treatise on American Popular Education* Kaufmann dealt with his topic in an orderly way but put what he had to say in very broad terms, so broad, in fact, that he presented a philosophy of education, a statement of its nature, assumptions, and major goals. He used several ideas he had previously presented in *Betrachtung über den Menschen* and also anticipated parts of his later major publication, *The Temple of Truth,* which overtly followed Hegel at key points.

Kaufmann saw education as a matter of highest importance and greatest moment because it directly served man's true goal in life, and "the end of man's existence on earth—as pronounced unerringly by God—through his three eternal voices: *'nature, reason and religion' is perfection!"* This end defined for Kaufmann all that might rightly be meant by happiness, prosperity, or welfare to which education is a means. But he did not think of education with this aim as confined to formal schooling. "The whole life of man," he held, "is therefore a school; and not only so the life of every individual man, but also the life and being of the whole human race, during the thousands of years of its existence on this globe, is *one perpetual living school.*"[12] As might be expected, Kaufmann saw language as particularly important and inseparable from the second of God's eternal voices, reason. It is not only a great social instrument of communication, and hence the mental lever of nations, but it is also "the universal repository of all that your entire existence presents, stamps you as beings endowed with *reason* and thereby distinguishes you from—and elevates you above—all other creatures of the Globe."[13] In particular, Kaufmann wanted a public education that would impart equal facility in both the English and German languages. Such an education would greatly promote unity of national character, be advantageous in many business uses, and provide a mental bridge for entering the vast literary treasury of two great nations. "Our national dignity," Kaufmann felt, "demands that we should at least know as much of other nations as they know of us."[14]

Revealing his interests in political philosophy and history, Kaufmann argued that education was especially important for "free or republican institutions" in view of the fact that civilized life is itself a species of education in addition to what takes place in classrooms, and republican institutions represent "a higher degree of advancement in civilization."

Further, the history of Athens, Sparta, and Rome testify that wherever liberty expired it was due to the ignorance and degradation of the people. When the people of Athens forgot the teachings of their philosophers and the citizens of Rome became only satellites of ambitious wealth, freedom of the people was lost. But liberty further depends on equality, not equality in body or physical conditions, but equality of rights before the law, including equal rights in the distribution of knowledge and the cultivation of mental powers. Without such equality a society invites tyranny. With such equality there can grow that friendship and fraternity which is the true substance of patriotism. Here again Kaufmann thought that the lesson of history was clear:

> Athens, Sparta and Rome contrived to exist as Republics, so long as the amount of equality, and the thence emanating amount of friendly and brotherly affection or patriotism, preponderated over the opposite and antagonistic amount of selfishness and self interest. So soon as the latter preponderated, the tongue of the scale was thrown in the opposite direction and liberty found its grave. And this is also the doubly reflecting mirror, in which America can read its ultimate fate for *weal* or *woe* just as it shall, by its own choice and its own action, choose and prepare its own fate.[15]

Kaufmann did not believe, however, that education should be primarily or exclusively intellectual. Rather it should deal with all man's fundamental powers, namely, his intellect which seeks truth in the immutable laws of nature, his volition which is the seat of moral virtue, and his body which demands health and comfort but dreads disease and pain. Education, Kaufmann believed, should attend to all three capacities, to the whole man, by focusing on a pattern or ideal of perfection. Those who object that ideals are useless because they cannot be realized too often forget that what is impossible for a single individual may be relatively easy for the combined power of thousands or a million as shown in the fact that almost all institutions, including the American republic, were once ideals thought to be no more than dreams.

In his views on education Kaufmann remained an indefatigable idealist and perfectionist but gave less emphasis to the religious element in his thought and more to the political. His understanding of the basic principles of republican government, however, and particularly his emphasis on equality and brotherly patriotism, reflected the Christian impulse which led him to admire the Rappite Community and organize "The Society of United Germans at Teutonia."

Shortly after the publication of his *Treatise on American Popular Education* Kaufmann embarked on more serious and technical studies in philosophy during his spare time from *Der Vaterlandsfreund* and almanacs. Through a Philadelphia bookseller he purchased copies of the first volume of Schelling's *Philosophical Writings,* Kant's *Critique of Pure Reason,* Fichte's *Science of Knowledge,* and Hegel's *Science of Logic* in two volumes.[16] Thus equipped with the landmarks of classical German philosophy, he began a course of study and writing which was to culminate fifteen years later in *The Temple of Truth,* his *magnum opus.*

Kaufmann's more technical studies in philosophy, however, did not consume all his energy. He had energy left for reform efforts, even efforts of a highly eccentric type. In 1847 he visited the Trumbull Phalanx which had been organized four years earlier nine miles west of Warren, Ohio, on the basis of Charles Fourier's principles of "Industrial Association" as interpreted in America by Albert Brisbane. The Associationists, as they were called, had adopted a thoroughly democratic constitution with a version of Fourier's "groups" and "series" and a provision for "perfect religious tolerance" among all members.[17] Kaufmann made use of religious tolerance in the Phalanx to present his Christian perfectionism to its members. A letter from a member of the Phalanx urged Kaufmann to continue in "works of Love" and expressed an expectation of being "rejected from this institution for protecting our daughter and defending the principles you advocated when here." The letter-writer was apparently unhappy about the diversity of sects in "this Babylon."[18]

In his religious reform efforts at the Trumbull Phalanx Kaufmann had a powerful ally in one Andrew B. Smolnikar, a former Benedictine monk, who had announced in his native Austria that on January 5, 1837, at 5:00 P.M., Christ had designated him to establish a universal republic. Straightway, Smolnikar went to America to tell his story in five volumes and participate in several Associationist conventions.[19] Kaufmann drafted and published Smolnikar's call for " 'A Convention of Reformers' who are willing to become the 'Messengers of Christ' for the introduction of the New Era of Universal Peace amongst all mankind." The convention was held at Trumbull Phalanx, August 12, 1847, to instruct those attending in the millennial dispensation of universal peace, the nature of the true church of Christ, and steps to end Catholic celibacy.[20] Apparently little more came of this project than others that Smolnikar undertook, except perhaps to weaken the Associationist movement in Ohio more than the economic challenges of the frontier had already done. In any case, the Trumbull Phalanx carried on for at least four more years.

Kaufmann was seriously enough interested in the Associationist movement and its possibilities to be a regular subscriber to the *Harbinger* published at Brook Farm near Boston and to offer to join forces with one of its leaders in creating a true "Church of Humanity." In a letter to W. H. Channing indicating the true fountainhead of his concern for social reform, Kaufmann confessed that since the age of twenty-one he had been devoting his life to a " 'Christian Church of Love' which, like primitive Christianity from which I obtained my Idea of Christian Social Life" would aim at the emancipation of the whole human race from its present sin, misery, and degradation. When his mind was first attached to this idea, "nothing was known anywhere publickly of the various schemes of 'Socialism' and 'Communism' which since that time have found their way to the public eye by the writings and labours of Owen, St. Simon, Fourier, and others."[21] Kaufmann sent Channing some articles from his almanacs and offered to discuss with him and Mr. Brisbane a "Scheme of Divine and Eternal Logic" touching on the laws and method of intellectual discovery required by the "Great Reformation" then under way. Thus Kaufmann's interest in philosophical problems and principles was linked with his commitment to social reform, a commitment rooted in the pattern of society he saw in primitive Christianity.

Language and Knowledge

From the time he first acquired the major writings of Kant, Fichte, and Hegel, Peter Kaufmann labored long—almost two decades—to weave his views into the "connected intellectual fabric" of which he had written to Channing. Along the way he developed his ideas in philosophical essays for the almanacs he so successfully and numerously published. Finally in 1858 the "connected intellectual fabric" appeared as *The Temple of Truth or the Science of Ever-Progressing Knowledge,* published in Cincinnati and Canton in both English and German.[22]

In the subtitle of *Temple of Truth,* in the preface, and in a notice to the public promising other volumes along similar lines, Kaufmann made it clear that his interests in the specifically philosophical problems of knowledge, logic, and dialectic were instrumental to a larger purpose. They were instrumental to the improvement and ultimate perfection of humanity. In the preface Kaufmann referred to *The Temple of Truth* as "the condensed result of our most earnest and active research after *absolute truth,* prosecuted during a period of thinking existence and amidst an interior and exterior experience, infinitely copious and multiform in variegation, in extent and amount, of nearly a half a century in duration."[23] He felt that he had found the Archimedean fulcrum, "the foundation elements, and skeleton theory of a system of absolute and unassailable truth" for which mankind was waiting and which would finally yield peace, union, harmony, and perfection. In similarly complicated, vaulting prose Kaufmann's preface sketched out the main topics and chapter-themes for the whole of *The Temple of Truth.*

Kaufmann's basic method of arriving at "unassailable truth" was to be an inseparable combination of analysis and synthesis—inseparable because the human mind, like a typesetter, combines elements that have been separated in analysis and also because analysis and synthesis merely reflect the part-whole relationship which is "one unitary law" and one of the "permanent features of being and existence" as testified in mathematics and the natural sciences.[24] There were two collateral features of this method of gaining knowledge to which Kaufmann gave particular attention, namely, its linkage with language and relationship to idealism and materialism.

Kaufmann had a special interest in language, the complexities of its usage, and its relation to thought and knowledge. He had been a teacher of languages at the Rappite Community in Economy, Pennsylvania. As his writings and letters show, he was able to use Greek, Latin, French, German, and English. He saw the "miraculous medium of language" as indispensable to communication between persons, the growth of knowledge, and the progessive achievements of the whole of civilization—cities, steamboats, the press, the telegraph, locomotives, and books. "Language, then,—the divine, first-born immortal child of mankind's Reason—is thus a gift to man of value beyond price." Particularly, it is the "magazine of thought." Each word in language may be said to "represent the conjoint incorporated judgment of men living from the beginning of time, up to this day, upon the thought contained in the word."[25]

Since the object of language is to fix and specify our inherently volatile thought to make possible its communication and accumulation in knowledge, one must be especially alert to mistakes in its use. Like contemporary linguistic philosophers and semanticists Kaufmann not only stressed the unity of thought and language but also sought to show how misuse of words subverts the understanding. He noted that a given name, for instance the name "sun," stood for a three-fold modification of one and the same thing:

> 1.) it denoted *the word* as the term in language by which the luminary was designated by man; 2.) it denoted the *luminary itself* as it stood, brilliant and glorious above every thing else in nature, in the azure sky; and 3.) it denoted the *idea, thought,* or *mental image* of the sun, present in man's intellect as a distinct entity from either the word sun or the real sun itself.[26]

These three uses of "sun," Kaufmann insisted, must be made distinct and separate if we are to avoid intellectual confusion. Hence there follow as corollaries two basic rules to achieve clarity of thought: First, we must so discipline our thoughts as to be able to give them as unequivocal and concise expression as if they denoted a geometrical proposition.

Secondly, to understand the words of others in their exact meaning or denotation we must determine by inquiry and interchange "what they really aim at." Taking his own admonitions on language seriously, Kaufmann devoted lengthy chapters of his *Temple of Truth* to the constitution of language, parts of grammar, and different uses of the elements of language.

Kaufmann saw his method of analysis-synthesis—the method of arriving at "unassailable truth"—as requiring a combination of sensation and reflection. Without the senses man could not become "acquainted with nature, its forces, their qualities and mode of action." Furthermore, the mind can become acquainted with its own characteristics only after it has learned from the school of nature what knowledge, fact, and thought really amount to. If that which exists and is known through the senses is not distinguished from what is dreamed of, there can only be intellectual chaos.[27]

The idealist philosophers, Kaufmann maintained, have mistakenly slighted the senses just as the materialists have mistakenly discredited thought and reflection. In their quest for the unity of all existence, the idealists have arrogantly assumed that somehow multiplicity could not exist in and with unity. On the other side, the materialists have forgotten that man's mind never stops with impressions of the senses, but the understanding translates them into the shape of thought and moves to the higher tribunal of reason where relations are established which result in "science."[28] What is needed, Kaufmann suggested, is to fuse the data of sense with the classifying generality of thought and reflection. Then it will be fully apparent that multiplicity coexists in and with unity.

While Kaufmann made no mention of Hegel in developing these points, his view of knowledge as involving the generalized organization of sense-impressions, as producing unity which includes multiplicity, was entirely in the spirit of Hegel's "concrete universal." In explaining the relation of "the universal," the characteristic activity of thought, to sensation and sense-perception Hegel wrote:

> Sensible existence has been characterised by the attributes of individuality and mutual exclusion of the members. It is well to remember that these very attributes of sense are thoughts and general terms. It will be shown in the Logic that thought (and the universal) is not a mere opposite of sense: it lets nothing escape it, but, outflanking its other, is at once that other and itself.[29]

Logic and Dialectic

With his discussion of logic and dialectic Kaufmann made his indebtedness to Hegel explicit. He considered the mind's knowledge of itself and of nature through sense as adequate "to authenticate the facts of the case." But logic and dialectic are indispensable to the organization of thought. Logic is primarily concerned with the form of thought, particularly the form of its use. To elaborate the proper form of thought Kaufmann went to Kant's table of categories—particularly to the categories of possibility, reality, and necessity under Modality—out of which he derived, rather loosely, "the three highest laws of thinking" embodied in the syllogism, namely, that contradictory predicates may not be united, that everything must have a sufficient ground, and that every thought must belong to one of two contradictory terms.[30] Kant's categories, Kaufmann noted, were paired with forms of judgment, thus showing that language itself is logical in scope though at times defective in form. Language is not only a medium of communication but "the grandest system of logic devised by the intellect of the eternal reason itself." "The office and object of language as well as logic, and thus, again, their common aim moves them both to be in essence—*one*."[31] Hence thousands of people use logic who never heard of the syllogism, and many abandon "book logic" after leaving school to rely on laws of thought which are innate in reason and implicit in language.

Dialectic, in Kaufmann's view, was distinct from logic and went further. Whereas logic was concerned primarily with the form of knowledge and its use, dialectic aimed at "the essence of fact, knowledge, and truth." It was the superintendent of thought in regard to "the matter or substance of truth itself." This function of dialectic Kaufmann traced particularly to Hegel. Though Zeno of Elea might be regarded as the father of logic and dialectic, it was Hegel who made dialectic "the matter and substance of truth itself" as he extended logic to embrace "the whole field of so-called metaphysics."[32] Kaufmann thus recognized that Hegel had distinguished between the externality of formal, Aristotelian logic and the concreteness of dialectic as the movement of thought through opposition and conflict toward synthesis and wholeness—a movement expressing development in things themselves, the very process of actuality. Comparing the concrete universal or "notion" toward which dialectic moves with the formal relations emphasized in traditional, Aristotelian logic, Hegel wrote:

> If the logical forms of the notion were really dead and inert receptacles of conceptions and thoughts, careless of what they contained, knowledge about them would be an idle curiosity which truth might dispense with. On the contrary they really are, as forms of the notion, the vital spirit of the actual world. That only is true of the actual which is true in virtue of these forms, through them and in them.[33]

As Kaufmann expanded and applied his view of dialectic, his kinship with Hegel became more remote. The current intellectual confusion and strife of sects plus the absurd notion that things can be true in thought but untrue in practice convinced him that no reliable system of dialectic existed, so he undertook to construct one. Utilizing an idea he had first presented in his *Betrachtung über den Menschen*, Kaufmann stated the main elements of his dialectic as follows:

> The ineffable Being which ubiquitously fills every point in infinite space, having no beginning and ending and sustaining the existence of the grand order visibly prevailing throughout the universe, has spoken and is speaking to man in and through three distinct cardinal voices, none more or less, each one of which being actually a revelation or manifestation of God to man and the three constituting conjointly the only exclusive and all-embracing sources of knowledge which man ever had, can, and will have—these sources of revelations of God's truth to man are called: a.) Nature, b.) Reason, and c.) Religion, forming a trinal disclosure of the Being and attributes of the infinite Author of all things and man's relation to God, nature, and his neighbor.[34]

In further detail, the phases of this "trinal disclosure" were nature as revealed by the senses in science, reason as involving the collective thought of mankind, and religion as the relation of the whole race of men to its ineffable cause. All three phases or "voices" in "conjoint cooperation" are essential to truth. None can be left out or slighted. In Kaufmann's words:

> Remove, for instance, nature as the bottom upon which man stands and exists: how and where could he make use of and apply reason or revealed religion? Or let nature stand and take away reason: of what and for what use is and remain revealed religion and nature? Or let nature and reason stand and take away revealed religion leaving reason groping in the dark to

understand itself and the sphinx of nature: where will nature and reason be?[35]

On the basis of such a dialectic Kaufmann claimed to have taken the road to the "final ruling philosophy" which would lead to man's "all-sided perfection." Such a philosophy appropriated the certainty of intellectual consciousness from idealism, the revelation of the senses from dangerous materialism as mistakenly defended by Holbach, the certainty of achieved truth from dogmatism, and the suspicious distrust of error from skepticism.[36] Further, such a philosophy defined the supreme end of man in terms Kaufmann had already developed in *Betrachtung über den Menschen* and *Treatise on American Popular Education,* namely, "all-sided perfection" involving the harmony of all mankind. This was the core of the teachings of Christ whose disciples lived as brothers and sisters with all things in common.[37] Were it put into practice, there would arise a community of pleasant homes, education, and healthy labor lightened by machinery, instead of the existing selfishness, greed, and compulsion. By virtue of its size, resources, and republican form of government, the United States, Kaufmann ardently believed, is especially able to realize such a community and become "a saviour-nation," linking itself to all other nations and leading to a United States of the Earth in everlasting peace. Relating this view to his social perfectionism and revealing the religious overtones of his intense patriotism, Kaufmann wrote:

Of all countries existing upon this globe and of all forms of government that men have ever tried to govern themselves by upon earth, there are none which so evidently have by Providence designedly been prepared for the purpose of realizing a saviour nation as the land and institutions of these United States. The former is large and fertile enough to accommodate and sustain almost, if not fully, one half of the present entire population of the globe; and the latter, having made the people themselves the permanent depository of their own sovereign power, have therein preserved a door widely thrown open for the introduction of all and any improvements, surely not excluding the possibly best, which these sovereigns may possess the wisdom to see and the virtue and patriotism to demand introducing. Hence, even a whole host of various defects, which such people may have inherited from the past and which to remedy neither the time nor opportunity have yet been favorable, will, when that proper time eventually arrives, be overcome by conquering even difficulties apparently insurmountable. And as this youngest among the nations is placed upon a new continent lying amidst the great oceans that separate the two extremes of the ancient world, that very geographical position, so easily permitting access to and speedy intercourse with all countries of the globe, is beyond question a stubborn fact of prophetic significance. For the same nation which, first, by embracing and introducing into its midst Christ's whole love and full purpose, thereby establishing a perfect peace and heavenly friendship among all the members of its body and thus making itself a saving nation of all its own, that very nation will thereby likewise become the *model* and saviour nation of the rest of mankind by the double action as well of its power as of its transcending example. For a nation which becomes so divinely wise as to aspire through all its citizens and agencies and with the whole immense power at its control after consummate perfection in all its men, things, and institutions thereby makes itself "The city that is set on a hill; hence the light of the world, which can not be hid."[38]

Kaufmann's development of dialectic, it would appear, reflected as much of his long-standing social and religious perfectionism as specific adherence to Hegel. To be sure, it contained a reference to the "trinal disclosure" of "all-embracing Being" which roughly paralleled Hegel's system, and its view of the relation of logic to dialectic closely followed Hegel's position. Very likely Kaufmann was inspired by the comprehensiveness of Hegel's philosophy and its emphasis on the dialectical unity of all existence. But beyond these debts Kaufmann's ideas were largely his own. This may have been why one biographer referred to his Hegelianism as "undigested."[39]

Certainly Kaufmann was less indebted to Hegel than J. B. Stallo and was inferior in respect to the precision of his thought and his mastery of philosophical ideas. *The Temple of Truth* frequently relied on invective for argument, was needlessly repetitious in its twenty-six long chapters of fine print, and failed to make precise logical transitions from one major position to another. Such defects were noted by at least one of Kaufmann's contemporaries who had enthusiastically read the book three times but found its style "peculiar" and its treatment of materialism to be unjustifiably abusive. "Many of the men you may condemn as materialists," the critic wrote, "are much more likely to read your book and be with you in heart and soul, long before the man that goes to church four times on a Sunday 'and for pretense makes long prayers.'"[40]

A Public Philosophy

In spite of some of its peculiar features and limitations *The Temple of Truth* elicited wide interest from Kaufmann's contemporaries. This was partly due to the author's own initiative. Practical idealist that he was, he linked the sale of his book to an appealing project in educational reform. Immediately after the title page in a note "To the Public" Kaufmann announced that he was applying the net proceeds from *The Temple of Truth* "to the benefit of man and the relief of suffering humanity" by "the establishment of a model institution of education, more comprehensive, liberal and humanitary than any yet existing." Hence those who purchased the book and gave the names of two other buyers would acquire perpetual membership in an educational association devoted to an "all-sided model school," and their names would be carefully preserved in the school's archives. This offer resulted in over 750 listed purchasers of *The Temple of Truth* including J. B. Stallo, Moncure Conway, many prominent public officials, about 100 members of the Ohio legislature, and a number of people from outside Ohio, particularly from Washington, D.C., Wisconsin, and Iowa.

One eminent reader of *The Temple of Truth* was Ralph Waldo Emerson, whom Kaufmann revered to a degree "such as God alone could barely surpass." Kaufmann had written to Emerson from Canton in 1857 indicating his great admiration and also sent an eighty-page manuscript with details on his life, aspirations, and philosophical views. Emerson found the manuscript "full of interest and encouragement" and further said, with accurate perception of Kaufmann's practicality, "I am glad to see how this Franklin-like ability has been working all this while so effectually in Ohio;—glad at heart to see it combined with what is better than Franklin ever knew."[41] Late in May, 1857, Emerson and Kaufmann met in New York for conversation, a meeting which Kaufmann deeply appreciated as "well spent hours."

Soon after its publication Kaufmann sent Emerson a copy of *The Temple of Truth.* In response Emerson wrote that he was sure that the book "will approve itself good to all eyes as they come to it." He would have preferred "a book of results, in which you left us to divine the premises," but nevertheless he found a number of important formulas in it and intended to introduce it to some of the good readers in his neighborhood.[42] While *The Temple of Truth,* with all its detailed philosophical exposition, had no influence on Emerson comparable to Stallo's *General Principles of the Philosophy of Nature,* Emerson was able to praise the way it "marches with method, and, best of all, to a moral determination."

The Temple of Truth elicited enough attention among its author's contemporaries to be reviewed in twelve Ohio newspapers. *The Canton Democrat* fulsomely praised it as "The Book of the Age," "the Textbook of our America as a Nation," agreeing with Emerson's commendation and quoting ex-governor Corwin as saying, "I find this to be one of the books that require to be studied, not merely read." Four hundred Cincinnatians, *The Canton Democrat* observed, including "the élite of the intellect," had already purchased *The Temple of Truth*. The *Ohio Repository* and *Columbus Westbote* particularly noted Kaufmann's chapters on language, logic, and dialectic and the *Ohio State Journal* commented on the book's appeal to all "for whom '*die reine Vernunft*' has attractions." The *Ohio Statesman* of Columbus found *The Temple of Truth* particularly valuable for introducing "philosophy, hitherto confined to schoolmen, to the popular mind in comprehensible terms and method."[43]

Though *The Temple of Truth* was Kaufmann's *magnum opus* and the high point of his intellectual life, his last decade was by no means empty. His social idealism came to further expression in his chairmanship of the Stark County Workingmen's Union which was organized March 16, 1861, in Canton. Kaufmann took the lead in drafting its constitution which expressed some of his typical, lifelong views and was published in parallel columns of German and English.

The Workingmen's Union based itself securely on the fundamental principles of the American republic and sought to apply them to the situation of the laboring man. Hence its constitution called for a return of "the nation and government to their original purity and integrity" and a full fruition of "the rich germs of universal prosperity and individual happiness so profusely therein deposited but not, until now, as yet fully developed."[44] To achieve such aims and consummate the noble work of the fathers of the American Revolution, the Workingmen's Union stood for reduction of taxes, strict accountability of public officials, giving the worker "the sure and full value for his labor or its various products," open debate on all issues except party politics and religion, and promotion of peaceful good will until "the whole state and nation shall become one unitary band of affectionate friends and loving brothers."[45] Under Kaufmann's leadership, the Workingmen's Union was thus fully and unequivocally devoted to extending the principles of the republic, to extending democracy, through the organization and improvement of industrial labor.

In the six years before his death on July 27, 1869, Kaufmann was absorbed in the vocation in which he had spent so many years of his adult life. He was editor and publisher of another Canton newspaper, *Deutsche in Ohio.* Though he had earlier held a commission in the Ohio militia, he was apparently too old to join the Union forces in the Civil War. Neverthcless he closely followed the fortunes of battle and particularly the exploits of his fellow-Germans from Ohio. Colonel Robert McCook, formerly Stallo's law partner and commander of the Ninth Ohio Volunteers which August Willich had organized and trained, wrote to Kaufmann: "You have no idea how proud I am that I command a German Regiment, that is in reality German in command and in habits. You should be proud of them."[46]

Along with being a social reformer, an ardent proponent of popular education, and an assiduous but somewhat desultory student of philosophy, Peter Kaufmann was above all a publicist. To some of the readers of his many publications he undoubtedly communicated Hegelian ideas on truth and dialectic. To many more, however, and particularly through his example, he communicated an earnest social idealism, a lofty perfectionism, which engaged the aspirations and hopes of the time.

V

RELIGIOUS NATURALISM AND REFORM IN THE THOUGHT OF MONCURE CONWAY

THROUGHOUT THE WRITINGS and public views of Moncure Conway there were two interrelated and developing themes in which his particular ideas on religion, politics, and social reform were directly or indirectly grounded. These two themes were significantly shaped and directed during Conway's formative years in Cincinnati. The first theme was his religious naturalism, his view that Deity is to be found within the processes of nature and history, not in a separate transcendent realm made accessible by some special revelation or ecclesiastical authority. In the development of this theme the philosophical views of Hegel and David Friedrich Strauss were of major importance.

The second theme, reinforcing and providing evidence for the first, was Conway's view of nature as a dynamic unity manifest in the pervasive processes of evolution. On this basis he defended the indivisible unity and brotherhood of all men, the premise of his ardent support of the abolitionist cause and other movements for social and political reform. Further, his attachment to the theory of evolution led him to defend for religion and all social institutions the openness to new ideas, continuous inquiry, and responsiveness to rational evidence implicit in the scientific spirit.

Education of a "Natural Radical"

Moncure Daniel Conway was born near Falmouth in Stafford County, Virginia, March 17, 1832, of a long-established and prominent Virginia family related to the Taylors, Madisons, and Lees.[1] One of his ancestors had been a signer of the Declaration of Independence. Another had hated slavery and would have released his slaves from bondage had not Virginia law prevented it. Conway's grandfather had absorbed liberal religious views at the College of William and Mary from a band of rationalists named the "Illuminati" after the German society founded by Adam Weishaupt. Shortly after their marriage in 1829, Conway's parents were converted from the mainly defunct Episcopal Church to Methodism and became leaders in the Methodist movement in the area. Though they were active and regular in their religious observances, they remained detached from the more extreme antics at camp meetings. They were more interested in the Methodist commitment to humanitarian reform than in issues of dogmatic theology.

After a few years of elementary education in a neighborhood school, Moncure Conway attended the Fredericksburg Classical and Mathematical Academy for five years and in 1847 entered Dickinson College in Carlisle, Pennsylvania, a Methodist college with daily, required religious observances but a liberal curriculum. There he studied mathematics, natural science, Greek and Latin, English, and church history. His courses in chemistry and zoology were effectively taught by professors who later became nationally prominent. In addition to required studies Conway read widely in eighteenth century novelists and such American literature as he could find. He participated in the college philosophical society and at one of its meetings defended an unbelieving classmate who had been forced to give arguments for Christianity. Thus Conway was already sensitive to freedom of mind, though his religious views were still quite orthodox. Further, some growing questions about the moral justification of slavery came into his thinking as a result of his part in a protest against antislavery activities of a respected and admired professor. During his second year at Dickinson, Conway attended a series of prayer-meetings in a nearby church. Determined to be converted, he went forward to the altar and "*resolved* never to stop from that moment until I enjoyed religion in my heart, if there was such enjoyment to be had." Shortly thereafter he joined the Methodist Church.

After graduation from Dickinson College Conway returned to Virginia in an aimless mood. He began the study of law with a Colonel William Phillips, clerk of a circuit court in the county north of his family home, but also remained interested in journalism through the influence of his intellectually companionable cousin, John Moncure Daniel, who was editor of the *Richmond Examiner*. Conway's aimlessness, however, was resolved in 1850, a particularly important year in his life. It was the year in which his first extensive writing was published, a pamphlet surveying the deplorable lack of education in Virginia and advocating compulsory education in free schools. Further, 1850 was the year in which Conway discovered Emerson, whose views indelibly influenced his whole life. Reading an extract from Emerson's essay on "History" in *Blackwood's* magazine, Conway was deeply moved and immediately purchased a copy of Emerson's *Essays, First Series* in nearby Fredericksburg.

Emerson brought him a "revelation" and precipitated a "spiritual crisis." "I caught a glimpse," said Conway, "of a vault beyond the familiar sky, from which flowed a spirit that was subtly inbreeding discontent in me of faith in myself, rendering me a mere source of anxiety to those around me."

The impact of Emerson's views, however, had positive results in another event of 1850 in Conway's life. He decided to become a Methodist minister, and Emerson was at the bottom of the decision. Emerson's essays "did away with the bounds between sacred and secular by making both sacred." Free of theological negations, they leavened Conway's Methodism imperceptibly. They offered many points of agreement with the Methodist emphasis on the personal character of spiritual life and general indifference to dogma. "I cannot remember," Conway observed, "ever hearing a Methodist sermon about the Trinity."

Conway's appointment as a Methodist minister by the Baltimore Conference made him a circuit rider, first in Maryland and later in Virginia. His travels brought him into contact with some Hicksite Quakers whose spiritual self-possession and creedless religion much impressed him and reinforced ideas he had found in Emerson. As a circuit rider Conway both lived and studied out of saddlebags in which he carried, in addition to the Bible and Methodist Discipline, Emerson's *Essays,* Coleridge's *Aids to Reflection,* and Carlyle's *Latter Day Pamphlets.* Emerson's transcendentalism, denying any gulf between sacred and secular and viewing God as nature's indwelling presence, set Conway's feet firmly on the road to religious naturalism. This direction was reinforced by his study of Coleridge's *Aids to Reflection,* which had profoundly shaped Emerson's transcendentalism between 1829 and 1832.[2]

Coleridge's book aimed to present to the general reader some basic ideas in the philosophy of Immanuel Kant and use them in the direction Hegel's philosophy had taken toward unifying the realms of nature and faith. In particular, Coleridge utilized Kant's distinction between the sense-based, discursive judgments of the Understanding and the necessary, universal principles of Reason. Thus there was a distinction in kind between Understanding which beholds the material, phenomenal world and Reason which gives access to an intelligible, spiritual order.[3] But Coleridge did not take this distinction as final in relation to the spiritual order. Again following Kant, whom he revered with his "whole heart and soul," Coleridge looked to Reason in its practical or moral employment, Reason as embodied in conscience, to delineate the spiritual order of perfect freedom and ultimate ends. Hence, "Practical Reason alone is Reason in the full and substantive sense," whereas, "Theoretic Reason, as the ground of the universal and absolute in all logical conclusions, is rather the light of Reason in the Understanding."[4] Thus through Coleridge's *Aids to Reflection* Conway was exposed to basic ideas in "the critical philosophy" of Kant and the dualisms of thought which Hegel tried to synthesize.

Even during his first year as a Methodist minister Conway began wrestling with doubts and misgivings. He wondered what he could honestly preach. "The morally repulsive dogmas, and atrocities ascribed to the deity in the Bible became impossible." He wrote to Emerson of his misgivings as a "natural radical" on a Methodist circuit in Virginia and received a kindly answer noting that a "true soul will disdain to be moved except by what natively commands it." Impressed by an address of a Unitarian minister from Baltimore and further assailed by doubts of his Methodist ministry, Conway left his native Virginia in 1853 to attend Harvard Divinity School and, hopefully, to find truer intellectual bearings.

At Harvard Divinity School Conway found most of his professors trying to steer a middle course between Unitarian orthodoxy and "German rationalism," the critical interpretation of the Bible, inspired by Strauss, which viewed miracles as myths or results of natural causes. The more radical-minded students, including Conway, rallied around Emerson and Theodore Parker who became their real teachers. Conway established close personal relations with both Emerson and Parker. He was impressed by Emerson's aversion to creeds and his emphasis on "the supremacy of the present hour." He became interested in Goethe through conversations with Emerson and later used passages from Goethe's writings as texts for his sermons and addresses. In retrospect Conway saw Emerson as "the most sweeping radical of his generation." From his "Divinity School Address" dated "the whole movement of reverent Freethought in America" and his distinctive philosophy of life precipitated an intellectual and moral revolution. In holding that there is one mind common to all individual men, an all-embracing intelligence containing each man's particular being, Emerson taught that the powers and privileges of each belong to all. Such a view, Conway believed, emancipates man from all masters as it induces a genuine and appropriate humility.[5]

Conway deeply admired Parker as "the standard-bearer of religious liberty" and was fully aware that Parker's critical treatment of the various miracles in the Bible was rooted in "German rationalism" and Strauss's *Life of Jesus.* While Parker was teaching school in 1832–1834, "he entered," as Conway put it, "into the great deeps of German Thought and Theology, his acquaintance with which was not surpassed by that of any living man."[6] Further, on a trip to Europe in 1843 Parker spent much time in conversation with such men as Strauss, DeWette, Carlyle, and Martineau, who became his steadfast friends. Thus influenced by Parker, Conway joined those of his Divinity School classmates who wanted to have Parker address their commencement in 1854. Though Parker advised Conway and his associates to "get a liberal man less notorious than myself," they invited him anyway, only to have their invitation vetoed by the faculty, a move contrary to Harvard's rules and traditions. That year instead of a commencement address there was only "eloquent silence."

Some months after his graduation from Divinity School Conway became pastor of the Unitarian Church in Washington, D.C. Since the church had long shown a liberal tendency, Conway had nothing to fear on matters of dogma. But during his last years at Harvard he had steadily moved toward the abolitionist position in regard to slavery. From the very beginning of his ministry in Washington he spoke out against the evils of slavery and reminded his listeners of its incompatibility with the brotherhood and unity of all mankind. The sonship of God, he told his congregation, means the brotherhood of all mankind, including the least of men. There is no ground whatsoever for treating some races as inferior beings. "Man is one, and one member cannot suffer but all suffer; one cannot be a slave but all are to some extent slaves."[7] In thus taking a firm stand on slavery, Conway was merely applying the religious views he had developed under the influence of Emerson, Parker, and indirectly "German rationalism."

During his ministry in Washington, Conway became increasingly firm on the issue of slavery. After a sermon early in 1856 advocating peaceful separation of North and South to free the North of moral responsibility for slavery, he was "rebuked" by his congregation. Some months later and after some complications of committee action, he was dismissed from the church for persisting in the "desecration of his pulpit." Sensing the futility of further struggle, Conway accepted appointment to the First Congregational Church of Cincinnati in 1856 during a presidential campaign in which, as he saw the matter, "slavery and freedom had for the first time confronted each other."

Cincinnati and Miracles

Conway found the cultural life of Cincinnati much to his liking. It was "the most cultivated of the western cities." With a third of its population German, there were many musical societies, and in that respect Cincinnati was ahead of all other American cities except Boston. There were theaters which attracted actors of international eminence and a flourishing program of opera. In addition there were well-established, extensive libraries and lecture programs which brought such speakers as Emerson, Holmes, and Agassiz. There was a flourishing literary club which included among its members Rutherford Hayes, J. B. Stallo, A. R. Spofford, and a number of eminent jurists for whom Cincinnati was famed. Conway threw himself into these movements with enthusiasm. "I was adopted in the clubs," said Conway, "and wrote criticisms of the classical concerts, the picture exhibitions, the operas, and plays." When his activities as a "dancing and theatre-going preacher" began to arouse adverse comment, he defended the theater from his pulpit as one of the most important institutions for the culture of the community. An important personal result of Conway's active social life was his meeting of Ellen Dana, who had recently returned to Cincinnati with her family after being brought up in St. Louis. Conway fell in love, and after a period of engagement married Ellen Dana on June 1, 1858. Following their wedding trip on the Ohio River the young couple made their first home in a modest house at 114 Hopkins Street.

Conway was pleased to find the atmosphere of Cincinnati and its Ohio environment congenial to social reform, "to every new creed or social experiment." Remnants of Father Rapp's Harmonists, Owen's New Harmonists, and Fanny Wright's interracial community had all "found some nest in Cincinnati." Conway visited the remains of the Memnona community at Yellow Springs and defended its record against Horace Mann's attacks. Josiah Warren's community of "individual sovereignty," first organized in Cincinnati and Tuscawaras County, so impressed Conway that he travelled to Long Island to talk with Warren about his "entirely original sociology." Though Conway's congregation in Cincinnati contained many of the city's wealthy and prominent citizens, including Judge Hoadly, Alphonso Taft, and J. B. Stallo, it was firmly antislavery in sentiment. As a result Conway could speak to and work on other issues of social reform. As his sermons revealed, his thought centered on Jesus daily crucified in the poor, woman deprived of her rights, the prostitute unwillingly degraded, and the drunkard driven into misery. With his customary boldness he not only confronted his wealthy congregation with issues of social reform but frequently wrote newspaper articles on them and lectured to Cincinnati's Jewish societies and German Turners.

Among the Germans in Cincinnati besides Stallo, Conway was particularly impressed by August Willich. Noting Willich's Prussian background, the wide belief that he was of royal descent, and his impassioned leadership in the Baden revolution, Conway found Willich to be one of Cincinnati's most interesting citizens, an eloquent and vigorous leader of the labor movement. Under Stallo's persuasion, Willich had become editor of the *Republikaner* and "made it a strong and radical paper." Conway admiringly recalled how Willich headed a torchlight procession in the streets of Cincinnati to protest and mourn the execution of John Brown after the ill-fated attack on Harper's Ferry. "In after years when I saw Garibaldi in London," said Conway, "I felt as if I had met him before in the form of my old friend Willich."[8]

One effect of Conway's exposure to the Germans of Cincinnati, among whom there were numerous and vocal "freethinkers," was a change of view on Tom Paine. Investigating for himself, Conway found that the denunciations of Paine he had heard since he was a boy were largely mythology. On Paine's birthday, January 20, 1860, Conway preached a vindicating sermon on him to a crowded congregation. After that, Cincinnati's freethinkers frequented his church, and at the request of many citizens, including some wealthy and eminent ones who were not members of his church, Conway's discourse was published under the title *Thomas Paine, A Celebration.* Conway did not follow Paine in his view of God. He had already rejected supernaturalism and "had passed from all dynamic theism to the theism evolved from the pantheism of the poets." But Conway's vindicating sermon on Paine as a freethinker was important as the beginning of his lifelong study of the revolutionary leader, a study which was to culminate at the end of the century in a two-volume *Life of Thomas Paine* and a four-volume collection of *The Writings of Thomas Paine.*

There was another and perhaps more important effect of Conway's exposure to German thought in Cincinnati. That exposure reinforced and developed the religious philosophy he had largely derived from Emerson and Parker who in turn, Conway was aware, had been deeply impressed by Kant, Hegel, and Strauss. Emerson made several visits to Cincinnati for lectures and on one occasion stayed in Conway's home for a week. Parker also visited Cincinnati and addressed "very crowded audiences" in Conway's church. The *Cincinnati Gazette* testily branded Parker's views "a vigorous attack on the prevailing opinions in regard to the Godhead, to Christ, and upon most other received views on religious topics" but supposed that his large audience might have been expected "in these progressive days."[9]

In Cincinnati, Conway's "theism evolving from the pantheism of the poets," his view that Deity is to be found within the processes of nature and history so that there is no place for miracles of supernatural intervention, was reinforced by his study of Strauss's *Life of Jesus.* In the year before moving to Cincinnati, Conway had purchased from his Washington bookseller Strauss's book along with Goethe's *Wilhelm Meister* and the works of Channing. The atmosphere of Cincinnati, it would appear, encouraged him to study and absorb *The Life of Jesus.* Strauss's views amply reinforced Conway's distrust of the Bible taken literally and directly. Even during his first year as a Methodist minister he had found it full of "morally repulsive dogmas and atrocities."

In 1859 Conway preached to his Cincinnati congregation a fateful series of sermons against the credibility of the miracles recorded in the Gospels. In what was probably the last of the series he said:

> Each man has to choose between two Christs today,—the Christ as the Church has made him,—the Christ as God made him, as he really was. The Church's Christ is the God Almighty; the real Christ calmly affirms, "My Father is greater than I." The Church's Christ was one who performed prodigies, walked on the water, cursed fig-trees so that they couldn't bear

> but withered, appealed to men's faith through their love of the marvelous; the Christ of God boldly declared to a credulous and superstitious generation seeking after marvels, "There shall be no sign given!" Now, in the sight of God, choose ye which of these Christs shall be yours. If you choose the Church's Christ, the Great Magician, the Astounder of the World by miracles of physical performance, then I assure you that you shall never hear of such a being from this pulpit, so long as I am in it. I would rather never enter a pulpit again than enter it under the superstition of believing that the being I worship was one who established a religion by his ability to walk on water, or swear at a fruit-tree so as to wither it.[10]

Conway urged his congregation to eschew "the star-announced supernatural Christ" for Christ as the "Ideal Man," "the Great Master in Spiritual Law," whose life was so wonderful that subsequent generations could only view him as a supernatural miracle-worker. Such words were fateful because they alienated many of the congregation, and as a result the conservatives seceded to form the Church of the Redeemer. This development was the beginning of the end of Conway's Cincinnati ministry.

Further, *The Dial* magazine, which Conway edited in Cincinnati in 1860 as a successor to the earlier New England transcendentalist journal of the same name, testified to the increased influence of German thought, particularly of Strauss and Hegel, on Conway's views. In its "Catholic Chapters" *The Dial* printed excerpts from Schiller, Goethe, and Hegel along with noteworthy passages from Socrates, Emerson, St. Augustine, Shakespeare, Alcott, and Martineau. Its longest series of articles was one by Octavius Brooks Frothingham on "The Christianity of Christ."

Frothingham, a "later transcendentalist" and historian of the movement like Conway, had absorbed much of Hegel's thought. History was for him the essence of things and philosophy's primary category was "becoming" not "being." With "historical reason" thus pre-eminent, Frothingham's heroes were F. C. Baur and D. F. Strauss. He viewed their "Left-Hegelian" philosophy—"Left" as suggested by the seating of critics and radicals in the French Parliament—as the proper and authentic fulfillment of transcendentalism.[11] In his long, detailed, scholarly series for *The Dial* on "The Christianity of Christ" Frothingham tried to show, in the spirit of Strauss and with Strauss's critical method, how much of Christianity is *not* of Christ and how increments of dogma and tradition have been engrafted, due to a variety of historical causes, on the few simple and human teachings of Jews. Frothingham found those teachings noble, natural, and morally commendable but in themselves having nothing to do with traditional metaphysics and ecclesiastical dogma.[12]

Conway had undertaken publication of *The Dial* to further the cause of freedom in thought and belief. He felt that the old center of this freedom, Boston Unitarianism, was "suspended." Freedom needed a new lease on life in the West. Conway described the aim of *The Dial* as follows:

> *The Dial* stands before you, reader, a legitimation of the Spirit of the Age, which ASPIRES TO BE FREE: free in thought, doubt, utterance, love and knowledge. It is, in our minds, symbolized not so much by the sun-clock in the yard, as by the floral dial of Linnaeus, which recorded the advancing day by the opening of some flowers and closing of others: it would report the Day of God as recorded in the unfolding of higher life and thought, and the closing up of old superstitions and evils; it would be a Dial measuring time by growth.[13]

The Dial, Conway was pleased to report, had a large subscription list, favorable notices in Ohio newspapers, and words of support from Emerson, Longfellow, Charles Norton, and O. B. Frothingham. Conway was particularly pleased by the notice in the *Ohio State Journal* written by

William Dean Howells. With *The Dial,* Howells observed, Cincinnati placed herself beside Boston as a place "where the inalienable right to think what you please has been practiced and upheld," an accomplishment more noble than the production of pork and more magnificent than Pike's Opera House, of which Cincinnati was so proud.

The task of editing *The Dial* in addition to his regular duties became too much of a burden for Conway. His church had already had a secession over the issue of miracles and supernaturalism. In December, 1860, he wrote his farewell message for *The Dial* and later explained that it had really been slain at the end of its first year "by the Union war several months in advance of its outbreak." Since the first organ of transcendentalism, *The Western Messenger,* had appeared in Cincinnati, it was historically fitting that the last one should there end its brief but colorful life.

Debt to Strauss and Hegel

In a commemorative address published some dozen years after he had left Cincinnati, Conway indicated in detail what Strauss and Hegel had meant to him in the development of his philosophy of religion. He had already paid some of his respects to Strauss in a London sermon defending him against Gladstone as "the Premier of the Kingdom of Reason" who had decisively shown the incredibility of Gospel miracles as history and the need to "adore the grandeur of the universe as the shrine of the Supreme life-giving and law-making Reason."[14] The commemorative address with fuller homage to Strauss was published both in London, where Conway was leader of The Ethical Society, and in *The Index* for which he was a contributing editor. *The Index* was a weekly journal sponsored by the Free Religion Association, edited by Francis Ellingwood Abbot, and first published in Toledo, Ohio, from 1870 to 1873. While Conway was a contributing editor, *The Index* published a number of articles on German philosophy, including a long, laudatory essay by O. B. Frothingham on Ludwig Feuerbach, the "Left-Hegelian" whose views were later to leaven Conway's own "religion of Humanity."

In his commemorative address Conway noted Strauss's debt to Hegel who was "destined to create an epoch in the history of the human mind." Borrowing an expression from geology, Conway held that

> We are all living in the Hegelian formation; and this whether we understand that philosophy or not, and even if we reject its terms. For Hegel was as a great vitalizing breath wafted from afar, beneath which, as under a tropical glow, latent seeds of thought were developed to most various results.[15]

Conway precisely and accurately formulated the leading theme of Hegel's philosophy as follows:

> Its essence is the conception of an absolute idea which has represented itself in Nature, in order that by a progressive development through Nature it may gain consciousness in man, and return as mind to a deeper union with itself.[16]

Such a view of the world, Conway allowed, had been at least partially anticipated in the Hindu conception of a universal soul of nature. But Hegel's formulation was particularly adapted to Western thought and hence its central meaning was reflected "in the materialism no less than in the idealism of our age, and may be felt in the philosophy of Huxley no less than in that of its best exponent, Emerson."[17] Thus Conway not only identified Emerson's philosophy, which had influenced him so deeply, with Hegel's but also saw Hegel's emphasis on the world's unitary process as being well reflected in Huxley's evolutionary view. Hegel's philosophy fully and adequately expressed Conway's philosophy of religion, his view that Deity is to be found within the processes of nature and history, not in a separate transcendent realm manifesting itself in miraculous, supernatural interventions. Hegel's philosophy well formulated Conway's rational "theism evolved from the pantheism of the poets."

Conway saw Strauss as the one who best comprehended the bearings of Hegel's philosophy on theology. "Strauss proved himself to be the truest pupil of Hegel," Conway held, "by throwing off the mere form of his forerunner's doctrine, just as that philosopher had thrown off the formulas of his forerunners." Though Hegel thought of himself as an orthodox Christian, Strauss came to renounce orthodox Christianity. Though Hegel was designated an idealist, Strauss came to think of himself as a materialist. "But we must not," Conway warned, "be victims of the letter. Fruit is different from the blossom; but it is for all that, blossom in another form." Hence, from the "blossom" Strauss concluded that Hegel's philosophy was incompatible with miracles though it might leave room for mysticism. He studied the life of Christ as an historical phenomenon and found that the miracles of the New Testament were on the same footing as stories told about Isis and Osiris, Apollo and Bacchus. They were myths generated by the thought-patterns of an unscientific age, not literal historical facts. Nevertheless, they were important as representing humanity. As Conway formulated Strauss's view on myths involved in miraculous events:

> They were born out of the human heart in every part of the world, and were types of its aspirations, hopes, and spiritual experiences. That which could not be respected as history could be reverenced as a reflection of the religious sentiment.[18]

Hence where the church set an individual, Strauss would put humanity. In Conway's quotation from Strauss:

> Humanity is the union of two natures—God becomes man, the infinite manifesting itself in the finite, and the finite spirit

> remembering its infinitude; it is the child of the visible Mother and the invisible Father, Nature and Spirit.

Thus Conway found in Strauss foundations for his own view of miracles as well as his developing "religion of Humanity."

While Conway was generally correct in his estimate of Strauss's relation to Hegel, he did not elaborate the details of that relationship. He did not show, in particular, how Strauss's idea of "myth" had applied Hegel's view that in religion truth takes the form of "imaginative presentation" transmitted by the community. It was Hegel's view that apart from a fully philosophical or conceptual grasp of religion's truth, Spirit—the true substance and reality of all things—takes "the form of the universal self-consciousness of a religious community." In that community events of the past are kept alive in sensuous form through "imagination." "Imaginative presentation," said Hegel, "constitutes the characteristic form in which spirit is conscious of itself in this its religious community."[19] Strauss's conception of "myth" was merely an extension and application of Hegel's view of an historically- and socially-formed "imaginative presentation." In the mythical interpretation of Biblical history, Strauss wrote, the higher intelligence at work in putatively historical events is "the spirit of a people or a community" and this spirit, not an immediate supernatural agency, gives them "an absolute inherent truth," not a specific and literal historical truth.[20]

The secession precipitated in Conway's church over his series of sermons against miracles suggests that Cincinnati was far from being uniformly liberal or of one mind on this issue. In the years in which Conway was championing religious ideas such as he found in Strauss, Parker, and Emerson, another Cincinnatian, William Nast (1807–1899), was actively combating them. Nast became "the father of German Methodism" in a long, dedicated career as preacher, church-organizer, scholar, editor, and college president—a career linked with David Friedrich Strauss at some important points. At Blaubeuren Seminary in Germany Nast was Strauss's roommate, and together they studied under Ferdinand Christian Baur who, in Nast's eyes, was the immediate father of Strauss's myth-theory. In spite of doubts, Nast accompanied Strauss to the University of Tübingen, where Baur had become a professor. Strauss became absorbed in Baur's ideas and lectures on Hegel and Schleiermacher, but Nast "got lost in the labyrinth of Pantheism" and withdrew from the university after two years.

After emigration to America and conversion to Methodism, Nast became editor of *Der Christliche Apologete* in Cincinnati from 1839 to 1894. As early as 1854 he attacked his old roommate, Strauss, in the *Apologete* for spreading doubt as he floundered in "an ocean of philosophical disputation." A few years later Nast made a more systematic answer to "rationalism and infidelity" in general and Strauss in particular with a massive *Commentary on Matthew and Mark.* Strauss was fundamentally mistaken, Nast tried to show, in viewing discrepancies and miracles in the Gospels as unintentional fictions born of the Jews' messianic consciousness. Such a view would require one to believe that the substance of the Gospels was derived not from the Apostles and their associates, whose probity Strauss never questioned, but from some other group with which Jesus had little contact, which "does not appear in history, the existence of which is irreconcilable with all remaining records, . . . and which, therefore, was unknown to the world before its discovery by Strauss." "The secret of the mythical hypothesis," Nast concluded, "is the pantheistic denial of a personal living God, and the *a priori* assumption of the impossibility of a miracle."[21]

In his attack on Strauss, however, Nast tried to use Strauss's own method of historical criticism. Some of Nast's fundamentalistic contemporaries, in fact, were disturbed by his historical approach and saw it as "furnishing the basis of modern Universalism." Nast questioned the theory of verbal inspiration and was careful to insist that the Gospels are a human record—thus not infallible—of a divine event, trustworthy on "simply historical grounds," not "assumed inspiration." Thus Strauss and Hegel, whose "idealistic pantheism" Nast firmly opposed, left their mark on him. Nast's opposition to all that Conway stood for on such issues as the nature of God, supernaturalism, and miracles was an opposition with some hidden links.

Evolution and Religion

During Conway's years in Cincinnati the second major motif in his thought, his adherence to an evolutionary view of the world and the scientific freedom it implied, was crystallized and firmly grounded. This motif reinforced and provided evidence for the religious naturalism he developed under the influence of Emerson, Parker, Strauss, and Hegel.

Early in 1859 Conway "answered" for his Cincinnati congregation the Rev. Dr. Horace Bushnell's defense of supernaturalism based on supposed evidence from geology that life could not have existed in the first condition of the earth. In Bushnell's view life required supernatural creation. Conway cited what he had learned from Agassiz in Cambridge about embryonic development which pointed to "the derivation of one species from another," a conclusion Agassiz had rejected as leading to atheism. In the same year Conway's *Natural History of the Devil* brought forward the idea of "arrested and progressive development" which he had derived from Emerson possibly as early as 1853 or 1854.[22]

Conway regarded this idea as one of the most important in the pre-Darwinian history of evolution, showing that those who studied Emerson were building their faith on evolution before Darwin came to prove the foundations strictly scientific. Apparently Conway was unaware that Emerson's pre-Darwinian views on evolution had been significantly supported and shaped by the Hegelian book of his friend and fellow-Cincinnatian, J. B. Stallo.

There were other indications of Conway's evolutionary view of the world prior to the appearance of Darwin's *Origin of Species*. In "A Discourse on Truth" a few months after his "answer" to Bushnell, Conway proclaimed the unity of man and nature. Whatever is in nature, Conway held, is in man. Man is nature in quintessence. There are minerals in his skeleton, vegetable matter in his hair, and metal in his blood. "These things reappear in the human form because the Law of the Universe is *Ascent*." Man's roots lie deep in the strata of nature's laws but also stretch forth heavenward. In the realm of mind the truths of science—"and, rightly speaking, there are no others"—become knowledge without ranting and violent dispute. It is time that religion, Conway suggested, abandon its disputes for a quieter, surer, and stronger key to truth.[23]

With an evolutionary view of nature already entrenched in his mind, Conway hailed *The Origin of Species* in a sermon to his Cincinnati congregation with these enthusiastic words:

> Now comes Darwin and establishes the fact that Nature is all miracle, but without the special ones desired: that by perfect laws the lower species were trained to the next higher and that to the next—until
>
> Striving to be man the worm
> Mounts through all the spires of form.
>
> This formidable man, speaking from the shelter of the English throne and from under the wings of the English Church

> itself, did not mean to give Dogmatic Christianity its death-blow; he meant to utter a simple theory of nature. But henceforth all temples not founded on the rock of natural science are on the sand where the angry tides are setting in.[24]

A review of Darwin's book in *The Dial*, unsigned but in view of its content probably written by Conway, was similarly enthusiastic. After a summary of the principle of natural selection supported by quotations, the review concluded:

> We have given but the theme of this timely and excellent work, which brings with it inevitably the crisis of inquiry into this much discussed question of the origin of species. Owing to the theological exigency, which, finding historic records inadequate to the proofs of supernaturalism, has fled to an imagined series of "independent creations" miraculously carried on in the strata of the earth, naturalists have been intimidated and the people befogged on the question of their own origin. Chasms have been opened where God built bridges; insulations superseded continents—the lovers of truth were called on to dance to the pipes of discord and complexity. Where Reason had passed long since by her birthright to Music, lagging Science is now beginning to come; the walls which rise to such strains will endure.[25]

Conway's commitment to an evolutionary view of the world was not only rooted in what he had learned from Emerson but also found support in Hegel and Strauss. As already noted, Conway saw Hegel's central principle as the "progressive development" of an absolute idea through nature and the consciousness of man. In Conway's eyes the Hegel who was "destined to create an epoch in the history of the human mind" was preeminently the philosopher of evolutionary process before Darwin and Huxley.

Conway was particularly enthusiastic about Strauss's last book, *The Old Faith and the New*, which ardently embraced the theory of evolution and applied it to religion. Conway quoted the core of Strauss's position as follows:

> We perceive in Nature tremendous contrasts, awful struggles; but we discover that these do not disturb the stability and harmony of the whole,—that, on the contrary, they preserve it. We further perceive a gradation, a development of the higher from the lower, of the refined from the coarse, of the gentle from the rude. And in ourselves we make the experience that we are advanced in our personal as well as our social life the more we succeed in regulating the element of capricious change within and around us and in developing the higher from the lower, the delicate from the rugged. . . . That on which we feel ourselves entirely dependent is by no means merely a rude power to which we bow in mute resignation, but is at the same time both order and law, reason and goodness, to which we surrender ourselves in loving trust.[26]

Conway agreed with Strauss on the need to replace the old Deity with "the law-governed Cosmos, full of life and reason." Such a view, contrary to William Gladstone's misrepresentation of it,[27] demanded the same piety for the cosmos as the devout had always held toward a supernatural deity. "All that any worshipper can say of his God," Conway noted, "Strauss says of Nature."[28] He especially agreed with Strauss in opposing the traditional Christian dualism of soul and body, man and nature—an inevitable offspring of supernaturalism and failure to see that the issue between materialism and idealism is largely verbal since both endeavor to explain the totality of phenomena by a single principle, though their starting points differ. The dualistic view of the world engendered by supernaturalism, Strauss suggested to Conway on a visit to Heilbronn in 1864, reinforces superstition as the Siamese twin of political despotism. In striking at supernaturalism Strauss was aiming at the whole tree of political and social degradation.[29]

Always committed to liberal social reform, Conway returned to Hegel in explaining Strauss's apparent conservatism as a legislator. Strauss, as Conway put it, distrusted sweeping away a few snowdrifts when winter was still in the air. In this respect he correctly followed Hegel. "Those who study Hegel," Conway insisted, "know that his apparent conservatism was the crust outside a fiery radicalism." Hegel viewed history as the realization of liberty but also held that in modern times a Reformation was its indispensable prerequisite. The French Revolution, missing this prerequisite, had led only to formal, "external freedom." Full freedom, however, required basic institutional changes. Similarly, as Conway put it, Strauss broke with the popular movements of his day because he properly and wisely saw that the institutional conditions of concrete freedom were being left out of account.[30]

Language as Nature Humanizing

During his years in Cincinnati, Conway's sermons, addresses, and writings developed many ramifications of his naturalistic philosophy of religion, a philosophy largely derived from Emerson, Parker, Strauss, and Hegel and confirmed in Darwin's theory of evolution. In a sermon on Socinius, for example, Conway found his own major conclusions already adumbrated in the views of that sixteenth-century champion of tolerance who "had vindicated the right of private thought" in his own life. Furthermore, Socinius had seen the "humanity of Christ," the human sorrow and suffering and joy of the "prophet of man," as the true center of the Christian Zion. Jesus's office as mediator and helper could only be destroyed by his deification.[31]

Refusing to identify Jesus with the Deity, Conway was nevertheless ready to find in Jesus a reflection of the principles and values of his naturalistic philosophy of religion. For example, in *Tracts for Today,* published during his Cincinnati ministry, Conway saw Jesus as the greatest of freethinkers:

> I will take you to the bed of the greatest freethinker who ever trod the earth. It is a hard, severe one, and there is much agony on it. A terrible freethinker's end, you may say! It is only about eighteen centuries back. That death-bed is the cross—that freethinker is Christ. Never before had a spirit of doubt been let loose with such resistless power on this earth. His doubts led him to the doctors' feet at first, where his parents found him inquiring of them in the Temple; they led him to the wilderness, to the cold mountain, to the midnight air. He brought all the existing order into doubt. Pharisee and Scribe, Temple-service and Palace, Church and State bear witness that a fearful questioning of all things is at hand. Every drop of his blood is paid for free thought.[32]

Above all, Conway was concerned with the human significance of Jesus and not his status as defined in a supernatural or Platonic metaphysics. The road to God lay not in the intellect but in the heart, in the pulses of love to one's fellowman and brother. The mission of the church was essentially a mission to humanity, a dedication to the dignity of man and "a God identified with man."[33]

As he developed his naturalistic philosophy of religion and departed from supernaturalistic views on God, on the activities of Jesus, and on man's relation to nature, Conway could not but become aware of the problem of the shift in meaning of key words he was using in his sermons and addresses. He became sensitive to the relation of language and thought and to the perils of language in misleading thought, thus anticipating the current preoccupations of semanticists and prominent thinkers in Britain and America who see the main business of philosophy as the clarification of thought and the elimination of intellectual muddles through analysis of language.

As early as 1855 in Washington Conway had given addresses on the origin, uses, and misuses of words. He developed this theme in a sermon to his Cincinnati congregation and in a lengthy article for *The Dial.* Using "Hold Fast the Form of Sound Words" as his text, Conway introduced his sermon with a vivid warning from Bacon "that words as a Tartar's bow do shoot back upon the understanding of the wisest and mightily entangle and pervert the judgment." What was needed was "a philosophy of words," and though Friedrich Schlegel and the Humboldts, Conway noted in *The Dial,* had studied the bearing of language on race, "the naturalist of words" had yet to appear.

In Conway's view the use and development of language is characteristic of mankind, a specific and distinctive mark of humanity in contrast to animality. Further it is distinctly a social achievement. "Words are the fossil thoughts and experiences of a race." While Genesis might attest to the antiquity of language with the assignment of names in the Garden of Eden, the notion of "a supernatural gift of words from the Creator must be excluded" on the basis of "the frequent imperfections of words in expressing the true nature of their objects" as shown, for example, in the Old Testament conception of "firmament." Nevertheless there is a religious significance in language. With language nature begins ascent to God through man. "It is Nature humanizing."[34]

The various uses and derivatives of words show that they are only "symbols" of things. This is the first great principle of language. The word is not the fact itself. "The word *love,*" Conway noted, "can not do instead of loving; *truth* and *mercy* can mean nothing save to the merciful and true." As knowledge changes and grows, the meanings of words change, as shown in the meaning of "sunrise" since Copernicus's discovery of the relation of earth to sun. On the same basis, a misleading use of words may arise as in the case of "insane" and "lunatic," holdovers from a period of ignorance about the nature and causes of mental disorders. Conway found theology particularly prolific of misleading uses of words and full of "cant"—itself merely the use of unsound words—about "trinity," "election," and "orthodox." And many theological words have acquired emotional tones quite foreign to their origin, tones which widely mislead thought. "Heretic," for example, in its root meaning involved "choice," one's own decision as to what should or should not be believed but now leads people to shudder at unbelievers. The situation is similar, Conway held, in regard to "freethinker":

> The grandeur of the word free-thinker is written upon its face, and he who denounces free thought or rationalism (ratio-reason) must blaspheme God in his construction of the necessary functions of the human mind, and insult the noblest attributes of man![35]

Conway viewed his effort to be a "naturalist of words" as of great importance for the philosophy of liberal Christianity he was developing and propounding in his many sermons and articles. Such a philosophy particularly required clear thought and critical use of traditional ideas in the service of freedom and the dignity of man. Liberal Christians, Conway insisted to his Cincinnati congregation and readers, must especially seek sound meanings for the key words in their frame of thought. His clarification of his own naturalistic theology, however, made it increasingly difficult for him to remain in the First Congregational Church of Cincinnati, which had already split over the issue of miracles and supernaturalism. His antislavery position, moreover, was mounting in vehemence. He had seen Wendell Phillips assaulted with rocks and eggs following introductory words of J. B. Stallo. In spite of the violence—probably "the last literal stoning of an abolitionist"—Phillips was entertained in the homes of many prominent Cincinnatians and fulfilled his engagement to speak from Conway's pulpit. In these circumstances Conway readily accepted an invitation to join F. B. Sanborn to edit *The Commonwealth* in Boston, a strongly antislavery journal. On June 29, 1862, he preached his farewell sermon in Cincinnati and shortly thereafter left for his new residence in Concord, Massachusetts, to re-establish old ties of friendship from his Harvard days with Emerson, Alcott, and W. H. Channing.

Abolitionist and Liberal Minister Abroad

During his two years with *The Commonwealth* Conway's ardor against slavery became more intense. He became bitterly impatient with Lincoln, the only president for whom he ever voted, for refusing to act immediately and decisively on emancipation in the "golden hour" of opportunity to end slavery. In this mood Conway went so far as to attack Lincoln as a "tool," a "follower," and not a real leader. At a meeting in Massachusetts celebrating the freeing of slaves in the British West Indies, Conway lamented that God had given America stupid leaders, and in a moment of high-pitched excitement he was ready to welcome world revolution to sweep away all forms of tyranny.

To the abolitionists associated with *The Commonwealth* Conway, born in Virginia and militantly opposed to slavery, seemed just the man to convince the English that slavery was *the* issue of the war and win their sympathy to the Union cause. In 1863 Conway went to London where he conferred with literary leaders—unsuccessfully in the case of Carlyle—addressed meetings of the Emancipation Society and Workingmen's College, and blundered into a treasonable offer to the Confederate envoy "on behalf of the leading antislavery men of America," an offer to oppose further prosecution of the war upon immediate and complete emancipation of the slaves. Conway's blunder created much consternation in England and America. His sympathizers dissociated themselves from his offer, and the incident was finally closed when the President and Secretary of State accepted a letter of explanation convincing them of his personal integrity.

In spite of little apparent progress and a diplomatic blunder, the virulence of Conway's opposition to slavery was unabated. He not only fought for complete emancipation but went so far as to advocate intermarriage as the solution for the race problem, holding that intermarriage would result in a stronger people in every way. "The evening star of the epoch of separate races," said Conway, "is the morning star of Human Unity. Men we have, but not yet Man."[36] Finally, as Conway continued to attack Lincoln's policies for their weakness and called him the most detested President in America's history, those reponsible for *The Commonwealth* refused to accept his articles from London on American politics. He had become blinded, they thought, by the intensity of his feelings.

In the meantime Conway became associated with the highly liberal-minded Ethical Society meeting at the South Place Chapel in the Finsbury section of London. Following a series of addresses as guest minister, he was invited to be permanent minister in 1864. He accepted the Society's invitation, thus indicating that he preferred not to return to America in view of his embarrassing diplomatic blunder, his differences with antislavery men over segregated Negro regiments, and the prospect of an uphill fight to nominate Fremont against Lincoln. Conway remained in London as the permanent minister of the Ethical Society for over thirty years and made such a distinguished record that the Society's new meeting place on Red Lion Square now bears his name, Conway Hall. At the end of his first year the General

Committee of the South Place Chapel was well pleased with its selection of a minister. In the words of the Committee's secretary:

> A more earnest, interesting, instructive, and eloquent series of Services than Mr. Conway has presented to the Congregation throughout the year could scarcely have been hoped for by the most sanguine among us, reviving, in the opinion of many, in their deep philosophy, in their nobleness of thought, and in their stimulus to upright and useful conduct, the best memories of the Finsbury pulpit.[37]

That pulpit had earlier been filled by William Johnstone Fox, an outstanding radical Unitarian. In recent years it has been occupied from time to time by such eminent philosophers as C. E. M. Joad, Susan Stebbing, and Bertrand Russell. A few years after Conway came to the Finsbury pulpit the congregation approved his substitution of devotional readings for formal prayer. An All-Wise and All-Loving Father, Conway felt, "could not change one iota of his wise perfect laws for all the prayers in the Universe."[38]

During his years in London Conway maintained some close ties with Cincinnati. He returned twice, in 1875 and in 1881, for well-attended lectures in the city. On the first of these visits he persuaded the conservatives who had seceded from his church in 1859 to return and even consent to omit the word "Christian" from the society's name so as not to alienate Jews and freethinking Germans who were an important part of the old congregation. After his sermon at the first meeting of the reunited church, many old friends begged him to return to Cincinnati permanently.

Conway further maintained ties with his Ohio friends and associates through a series of lively letters from 1870 to 1883 to Cincinnati newspapers, mainly to the *Cincinnati Commercial*, edited by his good friend Murat Halstead. These popular, chatty, sometimes sensational letters revealed the versatility of Conway's interests as well as the boldness of his thinking.[39] He reported, for example, the details of the struggle between capital and labor and the valuable role of unions in the iron industry of Staffordshire. Writing of George Eliot's funeral, he gave details on her background, her relation to Strauss, and her liaison with G. H. Lewes. He reported on the opening of plays and art exhibits in London, activities in Parliament, the growth of the Chartist movement in relation to London poverty, the proceedings of an international prison-reform congress, the funeral of Darwin, the views of Russian nihilists living in London, new and old books, and the aims of a Secularist Congress meeting in Leeds. With attention to native and exiled "radical republicans" like Arthur Trevelyan and Louis Blanc, Conway used his letters from London to describe the refugees from the Paris Commune. He tried to explode the myth of their bloodthirstiness and sympathetically compared their views to those which had animated Brook Farm near Boston. Needless to say, these letters sometimes aroused strong feelings. Their "radical religious and political opinions" were often "answered" or attacked in Cincinnati newspapers.

Soon after Conway became permanent minister of the Ethical Society he began associating with exiled revolutionists in London such as Mazzini, Louis Blanc, and Karl Blind. He exchanged views with Blanc but was closer to Blind who persuaded him to give a series of addresses to "the working class" on "relations between employers and employed, co-operation, the elevation of woman, national education, sanitary reforms, etc." The Conways and Blinds shared social evenings, and Conway later tried to induce Blind to participate in a projected Conference of Liberal Thinkers. When Blind's stepson made an unsuccessful attempt to assassinate Bismarck, Conway wrote an article to vindicate the attempt as a deed of noble self-sacrifice. Blind, who had been a leading figure in the German republican Revolution of 1848 and thereafter close to Karl Marx for a decade, was prominent among the London exiles and won Conway's deepest respect. "I have felt," wrote Conway, "that with Freiligrath, Kinkel, and others the real Germany was being modelled around the table of Karl Blind where also Mazzini, Ledru Rollin, Louis Blanc and others are also brothers."[40]

These associations reinforced Conway's interest in German thought and culture which had been crystallized during his days in Cincinnati. Thus on the centenary of Alexander Humboldt's birth Conway gave an address reflecting his deep admiration for that great German naturalist and his continued preoccupation with natural science as the only genuine form of knowledge. Conway saw in Humboldt's *Cosmos* "a hymn to the unity and perfection of Nature," the keynote of the age. Humboldt clearly depicted the unity of man and nature. Conway was pleased to note that Humboldt was widely regarded as an "infidel" and that the present generation sitting at the feet of Strauss, Renan, Emerson, Mill, and Huxley was just as little to be called Christian.[41] With the outbreak of the Franco-Prussian War, in which Conway observed the grim reality of battle at Gravelotte, his sympathies were with Germany as fighting for a free fatherland which would resist any oppression Bismarck might impose on either victor or vanquished.[42] But Conway's sympathy for downtrodden humanity superseded his feelings for any particular nation. Soon he was writing in defense of exiles from the Paris commune and seeking aid for them in London in collaboration with Karl Marx.[43]

German Republicanism and Religion of Humanity

Conway's mature political philosophy was widely informed by what he learned from German republicans in Karl Blind's circle. In his book on *Republican Superstitions,* written with the special encouragement of Louis Blanc, Conway concentrated on those political "beliefs without evidence" which European and British republicans were in danger of borrowing from the United States. Though the fathers of the American republic, Conway believed, were singularly free of such superstitions and wanted direct popular government by an executive committee and Congress, compromises with property and state interests introduced elements of the British monarchical pattern in the presidency and two houses of Congress. As a result the Civil War was made inevitable, and the House of Representatives became an assembly of corrupt brawlers trying to get their "hands in the till."[44]

The defects of the American republic, Conway believed, were especially apparent in the presidency. In view of the corruption and high-handedness of the Grant administration and the mediocrity of many presidents, Conway concluded with J. S. Mill that the chief executive should be elected by the people's representatives in their sovereign assembly. Such a procedure would also avoid the possible tyranny of a separately elected executive and eliminate perpetual opposition between the executive and assembly. In this conclusion Conway found strong support from *Der Deutsche Eidgenoss* (*The German Republican*) edited by Karl Blind and other committed republicans such as Louis Büchner, Ludwig Feuerbach, Ferdinand Freiligrath, Friedrich Hecker, General Franz Sigel, and Gustav Struve, most of whom had been leaders in the German Revolution of 1848. Conway quoted the program of the German republicans at length:

> The Constitution of the United States, however excellent in other respects, still bears, in some measure, the traces of the monarchical traditions of Europe. According to truly Republican principles, the executive power ought to originate from the legislative power, and continually remain responsible to it. But

> in America the President is appointed by an electoral act *outside* of the popular representation. He therefore stands on a level with the latter; maybe, in opposition to it; in a certain degree, even above it.
>
> Such a provision is only void of danger if the character of the man so appointed contains all guarantees of trustworthiness. It is difficult, however, to look into the human heart. The Constitution of a Republic should consequently be so framed, that it acts as a strong check and preventative against every despotic inclination.
>
> The disadvantages of the mode of election in the United States are only mitigated in so far as the appointment of a Chief of the Commonwealth is brought about by an election with two degrees. Even this feeble protection against certain surprises—such as have sometimes occurred in the history of Free States—a Republican party in America, which otherwise belongs to the most advanced, proposed to abolish! In the name of "Radicalism," the Cleveland Convention demanded that, in future, the election of a President should be accomplished by the direct vote of the masses. This desire is in direct contradiction to a wise Republican theory. We have seen the result of such a direct vote in France, 1848. Through the conflict which broke out, in consequence of such a procedure, between the Legislative and the Executive, a Usurper made his way to arbitrary rule.[45]

Though in political practice Conway was sometimes loose in his thinking and unwilling to engage in "the art of the possible," in conviction he was unreservedly on the side of assured popular government, the equality of all citizens, and unrestricted freedom of conscience, speech, and assembly.

As Conway associated with British "rationalists" and increasingly sought to apply the doctrine of evolution to religious forms, religious freedom, and the problem of sin, his thought moved through the view that nature is the manifestation of mind and love, a "measureless organism of Reason," toward a "religion of Humanity," free of all traces of his former theism.[46] This movement reflected the influence of Strauss, whose views Conway so warmly praised in 1874, and finally was crystallized under the impact of Ludwig Feuerbach.

Strauss had not pursued the question of the psychological source of myths, the content of religion, but acknowledged in *The Old Faith and the New* that Ludwig Feuerbach, another prominent "Left-Hegelian," had found the answer.[47] In a parallel movement Conway, in 1880, turned to a study of Feuerbach's *Essence of Christianity*. The results were apparent in discourses he delivered in South Place Chapel.

In an address occasioned by the publication of George Eliot's translation of *The Essence of Christianity* Conway noted how Feuerbach had continued the effort begun with German research and Unitarianism "to reconstitute Christianity on a natural basis." In particular, Feuerbach found Christianity more interesting than Christ as a great chapter in the spiritual history of mankind. After critics like Strauss had worked on the myths and dogmas in the Bible, Feuerbach pursued the question of their origin, "the mental and moral facts beneath them." He found the roots of religion to be man's self-consciousness as a species. Hence God is the personification by man of his own higher powers as a distinct being. In Feuerbach's words:

> Man—this is the mystery of religion—projects his being into objectivity, and then again makes himself an object to this projected image of himself thus converted into a subject; he thinks of himself as an object to himself, but as the object of an object, of another being. Thus here. Man is an object to God. . . . Man is himself at once I and thou; he can put himself in the place of another, for this reason, that to him his species, his essential nature, and not merely his individuality is an object of thought.[48]

On this basis Conway concluded with Feuerbach that the more God is exalted in theological Christianity, the more man is degraded; the more God is reified as a transcendent, metaphysical being, the more is Christ's one supreme command, "Love," replaced by the divisive, hate-breeding rule, "Believe." Conway fully accepted Feuerbach's view of Christ:

> He who loves man for man's sake, who rises to . . universal love . . he is Christ himself. He does what Christ did, what made Christ Christ . . Where there arises the consciousness of the species as species, the idea of humanity as a whole, Christ disappears, but not his true nature.[49]

Sharing Feuerbach's attitude toward "faith" and the command to "believe" in theological Christianity, Conway welcomed the decay of faith as a liberation of humanity. "Every day," Conway was pleased to observe, "the Christ of superstition declines, and Christ becomes a name for human charity."

Relying on Feuerbach's ideas rather than principles of Comte's "positivism" which he found ambiguous,[50] Conway emphasized the moral implications of the "religion of Humanity." Feuerbach had stated the moral law corresponding to the scientific law Darwin had discovered and Emerson had translated into spiritual truth—namely, "Man has his highest being, his God, in himself; not as an individual but in his essential nature—his species."[51] On this basis, moral conduct is action in loyalty to the law of the species, a law requiring variation and individuality in the service of universal ends. This, in contrast to Jewish tribalism and Christian sectarianism, is the basis of a truly Catholic religion in which man "finds his saviour by becoming one." Such a religion, not faith in a supernatural being, is properly the "religion of Humanity" foreshadowed by Feuerbach. It "transfers to the moral and intellectual forces which are mastering nature all the piety that now worships personifications of the abstractions mastered."[52]

Shortly before his death in 1907, and after he had returned to America to spend his last years in New York at work on his memoirs and vindicating biographies of Paine and Edmund Randolph, one of his ancestors, Conway gave testimony to the lasting influence of Hegelian philosophy, particularly the "Left-Hegelian" philosophy of Strauss, on his thinking. In an address on "Dogma and Science" delivered at the Rome Congress of Freethinkers in 1904, Conway recalled how Strauss had seen that "all freedom must be preceded by emancipation from supernaturalism," the birthplace of superstition and hence oppression. Strauss had insisted that

> So long as men accept religious control not based on reason, they will accept political control not based on reason. The man who gives up the whole of his moral nature to an unquestioned authority suffers a paralysis of his mind, and all the changes of outward circumstances in the world cannot make him a free man.[53]

In the whole course of Conway's life and thought the views of Hegel, Feuerbach, and particularly Strauss were the major impetus for a "New Reformation" of religion, a reformation which is still going on in current movements to "demythologize" Christianity and find its "existential" basis in man's concrete experience. For Conway the "New Reformation" began with the "fifth gospel" of Emerson and Parker, linked German "rationalism" with the scientific outlook inspired by Darwin, and carried the abolitionist passion for freedom and humanity into movements for wider social reform—the elevation of labor, the improvement of democracy, and the achievement of world peace.

VI

AUGUST WILLICH'S LEFT-HEGELIAN SOCIALISM

Running through August Willich's views and ideas was a single thread—one might appropriately say a red thread—namely, socialism as an immediate task and promise for the future. His commitment to socialism, to "the social republic" as extending the principle of democratic self-government into all social and economic institutions, animated and shaped his whole philosophy of life. It permeated his views on man, history, religion, economics, and politics. It was at once the persistent, dominating theme of all his mature reflection and the mainspring of his action as a military leader, champion of labor, political organizer, and newspaper editor.

The red thread of Willich's thought, however, was not entirely of his own making. For some of its main strands and fibers he was indebted to the philosophy of Hegel, particularly as Hegel's thought had been assimilated, criticized, and revised in the views of Ludwig Feuerbach and Karl Marx.

Yet Willich added important strands and fibers of his own. What his social thought lacked in intellectual rigor and consecutiveness was partly offset by its independence and originality in regard to the proper role of unions and government in the social republic he sought for America.

Parentage and Childhood with Schleiermacher

August Willich was born November 19, 1810, in the village of Braunsberg, East Prussia, some thirty miles from Königsberg where the great pathbreaker of modern philosophy, Immanuel Kant, spent his entire lifetime. Willich's family was a distinguished one, going back on his father's side through a line of clergymen with large families to Peter Willich, an army chaplain and parish minister in Brandenburg from 1652 to 1701.[1] His grandfather, an official of the Lutheran Church on the Isle of Rügen, had been raised to nobility in 1786, thus adding a "von" to the family name, and his father, a captain of cavalry in a Hussar regiment, was awarded civil offices for his military services and wounds in the French wars. Through his mother, Fredericka Lisette Michalowska, Willich's ancestry was Polish. According to some reports she was an actress, but in any case she never engendered in her son much filial love or respect. Toward the end of his life Willich was heard to say, "My mother was a beautiful Polish woman—and how I hated her."[2] This relationship, one is tempted to conjecture, may have had something to do with Willich's permanent bachelorhood.

The lines of Willich's parentage, however, are clouded by the widespread belief among his contemporaries that his real father was a member of the Hohenzollern family, possibly Prince August, brother of King Frederick William III. Stallo, Conway, and many other Cincinnatians held to the story of Willich's Hohenzollern ancestry. In their private correspondence Marx and Engels referred to him as "The Hohenzollern Knight," and Engels said he had inherited the "treacherous Hohenzollern eyes" from his father, Prince August. Willich himself, on one occasion, gave support to the belief that he was of noble birth. Toward the end of his life in St. Mary's, Ohio, and long after he had dropped the aristocratic "von" from his name, he responded to a query about the Kaiser's appearance with a twirl of his mustache and the statement, "Look at me and you will see the Kaiser."[3] To be sure, the removal of the Prussian court to Königsberg a few years before Willich's birth and its previous reputation for "loose living" lend some circumstantial support to the belief in his royal ancestry. But the lack of any firm and decisive evidence—difficult to secure in the nature of the case—pushes the matter into legend, a colorful legend appropriate to Willich's colorful personality.

On the death of his father at Braunsberg in 1814, young August and his older brother went to live in the home of Friedrich Schleiermacher, professor at the University of Berlin, who was to become one of Germany's most eminent and influential theologians. Shortly before his appointment at the university Schleiermacher had married the widow of Willich's uncle who had been a pastor on the island of Bergen in the North Sea. The years Willich spent in daily contact with the distinguished professor, then lecturing in both philosophy and theology, were very likely more important in the formation of his character and thought than his family inheritance, royal or otherwise.

In philosophy Schleiermacher was particularly concerned with Plato, whose dialogues he translated, and with German idealism as represented in Kant, Fichte, and Schelling, Hegel's immediate predecessors whose views Hegel amended into his own. Schleiermacher's attitude toward the German idealists, however, was distinctly critical. He found their philosophical systems too formal and their view of the unity between knower and known much too abstract and stuck in antitheses. For Schleiermacher the unity of knower and known was to be sought in felt individual existence beyond the purview of analytic, dissecting intelligence. Hence he particularly favored the philosophy of nature advanced by his former colleague at Halle, Heinrich Steffens, who believed that throughout nature, from its lowest forms to progressively developing organic life, there is an individualizing tendency. The more individual any natural form becomes, the more it bears the stamp of infinity as it more richly embraces the differences and antitheses of its existence.[4]

Some faint but distinct echoes of this view of nature appear in Willich's later writings though he never overtly linked them with Schleiermacher or with his years in Schleiermacher's home. In those years he was almost certainly exposed to Schleiermacher's ideas and possibly also to a wide circle of scholars and professors from the University of Berlin. The circle, however, did not likely include Hegel with whom Schleiermacher differed on fundamental issues. Other facets of Willich's later thought such as respect for individuality and political independence may have been fixed during the years of his youth in Schleiermacher's house, and the memory of those years very likely entered into his decision to attend the University of Berlin five decades later.

Philosophy in the Prussian Army

At the age of twelve Willich began his education for a military career. For three years he attended the Cadet School at Potsdam on the edge of Berlin and after that spent three more years at the Cadet House of the Royal Military

Academy in Berlin in the period when Karl von Clausewitz was director of the Academy and beginning his rise to prominence as a military theoretician. On graduation from the Royal Academy in 1828 Willich was commissioned a second lieutenant and assigned to the infantry. In the 1840's he was promoted to first lieutenant and company commander in the 7th Royal Artillery Brigade stationed in Westphalia where, as in other Rhine provinces, democratic and socialist tendencies frequently came to expression in the public press and sometimes in open demonstrations. These tendencies left their mark on the military forces as well as the civilian population and contributed to a radical change in the course of Willich's life.

Around 1845 Willich became a leader in a circle of army officers devoted to the study of forbidden books and the discussion of social and political principles which increasingly generated opposition to the monarchy and the monarchical pattern of army life. The circle also included among its leading members Friedrich Anneke and Joseph Weydemeyer who, like Willich, were later to become active in the Revolution of 1848 and supporters of the Union cause in the American Civil War. In their studies and discussion the dissident officers paid particular attention to Hegel's philosophy. As one member of the circle wrote, "The study of Hegelian philosophy and political-social sciences led to a critical investigation of conditions and brought forth in the officer corps an opposition party."[5] Certainly Hegel's view of the "spirit of a people," his heavy restriction of the power of the monarch, his analysis of the economic class struggle within civil society, and his provisions for individual freedom in a fully rational state could have contributed to such a result. Within the circle of democratically-minded officers Willich was one of the oldest and most experienced. This made him keenest and most decisive in the art of wedding "word" and "deed."[6] Like others in the group who became "true socialists," *i.e.*, socialists dedicated to ethical principles and the realization of man's true humanity, Willich was always impatient with theory alone or any preference of theory to action.

In a move to eliminate the growing democratic and socialist sentiment in the officer-corps, Willich's superiors transferred him to the fortress of Kolberg in Pomerania and expelled Anneke from the army. Willich responded with an open letter to the king requesting permission to leave an army in which he could no longer in conscience serve as an officer. He explained his decision and the events leading to his release from the army in a fifty-page pamphlet, *In the Prussian Army*, which also revealed the direction of his philosophy in 1848.

In Willich's view the Prussian army of the 1840's had subverted the "spirit of the people" which Tacitus had identified with German freedom and which was dramatically manifest in the War of Liberation of 1806. Then the army which defeated France was "the people armed" and their leaders were fellow-citizens. By the 1840's, however, the officers who led the army were separate from the people. They were a special class whose position depended on birth, name, or family, rather than capability. As a result there arose the new idea that a man could be a soldier and nothing more. In Willich's view, however, an individual was first a man, then a citizen, and then a soldier. "Where human right contradicts state law," Willich wrote, "the state is wrong; where military law conflicts with state law, the military is wrong. Humanity and human rights constitute the foundation of the state as well as rank."[7] Where an individual's circumstances no longer permitted him to act in accordance with the "universal human consciousness," the principle of Humanity manifest in all religion, science, and law, he had no choice but to remove himself from those circumstances. On this basis Willich concluded, as he said in his letter to the king, that he could no longer have anything to do with a rank or position which was opposed in principle to the idea of Humanity and human dignity.[8]

Admitting his long friendship with Anneke whose views he shared; and recognizing that "communist sentiments" were part of the indictment against Anneke, Willich felt impelled to explain his own social views to clear up misunderstandings. Deeply disturbed by the "pressing need and demoralization of the working class" in face of luxury on the other side, he had been driven to study various communist and socialist systems. Usually he found them unrealistic or lacking in intellectual foundations. In some cases they were willing to rely on hate to achieve their end. But "as the means are," Willich insisted, "so is the end. The means through which something is accomplished also retain mastery over it."[9] After witnessing the proletarian bread riots in Pomerania and the struggle concerning the Prussian Diet, after being "taken with brotherly love into the circle of old and new friends in the Rhineland" on leaving the army, he was still disturbed by the notion that man is essentially egoistic and selfish. He turned his thoughts to "the essence of man and his relation to nature" in order to find the conditions of man's reconciliation.

Willich's search for intellectual foundations led him to see the universe as an eternal, self-existing, and moving Whole out of which physical things, chemical elements, and living things emerge as increasingly unified forms. With man, however, life is not only a specific form as with animals but "the feeling of totality" and the "thought of existence" as well. Thus there are two sides to the human individual—the drive toward the Whole and the drive toward self-perpetuation of the particular individual. The clash of these drives is suggested in *Genesis* and manifest in the long world-historical struggle of humanity. With both drives in his innermost depths man includes within him both death and immortality, time and eternity, egoism and altruism. "Man lives eternity in a moment and a moment in eternity."[10]

Where and how, Willich asked, is mankind to be reconciled with itself and truly unified? Reconciliation will not come through Christianity whose message of the unity of all life in God has become, after two thousand years, "mere words." Nor will it come through politics in its present form. This is only an arena of private egoism and self-seeking. It must be sought, rather, in labor, in man's working life. Only as the laborer controls his employment can the needs of community life be met and industry be humanized in a way that preserves the free will of the individual.[11] In a society of this type the state would initiate economic activities, but the young must be particularly educated for the control of their work-life. With the use of machines as slaves, work would no longer be drudgery but rather an all-sided human activity. Statesmen could then take seriously the common good in a unified working society. With such a reorganization of labor, man would necessarily find himself in the community and the community in him. When existing forms of selfishness and self-seeking are thus put to rest, Willich concluded, "the reconciled man, the man of the community" is born.

Several elements of this view of man's relation to nature and society faintly echo Schleiermacher's ideas. They reappear in greater detail and clarity in Willich's subsequent writings in the *Cincinnati Republikaner*. But it is already apparent that Hegel's influence had been felt, though Willich never overtly mentioned it. Like Hegel, Willich viewed the universe as a vast, eternal, infinite process whose particular elements are real in so far as they become unified or whole. With Hegel he saw this process as moving dialectically, as being a perpetual series of antitheses or clashes to be reconciled with one another.

Willich's particular view of the nature of man, however, bears strong traces of the thought of Feuerbach who had critically incorporated several aspects of Hegel's philosophy into his own and was the inspirer of the "true socialists" with whom Willich associated in Cologne after leaving the army. The true socialists, particularly Moses Hess, emphasized the wholeness of humanity and man's reconciliation with himself—the overcoming of his "alienation" in capitalist society—as the underlying rationale for a new, communistic social order.[12] Willich's ideas about the proper organization of society reveal that he had identified himself with the working class and saw socialism as a question of the control and organization of work by the workers themselves. This conclusion coincided with the view of the working class and its relation to socialism which Hess had adopted from Marx and Engels in 1846.

Worker and Revolutionary Leader

On leaving the army in 1847 Willich went to Cologne where he was "taken with brotherly love into the circle of old and new friends," a branch of the Communist League which included his "old friend" Anneke and was led by a "new friend," Andreas Gottschalk, a physician who practiced medicine in the working-class quarters of Cologne and had made the workers' cause his own. Gottschalk had jointly owned a clandestine printing press with Moses Hess and highly esteemed him as the intellectual mentor of the League's central committee. Since Cologne was the largest city in the most industrialized section of Germany, the League there was strong and active with a membership of some 7,000 workers. Willich became a leader in the League and early in 1848 was its president.[13] He had solidly identified himself with the working class by becoming a carpenter's apprentice and deliberately paraded with axe on shoulder and carpenter's apron in front of his former army associates to advance the cause of socialism among the military.

With the news of the French revolution the Communist League in Cologne organized a mass demonstration at the city hall on March 3, 1848. Gottschalk, Willich, and Anneke were leaders of the demonstration. In the name of the working class—"the fourth estate" and "most important of all estates"—they called for universal suffrage, free speech, freedom of the press and assembly, replacement of the standing army by a people's militia, improvement of labor, and free public education. After the municipal officials had fled through the windows of the city hall, an army unit arrived in time to arrest Willich. The following day Gottschalk and Anneke were arrested, but Willich was released. Marx and Engels, leaders of the Cologne Democratic Society which included the communists as its "left-wing," warmly welcomed the March 3 demonstration and considered its leaders their "new friends," the "three best people" in the struggle for democracy.

Around the middle of March Willich went to Heidelberg to join the democratic forces, particularly the "convinced democrats" who did not believe that parliamentary institutions could be established by gradual measures. After a meeting with Bakunin, the implacable Russian revolutionary, Willich assumed command of a unit of the republican army led by Friedrich Hecker and went into battle at Kandern. The republican forces were defeated, and Willich took his troops to Besançon in France to prepare for further fighting. Unemployed German laborers flocked to his unit which became known as the "Workers' Legion." The Legion lived in poverty and distress in Besançon, supported by a trifling dole from the French government. Beloved and trusted by his volunteers, Willich shared their poverty, took no privileges for himself, and never shirked from even the hardest manual labor. The dignity and discipline of the Workers' Legion in spite of adversities won the admiration of the people of Besançon. Its plight, however, did not secure it financial support from Marx's Democratic Society, and the more radical elements in Cologne who had identified themselves with the cause of the workers saw this as evidence of Marx's "opportunism." Marx held that the workers should support a capitalist revolution in Germany against feudal power to secure material foundations in industry for a new society. The proletarian revolution and transition to socialism could only come later. To this view the leading Cologne communists replied as Willich did a year later: Why should the workers spill their blood for "decrepit capitalist domination"?[14]

Entering Lyons illegally to find recruits for his republican forces, Willich was arrested, held prisoner, and finally escorted in chains to the Swiss border. With a further wave of revolutionary uprising in the spring of 1849 Willich returned to Germany to command a corps of volunteers fighting in Baden. Among the members of the corps was the poet Gottfried Kinkel with whom Willich was later associated in an effort to revive the German revolution. Willich's adjutant was Friedrich Engels, Marx's lifelong friend and collaborator.

In a letter to Marx, Engels described Willich as "brave, cold-blooded, skillful, and of quick and sound perception in battle but outside of battle a somewhat boring ideologist and true socialist."[15] This characterization was an implicit criticism of Willich's views. Engels was suggesting that for

Willich socialism was essentially a matter of high principles and the proper mental picture of a new social order with no provision for the real foundations of socialism in the ongoing economic developments of society. Engels was pointing out that Willich was preoccupied, as both he and Marx had been earlier, with socialism as a question of the "realization of Humanity" rather than as a movement of the economic forces and relationships of society. In brief, Willich had not gone beyond Feuerbach and Moses Hess.

In the fighting in Baden Willich's unit, composed almost entirely of workingmen, was one of the best in the revolutionary army. It fought hard to the very end and was one of the last units to be forced out of Germany into Switzerland. But in spite of the high hopes and hard fighting the revolution was defeated. Toward the end of 1849 Willich left Switzerland for London, the gathering-place for many of the leading republican exiles.

The Communist League

In London Willich immediately joined the workers' movement headed by Marx, whose writings he knew and whom he had met once in Germany. On Marx's initiative and with Engels' recommendation he became a member of the central committee of the Communist League. His attractive personality and selfless sharing of privation with the revolutionary exiles made him a popular leader. With Marx, Engels, Bauer, and Pfänder he founded a Fugitives' Aid Committee to assist political refugees who were coming to London in increasing numbers. The committee gave its aid freely, without restrictions based on specific political loyalties. At one meeting of refugees Willich put the question as to whether anyone whom the committee had aided had been asked whether he was a communist. The answer was decisively negative.

As a member of the central committee of the Communist League—along with Marx, Engels, Schapper, Bauer, and Eccarius—Willich co-sponsored a circular in March, 1850, calling on German workers to support capitalist and business elements in an imminent revolutionary uprising but at the same time "make the revolution permanent" until "the possessing classes have been forced out of power and state power has been taken over by the proletariat, and the association of proletarians, not only in one country, but in all the leading countries of the world has so far advanced that competition among workers of these countries has ceased and finally the most important forces of production are in their hands." To achieve this end the workers must be ready to push the ordinary democrats to measures of violence and demand that large feudal estates not be broken into small private holdings but converted into large-scale workers' colonies to establish the principle of common ownership.[16]

Not content with a proletarian revolution in Germany alone, Willich joined Marx and Engels, Julian Harney from the British Chartists, and two French followers of Auguste Blanqui, who favored insurrectionary action and proletarian dictatorship, in launching a World Society of Revolutionary Communists. The first article of the Society's charter, written by Willich in French in April, 1850, asserted:

> The aim of the Association is the overthrow of all privileged classes and their subjection to the dictatorship of the proletarians by maintaining the revolution in permanence up to the achievement of communism which is to be the ultimate organizational form of the human family.[17]

Other articles of the Society's charter welcomed all revolutionary communists willing to unite in republican solidarity, designated the founders as the executive committee of the Society, prescribed conditions for admission to the Society, and bound all adherents strictly to uphold the first article above. Apparently, however, the World Society of Revolutionary Communists was little more than a paper organization. It lasted for seven months, killed by the split within the Communist League between Marx and Engels on one side and Willich and Schapper on the other. Engels invited the French supporters to join him at his home in October, 1850, to witness the burning of the Society's charter. Like the Communist League circular of March, 1850, however, the charter of the World Society represented a point and period of unanimity between Willich and Marx on specific revolutionary strategy and communist goals.

With increasing prosperity in Europe during the summer of 1850 Marx and Engels concluded that the revolutionary tide had decisively ebbed and that the Communist League should revise its strategy accordingly. Willich differed with them about the prospects of revolutionary action and there resulted a split in the League. Even earlier in the year, however, Willich's differences with Engels had become so acute that a "court of honor" was established within the League to resolve the dispute. Willich refused to appear before the court in protest against its method of procedure. Finally in mid-September the majority of the League's central committee joined Marx and Engels against Willich, Schapper, Fränkel, and Lehman in voting to transfer the central committee to Cologne. Thereafter the two parties within the London League would remain as separate branches of the Cologne organization. Speaking for the majority, Marx formulated his own position and criticized Willich's as follows:

> In place of the universal perspective of the Communist Manifesto, the minority exalts German nationalism and flatters the patriotism of the German worker. In place of the materialist outlook of the Manifesto, the minority advances idealism. It makes will instead of actual conditions the primary factor in

the revolution. While we tell the workers that they must go through 15, 20, 50 years of civil strife to change conditions and fit themselves for power, you tell them to seize power immediately or they can go to sleep. Just as the Democrats used the word "people" as an empty phrase, so now you use the word "proletariat."[18]

The differences between Marx and Willich over questions of strategy were further complicated by personal factors. Willich was much more a man of direct action than Marx and was frequently impatient with theory. While Doctor Marx—Ph.D., University of Jena—studied in the British Museum, lectured to workers on economic theory, and enjoyed the reassurances of a wife and family, Willich lived among the refugee workers and shared their privations. Both their temperaments and their conditions of life tended to generate personal friction. With his long-range theoretical perspective Marx was amused and irritated at hearing Willich say, "It's all so simple." And Willich, in turn, felt that Marx regarded the workers as "zeros."

At one point the friction between the two factions in the Communist League became so intense that one of Marx's followers challenged Willich to a duel, which took place near Antwerp. After that, the division in the League was deeper than ever. One of Marx's friends described the circumstances of the duel and its outcome as follows:

> The differences with Willich's sect became bitterer and one evening Marx was challenged to a duel by Willich. Marx treated that Prussian officer trick for what it was worth, but young Conrad Schramm, a hotspur, replied by insulting Willich who challenged him in accordance with his student code. The duel was to take place by the coast of Belgium, pistols being chosen as the weapon. Schramm had never held a pistol in his hand before, whereas Willich never missed the ace of hearts at twenty paces. His second was Barthélémy. The day for the duel

> went by, we counting the minutes. Next evening, when Marx was away and only his wife and Lenchen were at home, the door opened and Barthélémy entered. He bowed stiffly and in answer to the anxious request for news announced in a sepulchral tone: "Schramm has a bullet in the head." Then he bowed stiffly again, wheeled round and went out. The fright of Mrs. Marx, who almost lost consciousness, can easily be imagined. An hour later she told us the bad news. We naturally gave up all hope for Schramm. Next day, just as we were talking about him mournfully, the door opened and in came the man we thought dead, his head bandaged, but laughing merrily. He told us that the bullet had grazed him and he had lost consciousness. When he had recovered he had been alone by the seashore with his second and the doctor. Willich and Barthélémy had just managed to catch a boat back from Ostend.[19]

In recounting the details of the duel a few years later, Willich noted that Schramm had had no personal grudge against him and had acknowledged his position in the League. The duelists and their seconds had parted, said Willich, "pleased with the happy outcome of the event."

Polemics with Marx

After the split in the Communist League Willich's branch continued to function for a time with Moses Hess as its secretary. Willich had not abandoned his belief in the immediate prospects of revolutionary action along the lines on which he, Marx, and the central committee of the League had agreed in March, 1850. Early in 1851 the Paris branch of Willich's League discussed revolutionary strategy and proposed a dictatorship by a central committee which would arm the workers, confiscate property of the nobility, replace courts by revolutionary tribunals, establish free schools, and furnish employment for all in the industries confiscated from their capitalist owners. The central committee would itself be composed of deputies elected by universal suffrage from various workers' organizations and would constitute the first step toward "free self-government," a truly social state.[20] According to some reports Willich's proposals for Germany were even more forceful. In copies of letters to Hermann Becker in Cologne—copies which Willich repudiated as "false" but Marx held to be reliable—there was a call for the immediate election of battalion and regimental councils within the homeguard troops of the Rhineland. These councils, subject only to their own electors, were to be the agencies of a new revolutionary government and were to be "invested with the image of omnipotence and inviolability." Any public official who opposed them was to be "court-martialled for high treason and shot." Only one newspaper was to be permitted in the area so as to "draw the individual to the common interest as his own." The military councils were to arrange civilian elections to "community and county councils" which would replace the previous government, stimulate revolutionary action in the rest of Germany and neighboring countries, and provide "a basis for the organization of the new society."

Willich joined Gottfried Kinkel in a project to raise a German National Loan of two million dollars "to further the coming republican revolution." Kinkel went to America in search of funds and in November, 1851, visited Cincinnati where he was welcomed by the mayor and the German community, many of whom were refugees from the revolutionary struggle in the fatherland. Kinkel succeeded in raising only a fraction of what was needed and, after squabbles in London over what he did raise, a thousand pounds sterling found its way into a Westminster bank to be used fifteen years later in financing the press of the German Social Democratic Party.

Marx and Engels, having withdrawn from political action with the League's removal to Cologne, were contemptuous of the German National Loan and Willich's "adventurous conspiracies" aimed at reviving the revolution. Certainly their assessment of the social situation and the prospects of revolutionary socialism proved to be more realistic than Willich's. Marx saw the necessity of historical development to lay the economic foundations for the transition to socialism. Willich's attitude was "now or never," much like the attitude of Lenin and the Bolsheviks in Russia's October Revolution of 1917.

The only immediate, positive result of Willich's continued revolutionary efforts and collaboration with Kinkel was to provide a model for one of the main characters in a novel written by Kinkel's wife, Johanna Mockel. In *Hans Ibelas in London* Willich was the model for the character Wildmann, while the hero's role went to Kinkel, portrayed as a delicate, sensitive artist with a weakness for the opposite sex. In the novel the hero is reconciled with his jealous wife in eternal love, but in real life the outcome was more tragic. In a fit of jealousy Johanna Mockel committed suicide by throwing herself out of a window.[21]

Two years after the formal split in the Communist League the issues between Marx and Willich came out into the open as Marx answered fabricated charges of the Prussian police in a book entitled *Revelations Concerning the Communist Trial In Cologne.* One chapter of Marx's book was devoted to "The Willich-Schapper Faction" in the Communist League which, said Marx, sought an immediate overthrow of the state while his own faction stood for the building of a proletarian party rather than "plots and conspiracies." Marx's faction aimed to build the "opposition party of the future" and was not to be identified with the German National Loan or Moses Hess's "Red Catechism." Marx specifically accused Willich of being an intimate friend of a police spy and receiving money from him.[22] The substance of Marx's charges about the political plans of the Willich-Schapper faction was borne out by the facts, it would appear, in Willich's efforts to revive the revolution after September, 1850.

Willich was not one to leave Marx's accusations in *The Revelations* unanswered. He replied from New York where he had gone in 1853 to work as a carpenter in the Brooklyn Navy Yard and organize political refugees for a military invasion of Germany, a project which took him to German centers in the Midwest, including Milwaukee, where he founded a *Social Turnverein* "to carry," as one writer put it, "the red flag of socialism."[23] Writing for the *Belletristisches Journal und New-Yorker Criminal Zeitung*, Willich answered Marx's accusations about his role in the defunct Communist League by a lengthy article somewhat sarcastically entitled "Doctor Karl Marx and His Revelations."

Willich took up Marx's charges page by page and line by line. To the charge that he had collaborated with a police spy Willich answered with details of his associations, claiming that Marx must have known that reports he had received about those associations were misrepresentations or outright inventions. Willich noted that some of Marx's accusations were based on documents he knew to be forgeries. Willich claimed that the division in the Communist League was a result of personal differences and particularly Marx's maneuvers to make the communist movement into his personal property—thus dividing all mankind into two classes, those with Marx and those against him. But there were clearly differences over Marx's view that the League should devote itself to building "the opposition party of the future."[24] Such a role for the League, Willich argued, left it nothing to do and rested on a false estimate of the power of the middle class in Germany. Marx's position would make the working class subservient to the petty-bourgeoisie and leave the existing oppressive regime intact. In Willich's view the required tactics for the working class were still those presented in the circular of the Communist League's central committee in March, 1850, including the recommendations there for the disposition of large agricultural estates. Marx's case, Willich concluded, rested on his clever pen, his wit, his ability to color events, and his sovereign self-esteem as the master of all ideas. His own was grounded in "living records," in the men who had fought at his side in the past and would do so again in the future.[25]

Willich's defense of his role in the Communist League drew sharp rejoinders from two quarters. Within a month three of Marx's friends in New York wrote an article in the *Belletristisches Journal* claiming that the split in the League had been more than a matter of personal differences and that Willich's faction had never had "firmly grounded principles" as shown in the fact that Schapper had broken with it and a whole new workers' association had burgeoned in Germany after the removal of the League to Cologne. That Willich should claim an independent viewpoint for his own party and even attempt to correct Marx's ideas was only laughable. The only really new idea Willich had mentioned, Marx's friends concluded, was "the integrity of his personal and political character" and readers of the *Journal* would perceive what little that amounted to.[26]

From another quarter and somewhat later, Marx himself answered Willich even more harshly and sarcastically in a pamphlet entitled *The Knight of the Magnanimous Spirit,* published in New York in January, 1854. Taking his theme from Hegel's idea in *The Phenomenology of Mind* that the magnanimous spirit necessarily turns into a low and mean one, Marx tried to show the groundlessness and perversity of

Willich's various points in the article published in the *Belletristisches Journal.* With supplementary evidence and references to Willich's own statements Marx tried to re-establish Willich's association with police agents. Marx quoted in full a letter from Engels to show that Engels' "very complimentary" references to Willich's part in the Baden campaign were not very complimentary in their context. Marx corrected Willich's references to various publications and his characterization of Schramm's second in the duel as "a former Russian officer." With particular care and detail Marx reproduced a letter from a former Prussian officer who had seen Willich's letters to Becker in Cologne, letters "in which the Great Field Marshal and Social Messiah [Willich] gave the order from England to seize Cologne, confiscate all private property, establish an ingenious military dictatorship, proclaim a military-social code of laws, abolish all newspapers but one to announce orders on daily thought and action, and a host of other details."[27] Significantly, however, Marx devoted only six lines to Willich's criticism of the role he had assigned to the League as "opposition party of the future," and those lines were hardly a clear refutation of that criticism. Marx objected to Willich's omission of the first and negative part of his statement that the League "aimed to build not the governing but the opposition party of the future."

From these manifestations of heated dispute between Marx and his friends on one side and Willich on the other it seems clear that in addition to differences of personal temperament there were also differences in regard to the communist program—differences which were rooted in divergent estimates of the prospects of revolutionary uprising in Europe. Marx's estimate of those prospects proved to be sounder and more realistic, and in the whole dispute Marx showed himself to be profounder in his social analysis than

Willich. In comparison, some of Willich's revolutionary efforts—particularly the German National Loan and his call for military insurrection in Paris and Cologne—seem to have been ill-grounded, if not foolish, no matter how well-intentioned they may have been.

An appropriately generous conclusion about the whole controversy would be to say with Franz Mehring that "sins were committed by both sides." Before a decade had passed, as we shall see presently, Willich had publicly identified his socialist views with Marx's in major respects. And when Marx prepared a second edition of his *Revelations* in 1875, he expressed misgivings about retaining the chapter on the Willich-Schapper faction. In a special preface he noted that revolutionary events and their aftermath warp men's judgment so that they "indulge in conspiracies and romantic revolutionism which compromise both them and the cause they have at heart." But, Marx added, "In the American Civil War Willich demonstrated that he was something more than a weaver of fantastic projects."[28]

Left-Hegelianism in Cincinnati

When the futility of efforts to revive the German revolution became decisively clear, Willich left New York and the Brooklyn Navy Yard for employment with the U.S. government in Washington, D.C. There he put to use for the Coastal and Geodetic Survey the knowledge of maps and charts he had acquired as a Prussian artillery officer. Sometime during 1858 in Washington he made the acquaintance of Judge Stallo, an acquaintance which subsequently ripened into a warm and solid friendship. With Stallo's intercession Willich became "responsible editor" of the *Cincinnati Republikaner* published by the Social Workingmen's Club in association with Wilhelm E. Brecht.

The *Republikaner* was a four-page paper published in six issues a week, Sunday omitted. Except for novels and stories which regularly appeared on the front page, the *Republikaner's* first and last pages were entirely devoted to advertisements for books, stoves, patent medicines, clothes, hotels, boat trips, and rail transportation. The paper's real content appeared on the inside. Page two of every issue carried an editorial, usually a column and a half in length. Besides the editorial there were regular accounts of events in the Ohio legislature and in Washington, reports of events in Europe, book reviews, and information on the local and national *Arbeiterbewegung*. Page three generally concentrated on local news with particular attention to cultural events such as lectures, theatrical performances, musical events, and advertisements for German books by Schiller, Goethe, and Humboldt. On April 20, 1859, Willich's editorial announced that "the *Republikaner* is free," and was henceforth to be sponsored only by the Social Workingmen's Club and German Institute. Thereafter it would be a paper "truly by and for workers," promoting the interests of "the producing class against swindle and betrayal." Henceforth the masthead carried the slogans which Willich frequently used in his editorials: "Value in Return for Value" and "To Each his Own."

Having previously been more of a man of action than words, Willich had not put his philosophical and social views into any systematic written form except for the pamphlet he wrote on leaving the Prussian army. As "responsible editor" of the *Republikaner*, however, he was required to formulate his views in regular editorials, six days a week. Hence he used events of the day, particularly the problems of the labor movement, as a springboard for presenting his ideas on the nature of man, religion, the pattern of history, and the future of freedom. In editorials on such topics as

"The Labor Movement," "The State," "The Organization of Labor," "The Struggle Concerning Capital," or "Capital and Labor" he advanced his specifically socialist views, his idea of a "social republic."

On a number of occasions Willich revealed his attachment to the views of Hegel to which he had been exposed in the study-circle of army officers around 1845. He quoted Hegel's aphorism that "the world's history is the world's court of judgment" as a clinching commentary on mistaken social policies. He respected Hegel above all as "the greatest philosopher of the nineteenth century." In connection with a review from another paper of Marx's *Contribution to a Critique of Political Economy*, Willich noted that what the reviewer, Friedrich Engels, had called "criticism" of Hegel's dialectical method was only proof of it through the science of economics. Though Willich had reservations about judging a book by its author, he conveyed Marx's relation to Hegel in the following statements from Engels:

> Marx was and is the only one who could undertake the work of extracting from Hegel's logic the kernel which comprised Hegel's genuine discoveries in this area and construct the dialectical method, divested of its idealistic trappings, in the simple form in which it becomes the only correct form of the development of thought. The working out of this method which forms the foundation of Marx's critique of political economy we consider a result scarcely less important than his basic materialistic perspective.[29]

Marx's work, Willich added, could nowhere find such recognition in Europe as among those in America who were familiar with American conditions.

Usually, however, in what Willich wrote for the *Republikaner* the relationship of his thought to Hegel's was less explicit. As in his earlier pamphlet on the Prussian army, his view of man's nature, particularly man's power of thought in relation to religion, reflected the influence of Ludwig Feuerbach who, like Strauss whom Conway so admired, was a prominent "Left-Hegelian." In the spirit of Feuerbach, Willich saw religion as expressing the drive for the preservation of life. Through thought man is "infinite," a "universal being" in humanity. This is the basis of the notion of "immortality of the soul." On the other side, however, man is particular, selfish, and egoistic. As Willich put it:

> The self-preservation drive of man presents itself as the thinking essence, the personal totality of the whole life of humanity and nature, in a necessary opposition to the self-preservation drive as single in man and nature. In the first form, the self-preservation drive is concerned with its maintenance as species, as universal individual, and thus the preservation of the whole. In the second, it appears as the single man striving to maintain himself in the struggle for existence. This opposition in the nature of man was perceived in the earliest ages of mankind and in one way or another appears in the consciousness of men as the opposition between God and the devil, heaven and hell, good and evil, light and darkness, truth and falsehood, reason and sensibility, sacrifice and selfishness. There is no experience or thought of mankind which does not contain in itself this opposition.[30]

Feuerbach had developed a similar view of the two sides of man's nature in his *Essence of Christianity*, though Willich did not overtly mention it. In Feuerbach's words:

> Reason is the self-consciousness of the species, as such; feeling is the self-consciousness of individuality; the reason has relation to existences as things; the heart to existences as persons. . . . The heart sacrifices the species to the individual, the reason sacrifices the individual to the species. Feeling, the heart, is the domestic life; the reason is the *res publica* of man. . . . The desire of knowledge is infinite; reason then is infinite. Reason is

> the highest species of being;—hence it includes all species in the sphere of knowledge. Reason cannot content itself in the individual; it has its adequate existence only when it has the species for its object.[31]

With a perspective closer to Hegel's dialectic of opposition and synthesis, Willich held that the whole of man's life and history should be viewed as a struggle between the two opposing sides of his nature, the universal and the particular, moving toward wholeness. "The life of the individual as well as humanity," Willich wrote, "consists only in working through both opposites to full harmony and unity. This struggle of opposites to reach harmony is the life-process of man, of humanity." In this process nature becomes mind manifest in man's reationality, and the whole panorama of human history can be seen as a series of necessary developmental steps toward the "harmony and unity in the infinite manifoldness of the universe and of life." Whereas Hegel saw the process of world history as manifesting the Divine Idea, Willich followed Feuerbach in centering it on man. For Willich all issues revolved around the development and realization of Humanity.

With his unswerving commitment to Humanity, Willich vigorously attacked Christian supernaturalism. He saw the dualism of spirit and matter, of soul and body, as reinforcing the cleavage between government and people, capital and labor. Only a view which sees life, thought, and spirit as immanent in nature can transcend these oppositions. Such a view, Willich held, is the true theoretical basis of community life and of the principle of a republic, namely, consent and self-government. He found "the religion of the future" in Alexander Humboldt's view of the universe as "a living whole animated by one spirit which comes to self-consciousness in man." Hence the memorial meeting in Cincinnati at Humboldt's death was for Willich "a *cultusakt* of the religion of the future, the religion of science and art."[32]

Though Willich endorsed the *principle* of Protestantism as reflecting the German spirit of freedom and self-government in opposition to Catholic "absolutism," he set himself against the organized church as an impediment to the cause of Humanity, diverting men's minds from real issues with hypocritical talk about "brotherhood." He often condemned the puritanism of "Methodist preachers," but his heaviest blows against organized religion were reserved for Catholicism as week after week he commented adversely on statements from the archbishop of Cincinnati, editorials in the Catholic press, statistics on Catholic growth, or the amount of money Cincinnati was exporting to Rome.[33]

A Social Republic for America

In his social philosophy Willich once again identified his thought with Marx's at a number of basic points, thus moving to close the breach which had arisen in the Communist League nine years earlier. As already noted, he endorsed Marx's proof of Hegel's dialectic through the science of economics. Soon after the publication of Marx's *Contribution to a Critique of Political Economy,* Willich urged readers of the *Republikaner* to get the book for themselves since "knowledge of political economy is the essential prerequisite for the self-government and self-management of a free people." Without such knowledge "the republican form of government becomes in many respects a mere illusion, as is the case with our republic, the United States." To acquaint his readers with the main features of Marx's book Willich reprinted nearly all of its well-known and much-cited preface in which Marx told how his materialist conception of history arose out of the study of Hegel's philosophy of law. In Marx's words:

> My investigation brought me to the conclusion that neither legal relations nor forms of state could be understood by

> themselves or explained by the so-called general evolution of the human mind, but that they are rooted in the material conditions of life whose totality Hegel, following the English and French of the 18th century, summed up under the term "civil society," and the anatomy of civil society is to be sought in political economy.[34]

Subsequent paragraphs gave Marx's description of the internal dialectic of capitalist society—the conflict between forces of production and relations of production—leading to a period of social revolution. Willich also reprinted Engels' observation that the materialist conception of history had shown, in opposition to other socialist theories, how nothing can be accomplished by mere phrases. With this conception of history "our party," the German proletarian party, had provided new theoretical foundations for a scientific economics.[35]

With such endorsements Willich shared Marx's labor theory of value and the related conceptions of exploitation and class struggle. "All social wealth," Willich insisted, "is only the product of labor and exists through the value of labor." Capital is not to be identified with money, but with "the totality of labor," a view which Marx had developed from Ricardo's economics but had earlier found in Hegel's treatment of wealth as "the continuously created result of the labor and action of all."[36] But capital, Willich held, is turned against the laboring class because its control is concentrated in a few hands, and various forms of monopoly, abetted by government, so manipulate money-values that the worker never receives the full value of his labor. The general remedy for this situation is not to gloss over the class struggle but to prosecute it by organizing the workers to take the power of government and industry away from the monopolists and into their own hands.[37] As Willich developed this view, however, he departed from Marx's political position of the 1850's and advanced an original idea as to how socialism should be achieved.

While Marx was distrustful of republican principles as a cloak for capitalists' self-interest—a defense of "the egoistic individual, of man separated from man and the community" —Willich emphatically identified them with socialism. For Willich socialism was essentially and specifically the implementation of republican principles. The idea that men are born equal and remain equal under law meant, in Willich's thought, that "No man is a means for another, but he is his own end." Further, the principle of a republic is diametrically opposed to that of "the state" in its traditional and historical form. In Willich's words:

> As the institutions of the historical state seek to safeguard the domination of individuals, the republic, as a state, is no more and no less than a mutually based insurance association on a large scale. What more the free community, the republic, has than such mutual assurance it has derived from the historical state. The free community is incorrectly called "state." The state is of a political nature, it has "political justice" and, therefore, also "special privileges" since the two are inseparable. In a republic we need no political authority because we have no opposing political rights to adjust. Insofar as such rights remain, our republic is still not a republic. In a republic we need only an administrative organization. To make this concept still more meaningful, one could also refer to it as a partnership of the assembled citizens.[38]

Thus expressing his distrust of centralized political authority as the instrument of class privilege, Willich identified republicanism with the freedom, development, and dignity of man in equal, cooperative association with his fellows. Time after time in his editorials Willich rested his case on an appeal to "human rights," "human welfare," and the cause of common

"Humanity." In this respect his outlook was linked, as Engels had suggested, with the "true socialism" inspired by Feuerbach and developed by Moses Hess. As noted earlier, Hess particularly emphasized the wholeness of humanity and man's reconciliation with himself—the overcoming of his "alienation" in capitalist society—as the underlying rationale of socialism.

But a republic, Willich further insisted, is a "humbug" and a "lie" so long as it leaves the control of capital in a few hands. Political and economic relations are inseparable, and the concentration of economic power only shows "the necessity to establish on the economic field as well as on the political and religious, the principle of the republic, self-government and self-direction of the people."[39] Accordingly, Willich put his support behind the American Workers' League headed by Gustav Struve, his comrade-in-arms in 1848. The League aimed at political unification of the working class to achieve a "social republic," a government embodying the principles of 1776 in economic as well as political relations. He also favored the development of cooperatives which, though inadequate to the decisive mastery of capital, were nonetheless valuable as "schools of self-help and independence."

With increased experience in the labor movement Willich arrived at his own original view as to how a "social republic" should be achieved and constituted. Workingmen, he urged, must proceed at once to secure what is due them by organizing or joining unions. Next they must take steps to connect their unions with each other through assemblies which can serve as legislatures with representation by occupation. A national assembly of unions would make the present congress superfluous and secure "the political and economic independence of the producing class which the brave Jackson designated as the outcome and goal of all political administrators."[40] Further, such a government would at once invite the formation of an international assembly of unions. This would be, in effect, a world "Republic of Labor and Intelligence" which would break down all national limits and put an end to war by eliminating the conflicts of monarchs and monopolists.

Contrary to the judgment of one biographer that Willich's thought was unoriginal and only negative, his "social republic" of union assemblies was an original view of the strategy and pattern of socialism. It anticipated by several decades major elements in the American socialism of Daniel De Leon and subsequent movements for "industrial democracy." In identifying socialism with assemblies of self-governing organizations of labor rather than nationalization of industry by the existing centralized state, Willich departed from Marx's position in the *Communist Manifesto* but anticipated his stand of 1871. Marx and Engels endorsed the short-lived Paris Commune as "a new and really democratic state" aiming to replace the old centralized government by "self-government of the producers," a federation of "communes" run by elected representatives of the working class and "one great union" of "cooperative societies" wherein workers managed the factories in which they were formerly employed. Noting in 1891 that many socialists were terrified by the phrase "Dictatorship of the Proletariat," Engels wrote: "Well and good, gentlemen, do you want to know what this dictatorship looks like? Look at the Paris Commune. That was the Dictatorship of the Proletariat."[41]

While Willich stressed the union movement at the foundation of the "social republic," he also urged political action. "The road to the full value of your labor," he told his readers in the *Republikaner,* "goes through the corridors of the city hall, state legislature, and capitol in Washington."[42] Accordingly he took leadership in the creation of a Labor Ticket for Cincinnati (including Rutherford B. Hayes as candidate for Solicitor) and called for support of the Republican party until labor could organize a national party of its own. There were, he allowed, important elements in the Republican party serving monopoly and privilege, but it was clearly preferable to the "Slavo-Democratic" party. In 1860 he championed the nomination of Fremont and Clay, the heroes of the more radically republican Ohio Germans. Willich did not hide his disappointment in the "compromise" nomination of Lincoln but nevertheless urged his readers to "battle for Lincoln" as "soldiers of freedom," confident that Lincoln was committed to the abolition of slavery and, by virtue of his background, to the laboring-man's cause as well. Willich had ardently and combatively allied himself with the abolitionists. The *Republikaner* devoted two issues to "Theodore Parker's Message" against slavery, and in spite of threats against his life, as Moncure Conway noted, Willich headed a giant torchlight procession through the streets of Cincinnati to protest and mourn the execution of John Brown.[43]

Toward the end of March, 1861, Willich announced the end of his editorship and his break with the Workingmen's League which sponsored the *Republikaner*. The League, he complained, had become dominated by a clique which wanted to abandon the principles for which it was founded and concentrate on matters like death benefits and health insurance. For two and a half years, Willich said, he had stood unequivocally for "the security of daily bread and the freeing of labor from external restrictions—the absolutely necessary conditions for the progress of humanity and the life of the mind."[44] His two and a half years as editor, however, had a more personal importance as well. They gave him the stimulus and opportunity to formulate his own philosophical and social views more fully and systematically than any other period of his life.

Through the *Republikaner* he expressly recognized his attachment to Hegel, and his major views were directly shaped by the "Left-Hegelianism" of Feuerbach and Marx. With Marx he saw material labor as the basis of a dialectical movement of history reflected in class struggle. With Feuerbach he put Humanity at the center of religion and politics. Combining and adding to these ideas, he championed a form of socialism which extended republican principles—the principles of a truly free human community—into economic relations through representative and governing assemblies of unions.

Civil War Leader

Shortly after Willich resigned as editor of the *Republikaner*, Fort Sumter lay under seige and the war between North and South became a fateful actuality. The Germans of Cincinnati responded quickly. At a mass meeting in the Turner Hall Judge Stallo called for an all-German regiment to support the Union. Within twenty-four hours the muster rolls of the Ninth Ohio Volunteers—*Die Neuner* as it was called—were filled. Four of the regiment's ten companies were recruited from the Workingmen's Hall. Willich expressed his democratic convictions and his feeling that the Union forces were already over-officered by enlisting as a private, but a week later he was elected adjutant, narrowly missing command of the regiment, which went to Col. Robert L. McCook. As adjutant, however, Willich became the "military father of the regiment" and took main responsibility for its training and drill in "undefiled High Dutch."

The Ninth Ohio Volunteers went into action at the battle of Rich Mountain, West Virginia, where the Union forces under Rosecrans made a forced night march to surprise the Confederates and win the battle. In another engagement in West Virginia a few months later the troops of the Ninth Ohio again "covered themselves all over with glory" by victory at Carnifex Ferry. During the West Virginia campaign Willich left the Ninth Ohio Volunteers to become Colonel of the Thirty-Second Indiana Volunteers, an all-German regiment inspired by and modeled after the Ninth Ohio. Under Willich's command three Indiana companies achieved a remarkable victory over 3,000 Texas Rangers at the battle of Rowlett's Station, Kentucky, on December 17, 1861. One Cincinnati newspaper called it "the most brilliant Federal victory yet achieved" and lavishly praised Willich for his leadership.

At the battle of Shiloh, the bloodiest ever fought in America up to that time, Willich took his troops to the point where the firing was heaviest. When Confederates attacked on the second day, Willich commanded his forces against them in an unusual, audacious move that won him the admiration of his superiors and shortly thereafter a promotion to brigadier general. Major General Lew Wallace, later author of *Ben Hur,* described the movement of Willich's troops as follows:

> They were but a regiment; yet at sight of them the enemy halted, about-faced, and returned to his position in the woods. There he struck out with a fire so lively that the newcomers halted and showed signs of distress. Then an officer rode swiftly round their left flank and stopped when in front of them, his face to the enemy. What he said I could not hear, but from the motions of the men he was putting them through the manual of arms—this notwithstanding some of them were dropping in the ranks. Taken all in all, that I think was the

> most audacious thing that came under my observation during the war. The effect was magical. The colonel returned to his post and the regiment, steadied as if on parade, advanced in face of the fire pouring upon them and actually entered the wood. I despatched an orderly to the colonel of the unknown regiment with my compliments, and asking his name, "August Willich, of the Thirty-second Indiana Volunteers," was the reply brought me.

In a report after the battle Willich briefly mentioned that he had had to drill the troops for a moment on the field because their firing had become "wild."

Willich used other unusual methods of fighting with the troops he trained so thoroughly and arduously. At the battle of Stones River he was captured and taken to Libby Prison for four months, after which he was exchanged and called to Washington to report to Lincoln on Confederate fortifications at Richmond. While in prison he thought up a military movement called "advance firing," possibly an extension of something he had learned at the Royal Military Academy in Berlin. In this movement the lines of the troops were put into four ranks, each rank advancing a few paces in front to fire and then stopping to load while the other ranks advanced alternately, thus maintaining a steady fire against the enemy. Willich trained his troops in "advance firing" and also introduced the idea of using water-tight wagon bodies as boats to cross streams but could not put this amphibious strategy into effect over objections of the corps of engineers.

At the battle of Chickamauga in September, 1863, Willich held his troops fast against powerful Confederate assaults, again drilling them under fire in the manual of arms to restore their confidence and order. This action helped General Thomas earn the title of "Rock of Chickamauga," and Willich's division commander praised him for having been "always in the right place," thus rendering his country great service by his individual daring. Again, Willich and his troops were outstanding at the battle of Missionary Ridge in late November, 1863. They were part of the division which climbed the rocky face of the ridge to rout the enemy in what was called "one of the greatest miracles in military history." Willich's report on the battle, confirmed by others, suggests that the troops under his immediate command were the first, along with the Sixth Ohio regiment, to plant their colors on the embattled mountain.

Early in 1864 Willich's brigade joined Sherman for the celebrated march to Atlanta. During an engagement with the enemy in Georgia, Willich was wounded in the right shoulder, with the result that his arm was partially paralyzed for the rest of his life. Recovering sufficiently from his wound, he became commandant of the Cincinnati military district for a time and later was ordered to Texas to establish the authority of the Union there. In October, 1865, he was mustered out of service at the rank of brevet major general.

Willich had the respect and affection of the common soldiers under him because he shared their privations, was always in the lead when the fighting was thickest, and treated them "like men, not dogs." He saw their efforts and sacrifices as part of the continuing great struggle for freedom and human rights, an extension of his aims as a revolutionary commander in Germany and crusading editor of a labor newspaper. Recalling how a twice-wounded soldier in his command immediately returned to the battle line and how another, surrounded by dead comrades, held his position until the ammunition arrived, Willich said: "The highest ambition of a commander must be satisfied by being associated with such men who, through patriotism and a love for the free institutions of this country, have attained a degree of efficiency which professional soldiers seldom, if ever, reach."[45] With such an attitude toward his command,

Willich considered it entirely appropriate to introduce another innovation in military affiairs, one which his officers could not but tolerate while his battle record was being acclaimed as "the finest," "splendid," and "brilliant." On returning to camp he would put his troops at ease, address them as "citizens," and proceed to a lecture on socialism.

Willich's social views were not only reflected in his conduct as an officer during the war but also in his judgment of military organization after the fighting was over. He formulated that judgment, highly critical in many respects, in a pamphlet published in Cincinnati in 1866 on *The Army, Standing Army or National Army?* In Germany eighteen years earlier he had challenged the cleavage between army and people. The Civil War made him condemn America's "class of officers alienated, by an exclusive education, from the national interest and impulse; estranged even from social relations with the people."[46] With such a "contrivance of monarchies" many Civil War battles were simple "free fights" in which citizen-soldiers had to compensate for incompetent professionals. Willich detailed the common and costly mistakes he had observed during the war such as detaching units to intercept a retreat before the enemy is beaten, failure to close over-extended and vulnerable battle lines, the ordering of murderous assaults on entrenched positions rather than contriving to outmaneuver them, and failure to deploy skirmishers to draw fire off the main lines.[47]

In contrast to a professional army of "soldiers by trade," self-government in a republic, Willich insisted, requires a different kind of military organization and one that will prove entirely adequate to the nation's needs as suggested in the success of the Swiss republic in protecting itself from surrounding monarchies. Instead of blind subordination on the monarchical model, a truly republican military force must have a different pattern of discipline, namely, "a self-determined harmony . . . in cooperation with the leading will" of the commander. In Willich's words:

> We have two opposite systems. The one is to crush out the will of all individual men composing the army, making absolute machines of them, and thus rendering them powerless to resist the commanding will, however deficient and inadequate to the end in view this will may be; the other is, to educate the will of the mass to a self-determined harmony, and in cooperation with the leading will, which system requires and presupposes a commanding will, identified with the object in view, and supported by intellect and skill. The former system has been used, and is that adopted in all regular armies and is taught and applied in all military schools, though partly under the disguise of "implicit obedience to orders," which means in fact nothing else than a blind subordination even to imbecility and brutality. The necessity of the latter system has always been recognized, when national armies rose from the midst of the people to defend their liberties and national independence. The one system is that of despotic States, the other that of Republics. The former subjects the intelligence of the army to even the most incompetent, while in the latter the man that excels in intellect will be gradually elevated to the military leadership. One system makes of the army, when in the hands of a traitorous chief, an instrument even against its own country; the other makes it the most efficient guardian of national liberty.[48]

On these premises Willich urged that the army should be essentially a militia of citizens prepared by the demands of workmanship, the battles of industrial life, training in military subjects in public schools, and regular rededication to the republic and the principle of self-government through "national festivals." Revealing his belief in the imperative need of a "national army" and his concern about social conflict in the future, he concluded:

> Certainly, this war is over, and one abnormity, slavery, has been enacted out of existence. But other intellectual, social and moral abnormities still exist in our midst, and their main reliance is brute force. This brute force is bound to be marshalled, under one color or another, perhaps very soon, perhaps later, against the genius of human liberty. Should we not bring our acquired intelligence to bear on such a contingency, instead of placing ourselves on a level with brutal force? A drop of sweat on the drill-ground will save many drops of blood on the battle-field. A judicious preparation will enable us to tame the wild beast, which otherwise may tear the Republic to pieces.[49]

Last Days in the People's Cause

In October of the year in which Willich published his views on the kind of army a republic should have he was elected auditor of Hamilton County on the Union ticket. Rutherford Hayes was the successful candidate for governor of Ohio in the same election. The Union party had been organized at the beginning of the Civil War as a coalition of Republicans and war Democrats with the Republicans in a predominating position. In 1866 the Union party won most of the state offices and Congressional posts as well. Willich was encouraged to run for auditor by Judge Stallo, who felt that the post could be just as well served by a one-armed soldier as a two-armed politician. Further, it was a lucrative office and would provide Willich, who never had "the luck of money-getting," with enough income to last the rest of his life. Willich's pension from the war, in spite of his wounds and brilliant record, was a pittance of $360.00 a year, the standard amount for volunteer officers in contrast to a vastly higher rate for regular officers. With his income from the auditor's office, for which there was no fixed salary—the auditor received what was left of collections above office expenses—Willich augmented his resources by some $30,-000.00.[50]

In his management of the auditor's office Willich followed the customs and practices of his predecessors in the position, but shortly after he left office in 1869 suits were filed in the Common Pleas Court against him and three of his predecessors for illegal payment of a bookkeeper's salary and an illegal fee for a tax omission clerk. Willich was represented by Stallo's law partner, E. W. Kittredge. After two years of legal action the judge ruled that there was "no question of fraud, but a question of legality," and finally the suits were allowed to die. Significantly, the suits were originally filed shortly before the election of 1869 when a reform movement headed by Friedrich Hassaurek wanted new faces in public office. There was animosity between Hassaurek, editor of the *Cincinnati Volksblatt,* and Willich stemming from previous political clashes and apparently aggravated by their rivalry for leadership in the German community. As a result of his war record Willich was immensely popular, but while he had chosen the hazards of battle, the much younger Hassaurek had been safely ensconced in the U.S. embassy in Ecuador, a reward for his services in rallying German voters behind Lincoln. On leaving the auditor's office Willich was given a farewell party at the *Arbeiterhalle* at which he announced his intention to leave soon for a visit to Germany, after which he would return to Cincinnati. With this announcement Hassaurek used his *Volksblatt* and connections with other German papers in the Midwest to suggest that Willich was leaving in fear of the lawsuits against him and was absconding with illegally pocketed tax money. Both Stallo and Willich responded to Hassaurek's tendentious charges, and around May, 1869, Willich left for Germany.

In Berlin Willich re-established contact with his older brother, Julius, from whom he had been estranged and without communication since leaving the army for the workers' cause in 1848. According to the report accepted in St. Mary's, Ohio, Willich's meeting with his "staunchly imperialist" brother, a colonel in the Prussian army, was highly unsatisfactory. This seems plausible in view of the fact, shown in subsequent events, that Willich had not substantially changed his social views from what they were when he was editing the *Republikaner*. According to another report, however, Willich's meeting with his brother was cordial enough to result in a brisk correspondence after his return to America.[51]

While Willich was in Berlin the Franco-Prussian War broke out, and he offered his military services to the fatherland. Apparently he was moved by the overwhelming sense of patriotism which engulfed his fellow-Germans of Cincinnati in 1870, and he may have felt as Conway and Stallo did that Prussia was defending itself against a corrupt, aggressive French empire to achieve a free fatherland which would resist any oppression Bismarck might impose on either victor or vanquished. Whatever his motives, his offer was declined on grounds of age—ample grounds since he was then in his sixtieth year.

With the prospect of military service foreclosed, Willich enrolled in the University of Berlin where his foster-father, Friedrich Schleiermacher, had been a professor of philosophy and theology. On October 18, 1870, he matriculated in the philosophical faculty corresponding to the liberal arts division of American universities and attended lectures during the winter semester on physics under Professors Dove and Erman, economics under Professor Wagner, Roman history under the eminent Professor Mommsen, and Natural Law under Professor Karl Michelet, one of Hegel's best-known pupils, who had written several books on his teacher's philosophy and assisted in the publication of his writings.[52] Willich received a departure-certificate from the University on March 31, 1871, and not long afterwards left for America.

On returning to America, Willich lived in Cleveland for a time, but with a strong invitation from his old friend and fellow-officer, Major Charles Hipp, he moved to St. Mary's, Ohio, a picturesque canal town with a heavy German population. There he spent the rest of his days in the Dieker House, now apartments at 117 South Spruce Street. His last years, however, were active ones. He was a frequent speaker at patriotic meetings and a lecturer to German-American societies. One of his lectures was presented at a meeting of the *Humboldt Verein* of Columbus, Ohio, in March, 1873, on "The Origin, History, and Destiny of Man in the Light of Humboldt's 'Cosmos.'" The advance announcement of the lecture described Willich as a leading fighter for freedom in 1848 and a prominent figure in the recent Civil War who was now winning for himself "a significant position in the field of Knowledge." The lecture, however, did not live up to expectations. The audience was small and, according to the *Columbus Westbote,* understood little of Willich's "long philosophical exposition," which used many unfamiliar words that were never clarified. Without such clarification, the report in the *Westbote* continued, the system of any German philosopher will make no contact with the masses. Willich's effort to expound Humboldt's views was characterized by the anecdote often applied to Hegel: "Only one of his students understood him and that one misunderstood."[53] Regardless of its poor reception, however, Willich's theme revealed that he, like Stallo, had turned from Hegel toward Humboldt for a science-based view of the unity and interrelated development of man and nature. His writings in the *Republikaner* at Humboldt's death had already adumbrated such a turn.

Willich was a delegate from Cleveland to the Liberal Republican convention of 1872 aiming to defeat "Grantism" and identify the Republican party with the interests of the common people. Meeting in Cincinnati, the Liberal Republicans nominated Horace Greeley in some political "deals" which drove Stallo out of the movement and crystallized his enmity toward Carl Schurz. With Greeley's defeat most Liberal Republicans regarded the movement as dead. Not Willich. On July 30, 1873, Liberal Republicans met in Columbus with some Ohio Democrats to form a "People's Party" committed to the welfare of the masses. Willich became an active and ardent supporter of People's Party candidates in the election that fall.

Speaking at a pre-election meeting in Batavia, Ohio, not far from Cincinnati, Willich described the platform and aims of the People's Party in terms very similar to those he had applied to the "social republic" in the pages of the *Republikaner,* even to the point of using some of his old socialist slogans such as "Value in Return for Value." At Batavia he told his audience that

> The present irreconcilable conflict is between free labor and monopoly. It is my opinion now also not more the question [*sic*] between the Democratic party and the Republican party, but between on the one side the people, equal rights and general legislation, and on the other monopolists, privileges and special legislation.[54]

Willich condemned both the Democratic and Republican parties and their candidates, including Governor Morton of Indiana, who had appointed him commander of the Thirty-Second Indiana Volunteers, as being instruments of special privilege and proponents of special legislation that could only be detrimental to the interests of the ordinary farmer and workingman. Noting that Governor Morton had said there was nothing that his party might not change "except the general system," Willich argued:

> It is this general system we regard as the root of all economical and moral evils growing in our country and disintegrating society. It is this system of taxing the people for the benefit of private business, under the false pretense of protecting home industry. It is this system of giving the money of the people without equivalent to bank companies, under the pretense of facilitating the business of the country. It is this system which gives to private companies the domain, money and credit of the people for railroads, under the false pretense of increasing the wealth of the nation. It is the system of giving steamboat companies, etc. the people's money as subsidies for private business, under the false pretense of increasing the lucrative business of the country.

Willich concluded that the Republican party was a "bogus Republican party" because it was only "the voting power of the monopolists" and the party of special legislation. His view of the Democratic party, with its internal confusion and silence on major issues, was equally unfavorable.

By contrast the People's Party, not misled from fundamental issues by those who talk of Christian principles and prohibition of alcoholic drinks, would seek to educate the public on the economic principles of free labor. It would seek to elect a Congress "that not only abolishes the ruling monopolies, and saves of their former plunder of the people's property as much as may yet be reached" but also abolishes its own power to enact special legislation, confining itself "to its legitimate sphere, to general legislation—the same for all." Thus Willich saw the People's Party as carrying on the same fight in the same direction he had earlier sought for an independent American labor party.

Willich brought to St. Mary's an interest in the arts and was widely respected as a leader in cultural affairs. He organized a club to read the plays of Shakespeare, his hobby and favorite author, and from time to time entertained his many friends by singing Schubert's *Lieder*. He was even on close enough terms with many of the young ladies who joined him in reading Shakespeare to give them advice on proper posture, but this unexpected use of Prussian military training apparently never imperilled his bachelorhood. The Shakespeare circle eventually became a formally organized club which continued on the pattern Willich had established and took initiative in founding St. Mary's public library. Even today the Shakespeare Club is the center of the community's cultural life and each year recognizes "the General" as its true founder.

On January 22, 1878, Willich was found dead in his room at the Dieker House. At his funeral there were fully 2,500 persons in attendance, including deputations from various Civil War regiments and many friends from other towns and cities. Among the pallbearers were Judge Stallo, his steadfast friend since 1858, and Adolf Metzner of Indiana, an artist who had depicted Willich's Civil War exploits in a series of on-the-scene paintings. Graveside eulogies in English and German portrayed his noble character and lifelong fight for freedom on two continents. One memorial statement noted that Willich was not only a soldier but "also a philosopher and remained one all his life," though his views were heavy on the side of "humanitarian rhetoric." Above all he was "a man of action," and "while others talked of equality and the rights of labor he doffed his officer's uniform and went to work, committed to the people, freedom, and brotherhood."[55] Thus was marked the passing of a beloved and colorful figure, a lifelong bachelor who always had candy in his pocket for the children of St. Mary's and was remembered as saying, "*Alle amerikanischen Kinder sind auch meine Kinder.*"

VII

HEGEL IN THE LIGHT OF HIS FIRST AMERICAN FOLLOWERS

In hegel's own time and the decades immediately after his death his views incited controversy and dispute. While he lived, they were denounced by Schopenhauer as charlatanry. After his death they gave rise to rival camps, Right- and Left-Hegelians, each claiming to be true continuers of his philosophy in its essentials.

Today Hegel's thought is still a highly controversial subject. His very name, it has been observed, is "surrounded by a fog of emotion." His philosophy has been cited as the prototype of logically irresponsible speculation, and his language has been ridiculed as logically criminal or at best an offensive form of poetry. His "system" has been dismissed as a glittering empty palace beside which Hegel himself lived in a hovel. The ideology of the "closed society" manifest in both fascism and communism has been laid at his doorstep with the battle of Stalingrad characterized as a fight between the Right- and Left-Hegelians.

On the other side, Hegel has been praised as the father of modern dialectical thought, making possible the humanly relevant insights of *Existenzphilosophie* and the social penetration of original Marxism. He has been judged the outstanding philosopher of the nineteenth century whose wealth of insight is exceeded only in Plato and whose dissolution of the dualisms of subject and object, matter and spirit, nature and supernature, set the characteristic problems and tone for twentieth century philosophy.

Some of the controversies over Hegel's thought, of course, have been nurtured by ignorance and failure to read closely and carefully. Others have germinated in his dialectical method which never says a full "yes" or "no" to any viewpoint but seeks to preserve it in the synthesis of a wider perspective. With such a method and Hegel's emphasis on truth being found in its "working out" more than in specific results, his conclusions often seem to be "all things to all men" and particularly opposing things to opposed thinkers.

But if Hegel's method is often at the root of controversies, it is equally the source of his "insights," *i.e.*, aspects of his thought which may be defended and prized as relevant to current philosophical issues. What follows is concerned with some of Hegel's insights in this sense. It also aims to show how those insights were signalized a century ago in Ohio by J. B. Stallo, Peter Kaufmann, Moncure Conway, and August Willich, who were informally associated with one another as acquaintances and in some cases close friends. This chapter, then, will recapitulate and review major ideas of the Ohio Hegelians as they highlight aspects of Hegel's thought which are of current interest but have often been misrepresented or ignored. The concern here is with interrelationships of ideas which suggest something of the current relevance of both Hegel's thought and Ohio Hegelianism.

Rejection of Transcendent Metaphysics

One aspect of Hegel's thought which has been frequently ignored or misrepresented but was emphasized among the Ohio Hegelians was his unqualified rejection of transcendent metaphysics, the view that there is an independently existing order of entities or things-in-themselves beyond the phenomena we experience and think about. This rejection was especially apparent in the early writings of J. B. Stallo, the closest student of Hegel and the most penetrating philosopher among the Ohio Hegelians.

Stallo made particularly clear that for Hegel the "real nature of things" does not lie in a separate realm, a "beyond," which observed phenomena somehow imperfectly mirror or copy. Rather, it is implicit in the phenomena themselves as they are truly found to be through persistent experience and reflection, namely, interrelated and connected in lawful, rationally-patterned wholes. The truth about any particular observed object or event, its "real nature" and reality, is simply the whole phenomenon. Thus Hegel, far from defending any form of transcendent metaphysics, was the proponent of a concrete phenomenalism, "concrete" in his sense as meaningfully related and fully in context.

In this respect Hegel's views are akin to current "philosophies of experience"—empiricism, phenomenalism, positivism—which vigorously criticize transcendent metaphysics and seek its elimination from responsible thought. To be sure, some of Hegel's references to "the Absolute" and "Spirit" give the impression that he was simply pouring new wine into old metaphysical bottles. And his references to Reason in substantive terms have led some empiricists to dismiss him as belonging among the old metaphysicians. But the very title of his first book, *Die Phänomenologie des Geistes,* which he regarded as the basis of his whole philosophy, should rather pointedly suggest that he favored a form of phenomenalism.

Stallo's awareness of Hegel's phenomenalism and opposition to transcendent metaphysics is apparent in his *General Principles of the Philosophy of Nature,*[1] the fullest exposition and analysis of Hegel's thought that had yet appeared in English at the time of its publication in 1848. The second part of *General Principles* paraphrased and quoted from major writings of Kant, Fichte, Schelling, Oken, and Hegel; but half of that part, a total of 150 pages, was devoted to Hegel with particular attention to writings which emphasized his phenomenalism in relation to Stallo's special interest, philosophy of science. Hence Stallo carefully summarized sections of *The Phenomenology of Mind* on "The Certainty of the Senses," "Observation," and "Force and Understanding–Phenomenal and Supersensual World." In the last of these sections Hegel's phenomenalism and rejection of transcendent metaphysics are prominent in Stallo's summary:

> We look into the interior of things only through the phenomenon; the interior itself is transcendental, a "beyond" for our consciousness. This transcendental interior, however, reveals nothing whatever to consciousness; no more, to use Hegel's own simile, than *pure* darkness or *pure* light reveals any thing to the gaze. But the supersensual "beyond" results from mediation; it proceeds from the phenomenon, and the phenomenon is its reality. The Supersensual is but the Sensual[2] taken in its truth, taken as a phenomenon, and not as a permanent reality, which it has amply proved itself not to be. We behold the play of the forces, a continual shifting of determinate appearances, whose truth consists merely in the law which manifests itself there. The *law* is the permanent image of the fleeting phe-

> nomenon. The supersensual world is a quiet realm of laws, indeed beyond the world of observation, since this exhibits the law only in continuous change; but it is nevertheless *present* in the world of observation, and its immediate type.[3]

But Stallo did more than summarize the primary source to acquaint his readers with Hegel's phenomenalism. He also defended and interpreted it in the first part of the *General Principles* where he presented his own philosophy of nature and pointedly acknowledged his indebtedness to Hegel. Stallo frequently criticized the "old dualism" between "the Material and the Spiritual, the Objective and the Subjective" as represented in Kant. But their unity, he warned, is not to be achieved through "a mere hypostatic notion of universality."[4] It is not, in other words, to be achieved through any form of transcendent metaphysics. To move in such a direction, Stallo believed, is inevitably to court failure as amply shown in the materialists' attempt to deal with the variety of phenomena and processes in nature. To move in such a direction leads to "a firm immobile principle," "a rigid substratum," from which nothing can be inferred and to which the phenomenal world can only be appended as an otiose existence. The unity of things, rather, is to be found in motion or activity, "not rest as a substance." Stallo's view of how this activity—ultimately the essence of Mind or Spirit—is to be known, clearly reveals his adherence to Hegel's phenomenalism. Stallo wrote at the end of his analysis of Conscious Mind:

> The foregoing course of mental action may be resumed in these few words: *perception* gives the immediate certainty of the object in its space and time; observation determines its *general*, but distinct *predicates*, which are finally resumed in the ideal unity of the object (or, speaking with reference to the predicates, the *subject*). Once more: the predicates *are* the subject; they are not glued, plastered upon it, and torn off, when the

> subject is idealized. Everything exists *in* its properties, not *beside* them.[5]

Stallo's words here, it might be noted, endorse Hegel's dialectic as well as his concrete phenomenalism and further suggest that the former, in some respects, is logically inseparable from the latter.

Stallo's later book, *The Concepts and Theories of Modern Physics* (1881), was praised by Ernst Mach, leading pioneer of modern scientific empiricism, as closely approximating his own views. In that book Stallo *seemed* to break completely with Hegel's thought. He expressed regret for the "ontological reveries" of his *General Principles* and condemned Hegel's "old metaphysics" as an erroneous effort to evolve all things from "pure Being" which is "wholly devoid of attributes."[6] The close reader, however, will find Stallo's break with Hegel more apparent than real. At a number of key points in *Concepts and Theories* Stallo simply puts ideas he had previously credited to Hegel in a new context or attributes them to someone else. For example, he emphasizes the point learned from Hegel that objects are known only through their relations and have no attributes except through their relations. "In mathematical phrase," as Stallo now prefers to put it, "things and their properties are known only as functions of other things and properties. In this sense, also, relativity is a necessary predicate of all objects of cognition."[7] In 1848 Stallo found such relativity of properties in Hegel's *Phenomenology of Mind,* but now it is explicitly attributed to Helmholtz with reference to the theory of vision.[8]

An even clearer illustration of Stallo's lingering debt to Hegel's concrete phenomenalism is found in a discussion of the relation between "the Real" and "the Phenomenal." While the old metaphysics, Stallo notes, had separated them and made them opposites, "The true distinction between the Apparent and the Real is that the former is a partial deliverance of sense which is mistaken for the whole deliverance. The deception or illusion results from the circumstance that the senses are not properly and exhaustively interrogated and that their whole story is not heard."[9] With less emphasis on the senses and with "Absolute" substituted for "Real," Stallo had earlier developed the same view with reference to Hegel for whom truth was the "Whole in its development," not abstractly taken, but involving "phenomenal existence" and the materials of natural science.

It would appear, then, that Stallo was permanently indebted to Hegel's phenomenalism. His break with Hegel was, in major respects, only apparent. Those who have suggested that Stallo, like Hume, wrote only one book in philosophy—in Stallo's case, *The General Principles* based on Hegel—would seem to be substantially correct.[10]

Among the other Ohio followers of Hegel, Conway and Willich adopted views consonant with the concrete phenomenalism so fundamental in Stallo's thought or indicated their sympathy with it. Conway found the essence of Hegel's epoch-making thought to be "an absolute idea which has represented itself in Nature." It is equally expressed in materialism and idealism, in the thought of Huxley no less than Emerson. Thus in Conway's view the absolute idea was no "thing in itself" or transcendent entity behind phenomena. It was, rather, their pattern of wholeness, and its existence was exhausted in its manifestations. Conway particularly felt the consonance of Hegel's absolute idea with the process of organic evolution, one of his major interests. Evolution provided him evidence that the universe is "*vernünftvoll*," as Strauss, a "Left-Hegelian," had strongly maintained. "Our highest idea," Conway agreed with Strauss, "is the law-governed cosmos, full of life and reason."[11] August

Willich, it would appear, was also sympathetic with the main aspects of concrete phenomenalism. What attracted him in Marx was the observable and tangible manifestation of Hegel's dialectical process. Further, as managing editor of the *Cincinnati Republikaner* he devoted three long columns to an address by Stallo which expounded phenomenalism against materialism.[12]

Hegel's Process Philosophy

Hegel's radical and pervasive emphasis on process, movement, and evolutionary development is a second major aspect of his thought which is frequently missed or minimized but was stressed by his Ohio followers. This emphasis is missed when attention is too exclusively focused, contrary to Hegel's own warnings, on the structure of his system as outlined in *The Encyclopedia of Philosophical Sciences*. It is also missed when Hegel is viewed as some sort of a deductive rationalist like Spinoza with all his conclusions already stacked into his premises and initial conceptions. That Hegel was not such a rationalist has already been suggested in the previous section. But stereotypes die hard, and it is not difficult to find references to Hegel's "panlogism," his "archrationalism," or his "block universe," as static and motionless as a marble palace.

In terms of the main thrust of his writings, however, Hegel's view was pre-eminently the "process philosophy" of the nineteenth century. The most static part of his philosophy, his logic, admittedly dealt only with the interrelation of concepts in a "system of pure reason" apart from their actual manifestation in nature and society. But the first adequate concept in the logic, it should be noted, was that of "becoming." As the unification or synthesis of "being" and "nothing," which reflective analysis reveals as unable to stand by themselves, "becoming" is implicitly the model of all subsequent syntheses—all other adequate and sufficient concepts—set forth in Hegel's entire logic.[13]

Again, the emphasis on process is particularly apparent in *The Phenomenology of Mind* where Hegel differentiates his own philosophy and its method from that of his predecessors. The basic elements of his view are all defined in terms of process. Spirit, in Hegel's view, is not to be understood as an entity or determinate substance but rather as "that being which is truly subject, or, what is the same thing, is truly realized and actual solely in the process of positing itself, or in mediating with its own self in transitions from one state or position to the opposite."[14] Similarly, "experience" is the process whereby what is immediate in sensation and reflection leads to something else and then also returns to itself to yield a whole which is truth for that movement. "The truth is the whole," says Hegel in a familiar passage. "The whole however is merely the essential nature reaching its completeness through the process of its own development." Thus involving process, "Truth is a bacchanalian revel, where not a soul is sober." With such a perspective on the nature of Spirit, experience, and truth, Hegel insists that the real subject-matter of philosophy "is not exhausted in its purpose, but in working the matter out; nor is the mere result attained the concrete whole itself, but the result along with the process of arriving at it."

Thus Hegel not only introduced into his logic, for good or ill, the factor of time and tense implicit in process, but also saw the whole realm of society, history, and nature as manifesting the evolution of Spirit. While his *Naturphilosophie* rejected the doctrine of historical organic evolution later made prominent by Darwin, he could easily have adopted it in principle if he had known about it. Many of his professed followers did adopt it, directly and enthusiastically.

Stallo more pointedly shared and expanded Hegel's idea of process than any of his other Ohio followers. The far greater part of Stallo's statement of his own views in *The General Principles* was included in a long section on "Evolutions" which traced "phases and processes" in the solar system, heat and sound, chemical combinations, forms of organic life, the human mind, and the functional divisions of society. His general premise was that the world of all existences—Spirit, Absolute Mind, the Deity—is an intrinsic process, a "self-unfolding development," which comes to itself by a movement of self-projection into matter and self-recovery in a richer unity.[15] In this conception of Spirit, Stallo's debt to Hegel, even to Hegel's language in translation, is too patent to need comment.

Stallo applied his notion of evolution or "self-unfolding development" in detail to the whole of the natural world. The solar system, he found, shows no original matter at rest on which motion is conferred. The vibratory nature of heat shows there is no such thing as "caloric matter." Organic phenomena show individual acts as reflecting "the formative evolution of entire nature." In short, "Every individual existence is but a living history, and its truth, its real being, is its entire development through all its phases taken as a unity."[16]

Writing in 1848, Stallo did not, of course, mention the Darwinian theory but used the ideas of Lamarck and Goethe to reinforce his position. The circulation of Stallo's view of evolution, then an entirely novel idea to most of his contemporaries, was important in preparing the public mind for the advent of Darwin's theory and led Emerson, in the early 1850's, to see nature as rhythmic "unfolding" and true liberty as "spirit's realization of itself."[17]

Just as Hegel particularly emphasized evolutionary process in history, so did all his Ohio followers. They saw history and social life not as cycles of changes, circular movements, or a linear departure from some golden age, but rather as a patterned process of growth in which later stages have new features as they burgeon from previous epochs. In Stallo's view, the Infinite moves only in and through history, not apart from it. Like Hegel, he saw the "progress of history" manifest in Greek, Roman, and Christian epochs, the last extending into the present time.[18] Moncure Conway saw Darwin's theory as properly undermining supernatural creation and was concerned, as a corollary, with the evolution of religious ideas from belief in tribal deities to the recognition of Humanity as Christ, a token of the increasing unity and harmony of all religions.[19]

August Willich saw history as a dialectical process expressing a contradiction between what is particular in human nature on one side and what is universal or infinite on the other. Suggesting a debt to Hegel, Willich wrote: "The general comprehension of world history as the battle to overcome this contradiction is only a result of modern times, though a similar depth may have been achieved by thinkers of the ancient world and expressed in particular aspects. Only in modern times has cultural history been grasped as *history itself*."[20] Peter Kaufmann of Canton, Ohio, viewed history as a patterned process of growth but only vaguely akin to Stallo's strongly Hegelian position. Real religion, he thought, incorporates the truths of reason and science so that religion, reason, and science become the three conjoint voices of God, guiding man toward increasing perfection. In the movement toward perfection America has the special role of "saviour nation" for the world.[21]

In various ways, then, all the Ohio thinkers who were particularly influenced by Hegel impressed their contemporaries with a viewpoint which their daily experience confirmed—namely, that their total social and natural environment was a movement, flux, and process in which they participated and with which they would have to come to terms.

Philosophy and Language

Stallo, Kaufmann, and Conway had a strong and strikingly contemporary interest in the relation of language to thought and to philosophical thought in particular. In the case of Stallo and Kaufmann this interest seems to have originated as much in the fact that both men taught languages for a time—the former at St. Xavier's College in Cincinnati and the latter at the Rappite Community near Pittsburgh—as through anything they may have learned from Hegel. Stallo's summaries of Hegel's writings in *General Principles of the Philosophy of Nature,* however, did touch on those books and chapters where Hegel discussed language. Conway's interest in language seems to have grown out of practical problems of persuasively communicating his advanced religious views. Though he had studied the writings of Friedrich Schlegel and the Humboldts on language and Emerson's transcendental consideration of language in "Nature," he was not satisfied with their views.

Hegel's own complicated and involved use of language, often declared to be unintelligible if not preposterous, has discouraged most readers from seeking any insight in his writings on the relation of language to thought. His style has been called "barbaric" and "tortured." "To read Hegel," a sympathetic interpreter has recently confessed, "is often to undergo an intellectual crucifixion." The interpreter adds, however, that "one seldom feels that such a crucifixion has not been worth while."[22] In spite of this obstacle a number of Hegel's views on language are worth brief attention, and some of them parallel ideas disseminated by Stallo, Kaufmann, and Conway.

Like a number of influential contemporary philosophers, Hegel strongly emphasized the unity of language and thought. He viewed the symbols of language as being an externalization of thought while thought itself is an internalization of language. Referring to the relation of intelligence to signs which are "natural" as being sensible and perceptible, Hegel concluded: "The vocal note which receives further articulation to express specific ideas—speech and, its system, language—gives to sensations, intuitions, conceptions, a second and higher existence than they naturally possess—invests them with the right of existence in the ideational realm."[23] On this basis Hegel insisted that it is impossible to think without words. We only have definite thoughts when they are objectified as words, and, equally, words are manifestations of inward intelligence. The material of language is not a collection of imitative sounds, interesting as they may be, but rather sounds inwardly assimilated by thought. The formal element of language is precisely "the work of the analytic intellect which informs language with its categories." With such a view of the relation of thought to language it is not surprising that Hegel preferred alphabetical writing to hieroglyphics, which are static, inflexible, and restrictive of intelligence. Further, it is not surprising that Hegel attached high importance to ordinary language since both its matter and form particularly manifest the efficacies of thought.

Hegel was well aware that language has a variety of uses, that the norms of reflection differ with different uses of language, and that mixing and confusing those different uses can give rise to serious confusions of thought. This is particularly suggested in his treatment of the relationship of religion to philosophy. Both of these human enterprises, he believed, have substantially the same content, truth as the Absolute Idea. But it is essential for the Absolute Idea in its fullness to have differing and distinguishable aspects. Hence in religion the Absolute comes to expression in the form of imaginative representation while in philosophy it is manifest in logically related concepts. In Hegel's words:

> The genuine Idea of the intrinsically concrete mind is just as essentially under one of its terms (subjective consciousness) as under the other (universality): and in the other it is the same substantial content. Under the subjective form, however, fall feeling, intuition, pictorial representation; and it is in fact necessary that in point of time the consciousness of the absolute Idea should first be reached and apprehended in this form: in other words it must exist in its immediate reality as religion, earlier than it does in philosophy.[24]

The implication of this position is that religious words and utterances differ significantly from those in philosophy in both form and norm, and to identify or mix the two is only to invite intellectual confusion.

Again, Hegel saw language as a distinctly social phenomenon which at once serves to demarcate the individual self in relation to others and hide or mask the real content of social relations. Thus language has differing social uses which require analysis and interpretation by the philosopher. As spoken word and utterance, Hegel believed, language "is the existence of the pure self *qua* self; in speech the self-existent singleness of self-consciousness comes as such into existence, so that its particular individuality is something for others."[25] At the same time, however, language masks the social relations of the self and hides the truth about its part in the creation, for example, of a community's wealth and the power of the state. It does this by verbal rituals of flattery, jealous gossip, and witty chatter such as characterized the eighteenth-century French salons.

These views on the relation of language to thought and the different uses of languages have led J. N. Findlay to find a kinship between Hegel and current preoccupations of British and American philosophers. Addressing the Aristotelian Society, Findlay remarked:

> I found echoes of Hegelian dialectic in Wittgenstein's dissolution of philosophical puzzles: the very words he used sometimes had a Hegelian ring. Thus Hegel, who thought ordinary language to be "divine" and who held that it sometimes turned men's meaning in other directions than they intended, might very well have said that "the problems arising through the misinterpretation of forms of language have a character of depth" . . . are "deep disquietudes."[26]

Stallo and Kaufmann were particularly sensitive to the unity of language and thought and impressed their readers with the need for a critical philosophy of language. At the very beginning of his first book, heavily devoted to an interpretation and exposition of Hegel's views, Stallo noted the problems of putting the important idea of process into the English language. "In English," Stallo observed, "we have names only for the established results of a process; rarely a word expressive of the process itself." Hence a philosophy which seeks to deal with "everything in the process of its origination" encounters special difficulties and perils when its vehicle is the English language. But with German, Stallo's native language and the medium of his first philosophical reading and thinking, the case is different. "The German can use his verbs substantively, thus making pure actions the subjects of a sentence in order to enounce their predicates."[27] Thus Stallo suggested that the basic conclusions and categories of a philosophy are inseparable from the language in which they are put.

In his later writings, however, Stallo came to emphasize the perils which lie in the unity of thought and language.

Having studied comparative linguistics, he concluded that "every distinct form or system of speech involves a distinct metaphysical theory" and that scientists as well as philosophers and ordinary men make serious mistakes in their thinking as a result of language habits. Stallo had in mind particularly the hypostasis of concepts, the conversion of general ideas into distinct and self-subsistent entities, with the result that observable qualities are mistakenly thought to inhere in a fixed, immobile substratum. A critical approach to language, enlightened by the science of comparative linguistics, could resolve many of the perplexities of physics as well as philosophy. Stallo's *Concepts and Theories of Modern Physics* was an attempt to apply such a critical understanding of language to many of the outstanding puzzles and paradoxes in physics. Along the way, however, he also applied it to philosophy and to Hegel's philosophy in particular. Forgetting the rejection of transcendent metaphysics he had earlier found in Hegel's *Phenomenology*, Stallo sharply dismissed Hegel's concept of "pure Being" as merely a reified *summum genus*. It converts a general common property into a thing. " 'Pure Being,' " Stallo wittily concluded, "is simply the specter of the copula between an extinct subject and a departed predicate. It is a sign of predication which 'lags superfluous on the stage' after both the predicate and that whereof it was predicated have disappeared."[28]

Writing with a more general didactic purpose and for less sophisticated readers than Stallo's, Peter Kaufmann emphasized both the unity of thought and language and the misuses of language. Language, in Kaufmann's view, was essentially "the magazine of thought." Without language there could be no accumulation of thought in knowledge, no communication, and no analytical discrimination of objects one from another. "Language, then,—the divine, first-born immortal child of mankind's Reason,—is thus a gift to man, of value beyond price."

Like all words, names have a threefold aspect which must be understood if thought is to be clear and disciplined. The name *sun,* for example, may denote (1) the word as a term in language, (2) the object itself as in nature, and (3) the idea or mental image present in man's intellect in distinction from the word or the object itself. This complex character of language directly provided Kaufmann with two basic rules: First, we should so master our thoughts as to put them in words as unequivocal and precise as if they were in a geometrical proposition. Secondly, to understand the words of others we must try to "ascertain by thought what they really *aim at.*"[29] On the basis of these premises about the relation of thought to language, Kaufmann devoted lengthy chapters of *The Temple of Truth* to the constitution of language, parts of grammar, and uses of the elements of language. Thus was one Ohio thinker, over a century ago, seriously preoccupied with some of the distinctions and issues which have become currently prominent in semantics and linguistic philosophy.

In comparison with Stallo and Kaufmann, Conway was particularly sensitive to the way words can mislead understanding and judgment in religious and theological matters. He saw language as a distinctive mark of humanity in contrast to animality—a social achievement dependent on the cumulative experience of the race. Though it is not to be understood as a supernatural gift, there is a religious significance, Conway believed, in the fact that language is "Nature humanizing."

Conway found the first great principle of language in the fact that words are only "symbols" of things, not the facts being symbolized. Hence the word *love* "can not do instead of loving; truth and mercy can mean nothing save to the merciful and true." Further, the meanings of words change and shift with the growth of knowledge as shown in the current meanings of "sunrise," "lunatic," and "insane." Another fact about language of great importance in theology, Conway observed, is the way words acquire socially-induced emotional tones which becloud thought, as illustrated in misleading connotations of the words "heretic" and "freethinker."[30] Thus Conway moved toward a critical view of language which would at once formulate its natural roots and its relevance to a more adequate, and particularly a more liberal, philosophy of religion.

As noted earlier, neither Stallo, Kaufmann, nor Conway overtly concentrated on Hegel's philosophy of language, nor did they attempt specifically to popularize it in their writings. They did, however, introduce their contemporaries to ideas which distinctly paralleled Hegel's on the unity of thought and language, the different uses of language, and the dialectical linkage of language to social reality.

Liberalism in Hegel's Social Philosophy

With the appearance and historical repercussions of modern totalitarianism no aspect of Hegel's thought has aroused more controversy, provoked more violent feelings, or more readily lent itself to distortion than his political philosophy. Such reaction should surprise hardly anyone. The arena of politics is an arena, and in it men of differing or opposite interests contend for dominance, almost always with passion and sometimes with blood. Scholars too are men. In spite of their commitment to objectivity and detachment they are not immune to political passions and have frequently been led to distort or misrepresent Hegel's view of government.

Many hostile interpreters of Hegel's political theory have been singularly hypnotized by his statements such as, "All the worth which the human being possesses—all spiritual reality, he possesses only through the State," or "Whether the individual exists or not is indifferent to objective ethics" embodied in the State, or "The State is the Divine Idea as it exists on Earth."[31] When such statements are taken out of context and Hegel's particular meanings for "State," "Idea," and other key terms are ignored, he can be made into a spiritual father of modern totalitarianism, completely opposed to the emphasis on the worth of individual men and individual rights characteristic of liberal democracy. Thus one critic has asserted that Hegel's State is "totalitarian, that is to say, its might must permeate and control the whole life of the people in all its functions: 'The State is therefore the basis and center of all the concrete elements in the life of a people: of Art, Law, Morals, Religion, and Science.' " Another has stressed Hegel's attack on liberals of his day who wanted popular education and "more participation in government." Still another critic has claimed that in Hegel's "markedly anti-liberal" view the claims of the state precede those of the individual even if the individual must perish.[32] These interpretations of Hegel, it must be admitted, are significantly corroborated by his honorific references to monarchy, his criticisms of democracy, his antipathy to British political practices, and his opposition to the English Reform Bill shortly before his death.

Nevertheless there is in Hegel's political philosophy an important and ineradicable liberal element, a distinct effort to preserve and substantiate individual freedom, which was brought into the open and emphasized by his Ohio followers before the Civil War. This liberal element is a corollary of Hegel's premise that "In the State, everything depends on the unity of the universal and the particular."[33] This premise emphasizes unity as including diversity, unity as an organized whole of particular parts. Such a unity is implicit in Hegel's references to the state as an "organism," the true substance of ethical life, the divine Idea. On this basis he thought of the state not as the apparatus of government but as a genuine community akin to the Athenian *polis* he so much admired. But in spite of his admiration for the *polis* he did not find in it a full unity of universal and particular. It was deficient, as his criticism of Plato emphasized, in provision for "individual opinion, and individual will and conscience." This provision for "subjective individuality" is precisely the liberal element in Hegel's view of the state. It is the ground of his opposition to slavery in the name of "imprescriptible right" and his notion that "Man has rights because he is a man, not because he is a Jew, or Catholic, a Protestant, a German." It is the ground of his defense of the jury system, intellectual freedom, freedom of choice in employment, the individual's participation in government through various associations, and separation of church and state.[34] To eliminate these applications of liberal individualism as being mere "concessions" or "quibbles," as one interpreter has done, is to miss Hegel's fundamental premise and persistent themes in which he held that the state's unity must be "concrete," *i.e.*, organically whole as preserving and vivifying the individual parts.

Stallo, Conway, and Willich among Hegel's Ohio followers particularly brought out, directly or indirectly, the liberal element in his political philosophy. Their involvement in the partisan politics and social movements of their day whetted their interest in political theory. Through most of his adult life Stallo was engaged in partisan politics as a Democrat or Liberal Republican. He actively promoted defense of the Union in the Civil War to preserve its republican principles. Conway assiduously opposed slavery and while in England identified himself with radical republicans.

Willich championed self-government in a "social republic" as the answer to America's economic and social ills.

In outlining Hegel's "social morality" or "politics" in *The General Principles of the Philosphy of Nature,* Stallo referred to the spirit of a nation as the locus of self-conscious freedom. This spirit, however, is particularized "in *persons,* of whose independence it is the internal power and necessity" while at the same time it is their social end. The immediate form of this spirit is the unity of love in the family. A wider form is civil society, "a system of atomism" expressing mutual wants of many persons and families. The state, finally, is "the union of the principles of the family and civil society" in which "persons are maintained and promoted in their individuality" and at the same time absorbed in more universal relationships. Thus Stallo affirmed for his American readers Hegel's fundamental premise that "In the State, everything depends on the unity of the universal and the particular." But from this premise Stallo could not follow Hegel's view that "the power of the prince is the pervading unity." In fact, Stallo registered his dissent from Hegel and maintained that Hegel had violated his own premise. "As if the subjectivity of the state, or of anything organic," Stallo exclaimed, "could be something extraneous,—which the power of the prince always is,—something else than a reflex objectivity!"[35]

What Stallo made of the basic premises and principles of Hegel's political philosophy becomes clear in the section of *The General Principles* on "Evolutions" in relation to the state. There Stallo saw law as "nothing more than the universal reason slumbering in every individual mind, which manifests itself in the collective evidences of the Spiritual through its separate impersonations." On this basis the State is nothing more than society organizing itself, and a truly lawful state is essentially democratic in its fundamental character and relation to individuals. As Stallo put it:

> It is the destiny of the individual to identify his private reason and will with universal reason and will; and, obviously, this can take place only if the latter, in the form of law, be in the consciousness of the individual, and reproduce themselves *in* and *from* him. The organization of society is, therefore, essentially democratic.[36]

No government can be genuine or embody the life of society if it proceeds from a few individuals only or is imposed from without. Thus Stallo, from premises and principles essentially the same as Hegel's, persistently provided for "individuality" in his view of the state and even turned Hegel's principles to the defense of democracy. Later in his life Stallo came to stress the "dialectic process" in society and on that ground defended freedom of mind and separation of church and state as essential requirements for social growth and development.[37] In several ways, then, Stallo underlined and emphasized the liberal elements in Hegel's political philosophy.

In Cincinnati, Moncure Conway was mainly concerned with Strauss's development of Hegel's philosophy of religion as implying a denial of miracles, a mythical interpretation of Scripture, and a reinforcement of the theory of evolution. Later, however, Conway paid specific attention to Hegel's political philosophy in a commemorative article on Strauss published in both London and Boston. In Hegel's thought, "destined to create an epoch in the history of the human mind," Conway found a clear-cut affirmation of political freedom. "Those who study Hegel," he insisted, "know that his apparent conservatism was the crust outside a fiery radicalism." To prove his point Conway quoted at length Hegel's explanation of "how the history of the world is a record of the endeavors made to realize the idea of freedom and of a progress surely made, but not without many intervals of apparent failure and retrogression."[38] The French Revolution, in Hegel's view, was a failure because it sought "a boundless external liberation" without the indispensable condition of a religious reformation. Conway thus understood Hegel to be an unqualified champion of freedom but one who particularly stressed its institutional prerequisites and requirements. In this way Conway, like Stallo, emphasized the liberal aspect of Hegel's political philosophy.

August Willich admired Hegel as "the greatest philosopher of the nineteenth century," studied his social philosophy before coming to America, and occasionally quoted him in the *Cincinnati Republikaner*. But Willich's Hegelianism was also mediated through Feuerbach and Marx. In an internal criticism of Hegel, Feuerbach had concluded that concepts or ideas are not self-subsistent realities; rather they are derivatives or abstractions from the primary experience —from sensations, feelings, and wants—of individual men. It was this humanistic emphasis in Feuerbach which attracted Marx and turned him away from Hegel's treatment of Idea, Spirit, and Concrete Mind. It led Marx to condemn the degradation of human beings under capitalism and defend socialism as "an association in which the free development of each is the condition of the free development of all" and "the development of human power is its own end."[39] Similar themes frequently appear in Willich's writings. The motto of the *Republikaner* under his editorship was "Value in Return for Value" and "To Each His Own." Willich saw socialism as extending into the economic field the principle of a republic, namely, consent and self-government in which "No man is a means for another, but he is his own end."[40] Though Willich never overtly stressed the liberal element—the emphasis on individual freedom and individual rights—in Hegel's philosophy, his "Left-Hegelian" views might give pause to those who would label Hegel an anti-liberal totalitarian.

A year or two before Conway found in Hegel a "fiery radicalism" committed to individual freedom, other publications called attention to the liberal elements in Hegel's political philosophy. In one of a series of articles in *Harpers'* magazine reaching a half a million readers, Hegel was specifically linked with the growing republican movement in Europe. Emilio Castellar saw in Hegel the "true philosophy of progress" manifest in "the self-development of Being from indefiniteness to perfect fullness of life, to self-possession." On this basis Hegel's true heirs were those who fought in fields and parliaments "to incarnate the individual and the independent spirit of Germany in the republican organism." Hegel's own defense of monarchy, Castellar believed, was essentially a contradiction of the basic teaching of his philosophy and must be understood as a convenient accommodation whereby Hegel could be left alone for his work.[41]

A closer defense of Hegel's liberalism was presented by Karl Rosenkranz, eminent Hegel scholar, in the pages of *The Journal of Speculative Philosophy* sponsored by the St. Louis Philosophical Society whose leader, W. T. Harris, put at the foundation of his theory of education and his defense of democratic individualism—at times even a socially callous individualism—the concept of "self-activity" derived from Hegel.[42] With detailed evidence Rosenkranz noted the gross discrepancies between Hegel's view of the state and the existing Prussian monarchy, his limitation of monarchical power to dotting *i*'s and crossing *t*'s, his separation of church and state, and his provision for individual rights. "When Hegel is represented," said Rosenkranz, "as though he had in mind a centralized or bureaucratic state in which the omniscience or omnipotence of the government destroyed all individual vitality, as Fichte did in his exclusive, commercial state, he is entirely misunderstood."[43] These interpretations of Hegel confirm the earlier suggestions in

Stallo and Conway that there was an important and ineradicable liberal element in Hegel's view of the state.

Several aspects of Hegel's political theory emphasized by his Ohio followers in the mid-nineteenth century are relevant to present issues, with allowances being made, of course, for a changed social *milieu.* Hegel's central concept of the state as involving an organic unity of universal and particular underlines a host of social problems connected with the ideal of "community." Like Hegel's Germany and nineteenth-century America, the United States is today still ardently, sometimes feverishly, groping for self-identity. It is trying to find the particular tone and flavor of its universality, to use Hegel's expression, both as fact and ideal. The search is complicated by an inherited tradition of particularity which is more often alive in slogans and myths about individualism than in social realities. Nevertheless, that tradition evokes an ideal held widely enough and seriously enough to be indispensable to America's self-identity.

Along with its tradition of individualism the United States is also trying to determine how it is and should be a community, *i.e.*, a mutuality which preserves and nurtures particularity. Its groping and indecision are reflected in public controversies over the proper scope of freedom of speech in relation to national security, governmental support of religious schools, the relation of individual citizens to the economically enforced "togetherness" of giant corporations, and the extent to which freedom as a corollary of laws and institutions must invertedly generate restrictive conformity. On similar issues Hegel had something important and suggestive to say, his Ohio followers believed, for the mid-nineteenth century. In relation to "community" his principles are still important and suggestive for the twentieth century, though the issues have altered and in some cases have even been reversed.

Appendix: Key Writings

From *General Principles of the Philosophy of Nature*[1]

BY JOHN B. STALLO

PREFACE

I cheerfully acknowledge, that for many of my views I am indebted to the study of Hegel's philosophy, although, generally, these views are as independent of Hegel as Hegel is (if it be permitted *magnis componere parva*) of Schelling. It is, of course, altogether foreign to my purpose, as it is out of my power, to give a complete genetic history of German philosophy with the whole variety of its evolutions, in which the succession of the few names, Schelling, Oken, Hegel, would be grotesque enough. What I have given is, in all cases, the fruit of a long and serious study bestowed upon the original works [vi] mentioned in the text; and as I was in search of the results to which the train of these philosophical ideas led, and not merely of a perspective view of their manifold bearings, I can scarcely regret that not a single one of the numerous critical histories of German philosophy has been accessible to me, excepting alone that of Hegel, which is however, altogether unavailable for details.

Unfortunately, the materialistic, utilitarian tendencies, which at present pervade every branch of science under color of a misconceived Baconism, have revoked every alliance between philosophical pursuits and the investigation of nature. Speculation is perfectly disavowed (sometimes justly, perhaps), and the very worst passport which a naturalist could carry about him is that of a metaphysician. The assumption, that the creative source of free thoughts, the mind, should be even distantly akin to the immutable forces which actuate the movements of the Universe, rear the invariable structure of crystalline masses, preside over the evolution of vegetable forms, and manifest themselves in the organisms and instincts of the animal sphere, is held utter abhorrence. Now the fundamental principle, upon which, according to my conviction, all true philosophy of nature rests, is, that the different manifestations of the vitality which bursts forth in nature's phenomena are comprehensively united, centred in the mind; that the implacable rigor of cosmic laws, which sways [vii] *extensive matter,* is identical with the eternal freedom of *mind in its infinite intensity.* I know but one way to reconcile the reluctant reader to this view: that of contrasting it with the current opinions to the contrary, and of first showing what difficulties, and again, what contradictions, the latter involve, when consistently carried out. I have endeavoured to place these difficulties in relief, in the exposition of Kant's philosophy, the acme of the old dualism, where the contrast between the Material and Spiritual, the Objective and Subjective, is salient in the extreme. The unity of the two, asserted by the "philosophy of nature," is not (though such is the very common charge) the unity of pantheism, or a mere hypostatic notion of universality.

I shall think myself happy, if I have in any manner contributed to introduce more distinct ideas respecting German philosophy among the American and English reading public. The words, "German philosophy," or "German idealism," are heard every moment; but the only sense attached to them (if there be any) is a medley of vague abstractions, or a series of distractive day-dreams. This obtains even [viii] with regard to the writings of the excellent Carlyle. (See, e.g., his biographies of German poets, his "Characteristics," his "Sartor Resartus," &c.). Much confusion has arisen from the circumstance, that certain pre-established English criteria have been applied to German philosophy. It is suggestive of the national characteristics of the Germans, and serves to discriminate between the spirit alive in them and that animating the French and English, that in the philosophy anterior even to Kant, the Germans, and among them Leibnitz and Wolf, always set out from *themselves,* from a few axiomatic notions relating to being, thought, ideas, the Deity, &c., and upon these synthetically constructed their system of science; whereas the English and French began with objective nature, analyzed it, and then by generalizations sought to arrive at absolute conclusions. The Germans could not *descend* to the material world; hence they became idealists;—the English and French were unable to *ascend* to the summits of the Absolute; on that account they remained materialists. This again leads to the important distinction, often so little kept in view, between the German and the English sceptics. The latter, dwelling in the sphere of the senses, doubted of every thing which was not the object of these, and therefore of the *ideality of the Real;* the former, lost in their own being, doubted of every thing that was not, as it were, born a thought,—they doubted of the correspondence of [ix] the material world with their subjective conceptions, of the reality of the Ideal. For an illustration, I simply refer to Hume and Kant.

I ought, perhaps, to apologize here for some anomalies of language, which, in treating of German philosophy, it has been impossible always to forego. In English we have names only for the established result of a process; rarely a word expressive of the process itself. There is the term "knowledge," but the act of acquiring it—*agnoscere, erkennen*—is nameless. We have no term corresponding to the Latin "*fieri,*" the German "*werden,*"—no verb designating the act of absolute origination; "to become" does not express it. The German can use his verbs substantively, thus making pure actions the subjects of a sentence, in order to enounce their predicates;—an Englishman considers this as not congenial to the spirit of his language. Now, as it is the characteristic of true philosophy to study everything in the process of its origination,—to comprehend that which is evolved, by observing the process of its evolution,—the obstacles encountered in an attempt to reproduce such philosophical movements in the English language must be numerous. [x]

VIEWS AND PROSPECTS

The Universe embraces the different individual forms as its organic constituents, all of which are subject to the activity of the same general laws (and it might be added, consequently to the same fundamental typification, the types being only the record of those laws). Taking life in its most general acceptation, of a process of phenomenal variations, bodying forth an unvarying, permanent principle of existence, it would not be difficult to show that life belongs to any of these constituents solely in virtue of their relations with the entire Universe; that all the manifestations of life—change, motion, progressive development—are but a process verifying the vital innervations of the Whole. As to the life in the solar system: there would be neither revolution nor rotation without the link of universal attraction, hence no seasonal vicissitudes, no succession of night and day; [13] without the cosmic influence of heat and light, the water would not evaporate from the ocean's surface; there being no disturbance of aerial equilibrium, no breezes would waft the distilled products to the continental plains; there would be no irrigation of the soil, no circulation of waters, no vegetation, no support of animal life. To descend to terrestrial forms: a mineral solution stands inert and shapeless, until the magic lines of light trace in it the word "*union* with the vivifying Whole," when at once polarization is induced, the molecules attract and repel each other, assuming the form of a crystalline unit, the threshold, perhaps, to the realm of separate organization. Similarly the warm breath of the Universe impregnates the terrestrial womb with vegetation forms, and the solar eye, as it were, *looks* them into distinct, individual existence. The same with animals. It is useless to adduce further instances to show how the proposition, that life only then appears, when the Whole energizes in a part, or when the Particular enters into relation with the Universal, might be disjunctively established.

The vital activity of nature is evinced (I give this as a "Baconian" fact) in the continual evolution of individual forms, each of them tending to an independence of constitutional arrangement, and (in higher forms) of vitality. Now, since (as has been shown) all vital development depends upon the energetic relation between Whole and parts, which relations are materially exhibited in each individual form, in the shape of organs,* it follows that vital development is greatest when the direct relationship is most multilateral, when the organization, therefore, is most complicated. A greater multiplicity of relations will condition a more variegated combination of organs, [14] a superior organization. Inasmuch, however, as the same universality is the principle of all organization, the type of each particular organism will be a document of that universality; the development and the organic structure reared thereby will, in consequence, be a repitition of the development and form of the great organic Whole. The general results, then, which thus present themselves, might be stated as follows:—

1. Every individual organism is the activity of all comprehending nature embodied in concrete unity, the life of the Whole reflected in a part;† or, since this life can manifest itself in no other way than in a reciprocation between the Whole and its parts, between World and Monad, every individual organism is a material exhibition of these reciprocating agencies in conspiring, harmonic operation.

2. The development of each particular organic form is a miniature reproduction of the formative evolution of entire nature; and, inasmuch as

3. the gradation of natural forms will depend upon the greater or less universality of the direct relations embodied in them, upon the greater or less perfection with which they represent nature in her totality, and with which the above reproduction is effected, it follows, that

* Organ I call the material medium through which the reciprocation of the Individual with Whole is established,—the totality of organs in each individual development constituting an organism.

† The words of Goethe are quite in point:—

"Willst du dich am Ganzen erquicken,
So musst du das Ganze im Kleinsten erblicken."

"If you wish to appreciate the Whole, you must see the Whole in the Smallest."

4. every higher organism must exhibit a progressive repetition of inferior organisms, both in its development, and in the material form recording it.

I might, perhaps go farther still. All development is, from its nature, progressive; absolute progression would characterize life absolutely independent. Every [15] particular organic form, however, appears in a twofold capacity,–that of a self-perpetuating unit, of a whole complete in itself, and that of a mere complementary member, a part of a superior whole, from the connection with which it derives its vital significance. Its development will not, therefore, be absolutely progressive, but characterized by evolution and revolution, advance and retrogression; it will be self-returning, as it were, circular. Yet, since a mere retracing of a previous course would preclude all actual advance, and consequently all real development, the term of any evolution will never coincide with its outset, but fall beyond it; the development of all individual forms will be spiral.* This great law has been repeatedly insisted upon by Goethe, Carus, and others. Otherwise expressed, all life is periodical,–night and day, sleep and waking, life and death, &c., &c., are phases that must succeed each other.[16]

GROUNDS AND POSITIONS

What is the constant principle, we ask, in the variations of existing things? What is the origin of the movements of the Universe? the source whence every thing emanates? [22] the ground of so many modifications? The mystery is the connection between the unity demanded by the mind and the variety given in experience,–between substance and its transition into modifications,–between the mere *quantum* and the *quale*. Reduced to its simplest elements, the difficulty stands between constancy and change,–between absolute rest and absolute motion.

We are driven from effect to cause. Inquirers have therefore

* It is, perhaps, superfluous to remark, that already the word "development" (more appropriately *evelopment,–devolutio, evolutio*) implies this. The spiral growth of plants, the spiral structure of animal bones, the spiral progress of foetal evolution, the recent theory of the spiral nature of celestial movements, &c., &c., are all well known.

generally sought to reason their way up to a final cause, where their inquiry ceased, rested, and, as they inferred, where every thing has its absolute foundation, where it rests, reposes.* Wherever there was movement, variation, change, they went beyond it to the cause, and so on,—*ad infinitum,* or rather until they abandoned the hopeless chase. The only resource then was to assert an ultimate unital cause in spite of the failure to arrive at it, and to fill the chasm by—a mystery.

There is an assumption in this. The logical cogency which pointed to a goal receding before them consisted in this, that the absolute repose, rest as such, was made the origin of all existences, that rest was made the bearer, the absolute condition, the source, the element of motion. In other words, they assumed a logical priority of rest to motion. But is this true? Is rest the element of motion, or motion the element of rest? Is rest the principle upon which motion can be explained, or conversely? Is motion a mere incident to rest, or rest an incident to motion? Is rest, absolutely, substantially taken, at all?

It is my object to bring the reader by the simplest possible means to the point of view to which long, earnest [23] thought has brought me. I shall attempt to remove all dialectical difficulties, save those which lie in the nature of the subject, and are superadded by the circumstance, that all things present a new face when the position is varied. When I appear to make a gratuitous assertion, I request the reader not to be too hasty, and to read twice.

There is nowhere absolute rest, but motion everywhere. All rest is but relative, or it is equilibrium. What appears at first sight to be stationary will prove not only to be whirled away in the great cosmic movements, but engaged in a process of origination and evanescence.† But this is not enough. It is impossible to conceive rest without the concomitant idea of equilibrium, and therefore

* In several philosophical books this is conceived, sometimes illustratively, sometimes in the strict sense of the words, as the reference of the whole Universe to an absolute fulcrum, an absolute centre of gravity, around which all motion occurs, and from which all motion proceeds.

† Had I any need of mere plausibility, which has nothing to do with truth, I might adduce such instances as the incessant heaving of granite (one of the most rigid substances known) recently observed by Doellinger.

of motion. It is impossible to construe motion out of rest; rest is an incident to motion, and consequently to be explained from the nature of the latter. There is consequently no logical priority of rest to motion.* That we are forced to seek an explanation of the existence of things means, we are forced to reduce every thing to the ultimatum, to the last element of thought,—to its simplest item, beyond which our thought cannot go. This last element is of course the absolute unit; since, however, it is a logical impossibility to conceive rest but as the product of motion, as arising from an absolute opposition,—mechanically expressed, but as equilibrium,—this is not the unity of absolute repose, but the unity of absolute motion within itself, or motion as unital, substantial.

It was an inevitable failure, when philosophers [24] assumed a firm, immobile principle, from which they attempted to find their way to the variety of existences. They postulated the unity of all things, not in an ultimate substance, but in a rigid substratum. From this substratum they could deduce nothing; they could only superinduce the phenomenal world, by which they virtually made the latter as absolute and independent as the former. —Are we, then, to renounce the substantial unity in question? By no means; but it is absolute motion, or activity, substantively taken, not rest as a substance, which constitutes this unity.

Motion in the sphere of finitudes, where it allies itself to the idea of succession, is but an analogon of absolute motion, of which there is question here. Origination, generation, activity, &c., are all adequate expressions only in so far as we exclude time. There certainly is a word which expresses that absolute, substantial, timeless motion in and through itself; that word is spirit, and I shall afterwards introduce it, when we have gained a clearer insight, which can be effected only through an analysis of the familiar idea of motion. —For another reason the term motion is inadequate. We shall presently see that activity, when existing, is self-opposition; now this is quite easily understood by motion in

* The trivial fact might be insisted upon, that in mechanics the theory of motion precedes that of rest; dynamics precedes statics.

the relations of quantity, but in quality the same obtains, and thus the common idea of motion is insufficient. Still, it is perfectly relevant, because it is rigorously an analogon.

The absolutely first and last, the principle of all existences, therefore, is the substantiality of motion,*—[25] movement within itself; absolute activity, absolute life,—the substance originating within itself. It is usually dangerous to employ technical language; otherwise we might designate the same as self-equilibrating motion.

Motion (activity) is in itself necessarily dual, or, universally taken, plural and unital at the same time. This is no paradox. Let the reader reflect upon the nature of motion. Let him try to conceive the transition of a body from one point to another. We must catch the body in the *act* of transition, for however near we place the points, a shift from the one to the other is to be made, and there is motion only during that shift. If we wish, then, to seize upon that act as an act,—as a unital, identical being,—it is at two points at once. Motion taken as a unital activity, therefore, is in innumerable points at once. The reader will perceive that the very duality or plurality of motion arises from our attempt to seize upon it as a unity. —The act of origination, of beginning, &c., leads to the same contradiction, which contradiction nevertheless results from the necessary identity of the act, from its unity. We grasp the act as a unity, and we have an unavoidable duality; we endeavour to retain that duality as absolute, and it is nothing without the unity. Enouncing this generally: the principle of existences is just as absolutely self-identifying,—unital,—as it is self-differentiating, self-repelling, self-exclusive. It is as necessarily intensity as it is extension, as necessarily an interior,

* I once for all remark, that I use words here in their general sense; if they are used in a new sense, the words assume it themselves in the course of deduction, and not I for them. The word "substance," for instance, is a growth of the old theories, and comes from sub-*sistere,* implying fundamental rest; but I retain the word for its general import, which is well understood, instead of framing a new one that would lead to embarrassment. In how far I shall, in general, accept the charge of a contradictio in adjectis, for which further on there will often be a better pretext than here, where a captious repetition of a "moving substance" would be a mere quibble, our progress will show.

spiritual principle, as an outward, material manifestation. (That which is self-exclusive, and therefore extended and impenetrable, I call matter.) [26]

I hope the reader will seriously reflect upon this. Activity, life, &c., which all involve motion, being the substance of every thing, must be taken as existing, and for that purpose be identified. In this identification the substance "before our eyes" differentiates, defines itself as a plurality.

I can now safely proceed to vary my expressions. The principle of all existences is a living unit, or an absolutely existing process. Had Spinoza and others succeeded in deducing the phenomenal world from a rigid substratum, they had succeeded in deducing life from the absolutely dead,—which would be the same as making the body generate its soul, which afterwards assumed unlimited sway over its own creator!

The Rigid Material, or what was formerly conceived to be the Substantial, is therefore the exterioration or manifestation of life and motion; motion (life) is not the manifestation of a reposing substance. Yet absolute life *is*, exists; and as existing, it is (according to the preceding paragraph) plural, self-excluding, self-extending. The actuality of life, then, depends upon extension, upon multiplicity; the manifestation of life lies in the *beside* and the *after*, in *time* and *space*. The Extended, Actual, Material, is therefore strictly affected by time and space; they are, as it were, born with it. It is consequently incorrect to say that the inner identity of life was prior in time to its outer manifestation; if I forcibly abstract from the latter, the categories of time and space are inapplicable to the former. [27]

Matter has no foundation either by or in itself. Its nature is self-repulsion, exclusion, extension; in virtue of this exclusion only it exists, or it exists only in so far as it denies, limits, other matter. It is essentially finite in space; hence it does not exist by itself. But matter, moreover, has no foundation in itself. It exists only inasmuch as the purely Active, Living, the soul of all existences, thereby effects its essential self-mediation,—as through the exteriorating Material this principle of life comes to itself. Attaining to an external object by means of a third one is mediation; here, however, the inner moving principle attains to itself, to its own reality, by outward material existence, and this I call essential self-mediation. Matter is the absolute means; it exists not in itself, but in virtue of, and with reference to its inner vitality. It is consequently finite in time, that inner vitality being absolute change, motion. [31]

I have above expressly foreclosed the supposition, that finite motion, which proceeds from and towards definite spatial points, was here made the Absolute. Motion, substantially taken, or the substance moving, acting in itself,—in a word, the living substance, absolute life,—is the ground of all things. The word Spirit or Mind has been subsequently introduced; I avoided it at first, because it would then have given rise to vague associations. Mind is the absolutely Restless in itself, the absolutely Creative, the absolutely Free. Mind is not the blank of abstraction, not the *caput mortuum* of the External. The Deity, the absolute Mind, is the absolute intrinsic process,—the substance which causes, produces itself,—gazes into its own eye. —I beg the reader's pardon for the repeated use of the word "absolute"; other expressions, such as *eternal*, &c., are associated with the idea of time, which is a category inapplicable to the Spiritual. —If I have said, that, to maintain and to assert itself in its identity, the Spiritual realizes itself as the Material, it will not be inferred that therefore the Material precedes the actual existence of the Spiritual as such; that would be the greatest misconception of every thing I have said. In, not after, the act, in which the plurality of the Material [43] breaks forth as the self-realization of the Spiritual, this likewise flashes up as the absolute Mind, as the light of eternal self-consciousness. I use the present tense here, because I cannot use the past, present, and future at the same time, or rather, because I have no tenseless verb. But the Spiritual becomes phenomenal essentially; it is its being to realize itself in the Material. Now the Material exists in the categories of time and space. Consequently, whatever is in the Spiritual as unital intensity is likewise found in material nature, therefore in time and space, as succession and co-arrangement. The absolute act of self-evolution will hence be disjunctively represented in its phases in the Material. We shall consequently have,—

1. The Spiritual as the absolute origin of all existences, abstractly taken.
2. The exterioration of the Spiritual, as the manifestation in existence, abstractly taken.
3. The Spiritual as thus sustaining itself, regenerated in its exterioration, or the Spiritual taken in its concrete identity and truth.

This is not an arbitrary division; the nature of the Spiritual presents itself thus as *explicit.* The Spiritual repels its own nature from itself, in order to have the infinite joy, as it were, of gazing into its own countenance, thereby to comprehend itself in the rapture of boundless love, and to be its infinite self-absorption, self-attraction.

The Spiritual is its own source, its own emanation, and its own direction; it is its own force, its own material, and its own structure; it is its own painter, color, and picture. Beside it, there is nothing; whatever exists exists only in and through it. Matter is not a hearth, upon which afterwards the flame of the Spiritual is kindled; [44] the Spiritual is at once the hearth, the process of combustion, and the appearing flame.

On this account we can comprehend material nature only as one with the Spiritual. The understanding may compare and distinguish, sever, and compose, chain and measure, ever so long; it will, after all, know nothing real. What is knowledge of a thing? If I truly know a thing, is it not then perfectly transparent to the Spiritual in me, to the mind?—is it not thoroughly luminous to the "mind's eye"?—does not the light of the mind fill the place or every part and particle of the thing? Does not thing, therefore, perfectly dissolve in mind, resolve itself into the Spiritual, when there is question of intelligence? Must not that which I know enter perfectly within me, become unreservedly my own, identify itself completely with my mind?

The so-called different modifications of the Material are, in conformity with the above, so many different phases of the Spiritual in its outward existence. In the old view of the nature of material bodies, a substance was first taken as the absolutely primum of all existence; then the qualities, invariably conceived as material likewise, were superadded. That is to say, to the material substance there was added, e.g., first, so much specific gravity, then so much latent heat, so much electricity, so much color, such taste and smell, &c., &c. Now let us take away once from a material body its gravity, its heat, its color, its taste and smell,—in general, its qualities,—what have we remaining? We will not even speak of the mysterious compenetration of these qualities,—of the circumstance, that, for instance, a roll of sulphur is throughout yellow, throughout of its peculiar smell, throughout of its determinate specific gravity, heat, &c. The non-interference of these qualities in the old point of view [45] must remain as necessarily, not a mystery, but a down-right contradiction and defiance of common sense, as Dalton's law, that gases, no matter how compressed, act as vacua with respect to each other,—that after having compressed the greatest practicable quantity of one gas into a closed space, we can further introduce of other gases successively just as great a quantity as if the first were not there at all,—or Doebereiner's, Mitchell's, and Graham's law of diffusion, that, if two or more gases each contained in a separate vessel, be placed above each other, the lighter uppermost, the communication between them being left free, they will mix, the lighter descending and the heavier ascending,*—laws which will remain an everlasting poser to the atomistical chemist. [46]

EVOLUTIONS

The Conscious Mind

The mind awakens to active existence by its reciprocation with the external world, in which it meets with its own laws and

* These two difficulties could be resolved into one, the latter law being made a consequence of the former, were it not, that, after all, the diffusion depended upon the densities, the velocity of the diffusion being inversely proportional to the square roots of the specific densities of the gases respectively.

recognizes its own existence,—where, consequently, it finds itself. The old quarrel respecting the existence or non-existence of innate ideas in the mind, and which has created so much ado in English literature since Locke's denial of them, evinces the grossest and most irreflective ignorance with regard to the mutual position of mind and matter. Material nature is nothing, if you abstract the mind; and the reality of the mind vanishes, if you destroy material nature. I shall not exhaust the reader's patience by expatiating upon the assumptions made by men who undertook to solve such questions without in any manner looking beyond them; it is enough for us to have been taught by our investigations what existence is and means, to be rid of these quibbles at once. The Aristotelian "*nihil in intellectu quod non prius in sensu*" is true enough, if meant to imply that the developments and determinations of the mind depend upon a reciprocation with nature. So the antithesis between intuitions and cognitions *a priori* and *a posteriori* likewise holds good no farther than in this sense. [130]

The mind, in verifying its relations to the external world, determines both the latter and itself; it converts the world into ideas, itself into reality, and both into reason. The conscious mind, in facing an object, first perceives its particularities—of time, place, &c.; it is perception. But these particularities, as I have before demonstrated, are not insular existences, but relations, whose "ensemble" expresses the idea of the object; in becoming sensible of an object in this light, consciousness appears as observation. Finally, then, the unity of this idea and of its relations, the complete object, becomes the property of the mind in *cognition.*

The three forms of the conscious mind, therefore, are:

1. Particular, immediate perception,—intuition.
2. Generalization,—observation.
3. Idealization,—cognition.

(1.) *Immediate Perception,—Intuition.*—Perception furnishes nothing more than the direct assurance, the object *is*—in this place, at this time, under these circumstances, &c. In this, the mind becomes certain both of the being of the object and of itself, for the immediate being of both consists in their relativity. The object becomes present to the mind, and the mind becomes present to itself. (In the Second Part we shall see that Fichte made this immediate self-distinction of the mind the starting-point of all philosophy.) —Things, as immediately existing, are the exteriorated; they exist, consequently, in *space* and *time,* and are immediately beheld as such. But the nature of both is absolute relativity; the bearings of this relativity are appreciated in observation. Thus, time and space are forms of *intuition,*—not, however, as if they did not equally exist without. —It is obvious that it were impossible for the mind to be affected by the particularities of the external world, if the [131] latter were not radically homogeneous with it. Perception is therefore not to be taken in the sense, that external objects in their figuration, solidity, &c., are engraven upon the mind, as upon a cartoon. The fixed existence and independent solidity of objects dissolves, not only before subjective reflection, but in itself. Objects are thoroughly relative; their being is a complex of relations, which, though a complex, nevertheless constitute the objective unity. The particularities of perception on their own ground change into general qualities, general relations, which interpenetrate in this unity; the particularity of the object spontaneously destroys itself. The object thus referred to generality is the object of

(2.) *Observation.*—Observation, then, takes the object in its relations, in its general bearings, dissolves it into universal existences. The object is now no longer something fixed, absolutely present, merely being, but its existence is apprehended in its *mediation.* Observation beholds things, not in their isolation, but in their *common* existence. Not that they are in a manner seized and thrown into a common pit; but generality, universality, is just as essentially the nature of an object, as particularity. Perception is not a pitchfork, with which existences are seized; and the categories of the mind are not labelled bags, where they are huddled together. The ordinary notions of the operations of the mind are materialistic and irreflective to an amazing degree. The whole sophistry of scepticism, of the impossibility to know the truth of objects, depends upon nothing more than the notion, that the mind is an instrument, with which we lay hold of the external world. Pray, who, then, is the subject using that instrument? It is astonishing that these sophists had confidence enough in the great "Artisan," who contrived both the subtile nature of objects and the mind, to be certain that [132] the structure of the latter would be cunning enough to seize upon all the delicate threads of the object's "real nature."

(3.) *Cognition.*—Cognition finally reduces these generalities to an individual unity, in which they interpenetrate, and to which they refer,—whose nature they express. The object is then a unity phenomenal in general varieties, an identity internally diffracting itself into general differences, and pervading them as their inner idea. Cognition idealizes objects, that is to say, it refers the multiplicity of observation to a One, and the One to its external multiplicity; it makes objects transparent, evolves the light of immanent unity from their dispersive aspects. In discussing the philosophy of Kant, I shall advert to this conversion of objects into ideas under other points of view; suffice it here to say, that our ideas are not in any manner copies of external objects, no images; they are the objects themselves, in their reproduced spiritual nature. It is stated in almost all the text-books on psychology and logic, that in the conversion of objects into ideas the particular qualities are eliminated, i.e., omitted. This is rank nonsense. If the particular qualities be omitted, what remains of the object? Certainly I should be at a loss to tell. The truth is, that it is the nature of the multiple relations to eliminate themselves, to reduce themselves to spiritual unity, because in this consists their true being, their essence; but it is, conversely, the nature of the unity to exteriorate itself in the Manifold. This compenetration of unity and multiplicity is the object of cognition; cognition deals with realities, not with shadows.

The foregoing course of mental action may be resumed in these few words: *perception* gives us the im-[133]mediate certainty of the object in its space and time; *observation* determines its general, but distinct predicates, which are finally resumed in the ideal unity of the object (or, speaking with reference to the predicates, the subject). Once more: the predicates are the subject; they are not glued, plastered, upon it, and torn off, when the subject is idealized. Every thing exists in its properties, not beside them.

The Thinking Mind

Cognition has effected the idealization of the object, which now stands as an individual idea. But the individual, insular idea is dependent for its determination upon the universal Ideal,—upon the Spiritual generally. The next task, then, is to rank this idea in its general connection,—to state it as a link in the whole spiritual tenor of the mind. The object is known,—it must now be thought.

The mind, therefore, is to establish the Individual in its relations to the totality of the Universal. In the first instance, these two present themselves as distinct from each other, and as such they are taken by the *understanding*. But they essentially bear upon each other; the Universal, being the movement *in* the Individual, diffracts itself into the latter, and determines itself thereby. The two mediate each other; and the syllogistic movement of mediation is the sphere of *judgment*. Finally, the absolute unity of the two is re-established by *reason*, which recognizes the Universal as necessarily individual, and the Individual as necessarily universal,—which maintains their unity in their difference.

(1.) *Understanding*.—In the understanding [134] the thinking mind keeps the Universal and Individual asunder, as separate and distinct. We know from the investigations of the first paragraphs, that the spiritual unity and its differences are both necessary for existence, and that they must both be kept in view. The understanding merely appreciates the differences, and abstracts from their unity. I have said in the beginning, all existences are relative; now every relation implies at least two terms. They are different *terms:* Consequently there is a higher link establishing their internal unity; they are *different* terms: hence they are separate and mutually external. The latter side is that which is isolated by the understanding. In the view of the understanding, the Infinite and Finite, the form and the material, the Universal and the Particular, &c., are utterly distinct; their relation to each other is barely external. Thus the abstractly Universal, the Ideal, is taken as an independent existence: form, idea, law, rule, axiom, genus; with this the Particular is contrasted as the informal, lawless, arbitrary, material; then the latter is construed by the former, externally referred to it, and thus understood. It is evident, that, were this method of the understanding the ultimate and real one, the intimate nature of the material thus formalized would remain perfectly incomprehensible,—a conclusion at which, indeed, several philosophers have arrived. The ideal form, being perfectly heterogeneous to the crude material, could, of course, at most throw light upon it, but not pervade it, make it perfectly transparent, make it ideal light throughout. —The ideal forms have been termed (as the reader knows) *categories* or *predicaments*. The Pythagoreans already seem to have examined these categories, although Aristotle for the first time enumerated them, and their determination has on that account been attributed to him. (His table embraced ten categories: substance, magnitude, quality, relation, space, time, situation, possession (ἔχειν), activity, passivity,—to which the Peripatetics added five: antithesis, precedence, succession, coexistence, and motion. For an enumeration of the Kantian categories, see my discussion of his "Critique of Pure Reason," in the Second Part.)

Since for the understanding existences are mutually external, the sphere of the understanding is finite. Whoever, therefore, circumscribes his mental action by the boundaries of the understanding, must despair of an insight into the Infinite. But the understanding is to be recognized as limited, and to be confined to its sphere, where alone it is valid. The understanding, nevertheless, is a necessary form of the mind; in the regions of the Finite, where most of our activities, our investigations, and endeavours lie, it is the proper criterion. The intelligent man must discriminate; he must be of keen understanding; he must distinctly see the position of things and his own.

The developed philosophy, as it were, of the understanding is contained in Mathematics; its triumph there is the sweep of form over all finite existences. In Mathematics, the ideal form is presupposed and found in the mind in the shape of axioms; to these, then, every thing is held up; with them all determinations are compared, and thereby defined. Such a comparison with an ideal form is called a demonstration. This depends upon nothing more than abstract coincidence and abstract difference; but even higher mathematics themselves show us (the Differential Calculus, e.g.) that these two abstractions as abstractions are nugatory,—a proof that all existences and forms, if you honestly follow them up, drive themselves into an ulterior sphere,—into the sphere of absolute relativity, the expression of movement. —The understanding does not rest on its own basis; its axioms and laws are not of its own making, nor open to its insight; [136] they root in the domains of *reason.* As Kant would say, the understanding is not autonomic. While, then, we acknowledge the relative validity of the understanding, we are bound to rebut its arrogance, when it obtrudes itself as the ultimatum of the mind.

(2.) *Judgment.*—The understanding takes the Ideal as the mere form to which the material is adduced. But according to our first paragraphs, the Ideal determines itself as the Individual; it splits of its own accord into its particularities, and regenerates itself therefrom. This movement, by which the unity discedes into severalty, and its resumption, is given in *judgment.* For the method of the judgment we are to look to the nature of the Ideal itself; we have seen that the complete movement comprises, (1.) the Ideal, which (2.) states its particularities, and (3.) identifies itself therewith in the Individual. The exhibition of this is the *syllogism.* Old logicians have already remarked, that every proposition contains a syllogism; the syllogism, then, is the unfolded method of judging. All the forms of argumentation may be deduced from this in the most consistent manner. I am not writing a system of logic, and give only the groundwork. That the mind invariably syllogizes is owing to this, that the mind is the Spiritual, whose whole life, ay, whose whole life, is syllogistic, and can therefore be mentally reproduced in syllogisms only. It is pitiful to imagine "That some other form would have done the mind as well," as the usual conceit has it. How often must we hear, "it happens, that the mind is so constructed, that from such and such data such and such inferences must be drawn"!

(3.) *Reason.*—The Spiritual, as unital and identical in the syllogistic movement, reinvolving itself in-[137]to its inner intensity, not from, but in, this movement, is the object of *reason,* and identical with it. Reason resumes the whole nature of the object,—its truth,—not as ideal only, nor as particular, but as the whole unital process of its development and life in its integral completion. Whatever is an identity in opposition and difference, a unity in multiplicity, can be comprehended by reason alone;—the Spiritual, life, the soul, the mind, light, electricity, &c., are all objects of reason. It is reason which comprehends the true nature of all existences. Reason is the silent understanding between the particular terms of existence, whispering the secret of eternal love, of infinite unity. It reunites what the finite understanding had separated, and reconciles what limited comparison had estranged. All nature is reasonable, and breathes upon us with the aspiration of thought, speaks to us the language of mind. But reason only, not the understanding, is alive to its teachings; reason only, not the understanding, has access to nature's sanctuary. We feel an instinctive horror against the idea, that the understanding, as with its mechanical constructions, should ever be enabled to resolve the discrepancies of the Universe, and justly: for the one great breath which animates us all, the one spiritual tone which resounds in us all, the one infinite love which binds us all, would then vanish. Nevertheless, we have not merely the incessant longing for removing the veil which interposes between us and nature, but the fullest confidence that we can remove it. We are sure that nature cannot remain a stranger to us; that nature is the depository of our own being, the revealer of our own secrets. We cannot quench the thirst after knowledge. We all summon the spirit of nature by its infinite name, and feel that the meaning of that name is written within us. We, our real "selves," are essentially reason—in our impulses to thought and action; our whole being centres there. [138]

Reason constitutes, or rather is, our freedom, for it makes every thing one with us, so that there is nothing strange, nothing foreign to our nature, by which we are determined and circumscribed. Only where there is opposition, there is necessity. Necessity is but partial freedom, freedom split, as it were. Animals are not free; in our particular impulses and passions we are not free,—on account of their particularity. Nature's material forms are necessary, for they are the mind in material diffraction; the mind itself is *infinite,* and therefore beyond all shackles. [139]

Nation, State, Law

The spiritual nature of man, which is cultivated in the family as *morality,* is enounced in the form of a positive assertion by the voice of society as *law.* The law is nothing extraneous, nothing foreign to man; it is nothing more than the universal reason slumbering in every individual mind, which manifests itself in the collective evidences of the Spiritual through its separate impersonations. The incorporated authority of the law, the *state,* is nothing else than society organizing itself; it is not a *machine,* of which the individuals are the material. The assertion has frequently been made, and is daily repeated by the wiseacres of this country, "that the *form* of government is a matter of indifference, provided men live in perfect conformity to law." As if the law were nothing more than an outward rule, according to which men are to shape themselves! The beau-ideal of a government would then be found, if a state had been devised in which every thing was perfectly *moulded* according to certain presumed divine criteria. The forms there would be of external derivation, society standing as the brute mass, to be circumscribed and defined by them. But this "brute mass" is the bearer of universal spiritual life,—this "material" lives and reasons,—this society thinks and acts spontaneously and develops itself,—in a word, exists as a spiritual organism! It is inherently, necessarily, a unity, not only for physical, but especially for mental [158] cooperation,—not because the lawgiver has by main force riveted the individuals together and bound them by the same command; nor even, as the theory of Rousseau has it, because the individuals accidentally consented so to constitute themselves, but because society is but *one* eternal spiritual life. The law, therefore, is the expressed consciousness of society,—the act of intelligence, in which society takes cognizance of its immanent universal reason,—the act of volition, by which it establishes the validity of the unfolded Spiritual as paramount to particular impulses and opinions and desires. In the law society writes its own thoughts, reads its spirituality, brings it to the consciousness of its constituent individuals, and proceeds to regenerate itself,—to think itself anew. The form is by no means adventitious; it is essential. Whatever is organic—lives,—can have but one form; the form is the thing, and born from the essence, not added to it. And that society lives and is organic will not be disputed, I hope. Society is progressive,—a progression toward itself, toward the Spiritual, of which it is the representative. —I have stated and shown that it is the destiny of the individual to identify his private reason and will with universal reason and will; and, obviously, this can take place only if the latter, in the form of law, be in the consciousness of the individual, and reproduce themselves *in* and *from* him. The organization of society is, therefore, *essentially democratic.* The objects of government are by no means barely to secure tranquillity, formal justice, stability of affairs, &c., as we are told by the prevalent theories of government; the object of government is to embody the life of society. And how could it embody the life of society in proceeding from a few individuals only, or in being superinduced from without,—in a word, unless it were democratic? A government, offering the strongest [159] guaranties for individual security, material prosperity, formal justices, &c., if it were not born from society, not the representative of the people's reason and will, would nevertheless be an abomination; for it would be a stronghold for the imprisonment of divinity in man. Government is not a means for any extraneous purpose at all; it is its own object and purpose because it is a concrete form, in which the Spiritual exists. Whatever is life cannot be construed according to a table of means and ends. Of course, government, such as it ought to be, *democratic government,* will likewise fulfill all these purposes, and be the most powerful warrant of the peace, prosperity, and happiness of the individuals,—a thing quite easily proven. We have a number of irreflective pedants in this country who bode downfall and destruction of our republic, "because Greece and Rome have vanished before us." There is no greater illusion in the world than the inference of an identity of things from an identity of names. Was Greece a republic, when it branded all those not born within the confines of Hellas as barbarians? And was Rome free, when it shouted, "Long life to the Republic!" only after having put its foot on the neck of another slave? Or was France a democracy, at a moment when revenge and blood had drowned all consciousness? But there is annually a day with us, when the heart begins to thrill and the countenance to brighten for a life to come, at the solemn enouncement of the simple words, "All men are born free and equal," which, I am assured, will soon be perfectly a truth.

But what are the guaranties of a democratic government? Whoever knows why he is a republican will disdain every other answer but this: the eternal reason, the Spiritual in man, which lives its life in that government. There is nothing higher than the Spiritual; you cannot [160] prop it, you can offer no other earnest of its prevalence, than its own infinite power, than the energy of its own life. Nothing material, no "balance of interests," nothing beyond this spiritual life, can give "bail" for the Spiritual. And to what do you trust, who come with a theory, that the will of the individual must be extinguished, and a set of external laws substituted for that will? Must not your laws be adopted by society? And ere they become effective, must they not agree with the will, and therefore, proceed from the consciousness and be sanctioned by the reason of society? Have your laws, therefore, any other strength, and can they afford any other security, but that of reason, of the Spiritual in man? Is the confidence in the prevalence of your laws, then, based upon any thing else than the faith in the power of reason in man? All governments, however despotic in appearance, are in reality democratic. Even the despot is the creature of the people's will. If the slaves of a despot collectively will to be free, has the despot any superhuman power to restrain them in their fetters? The only difference between democratic and other forms of government is, that in the former the will of the people is a conscious and rational will, in the latter unconscious and unreasonable; that in the former thought and action are based upon conviction, in the latter upon illusion (to which belong irreflective, "canine" loyalty, slavish terror, &c.) brought about by hypocrisy and craft and a systematic animalization of man; that in the former society dwells in the light of day, while in the latter it gropes in an artificial night; *that the former is a truth, the latter a lie.* It is a truism, to say that the universal tendency of society is towards democracy.

I have said, that government, like every organic bearer of spiritual life, cannot be valued and defined by outward purposes. An instance of this is the ordinary assertion, [161] "Democracy is unfavorable to the culture of the arts and sciences." No matter as to the falsehood of this; first let us see what are the arts and sciences. Nothing else than the flower of the life of society, the expression of healthy social vigor, of the energetic realization of the Spiritual in society. The arts and sciences are of no other value than this. Science must be a beam of intelligence from the eye of the social organism, art the flush of beauty on its cheek. Both must be at the same time the fruit and the germ of the whole organization; if they are not this, they are utterly worthless. The only thing we can do for the promotion of art and science among us is, to foster the life of society. Cultivate the plant, and its blossoms will greet the eye. It is a despicable, narrow view, to consider mankind as a set of craftsmen destined to daub so many yards of canvas, to write so many books, to strike off so many epics, to fulfill so many commandments, whose connection with the purposes of human nature is nowise discoverable, to body forth so many foreign, extraneous laws. There is no purpose for man beyond HIMSELF, i.e., his true spiritual life. As to the treasures of art, which in Europe accumulate in the halls of the rich, unseen by the eye of ninety-nine hundredths of society, they are just as important to mankind as the supposed treasures of gold at the earth's centre.—But to return.

The individual man, in obeying the universal will, simply obeys his own true will; he does not succumb to an external antagonist. He only meets in reality what was ideally prefigured in himself. His own true being already demanded for him and in his name what is exacted from him by the law. His rights, therefore, perfectly coincide with his duties, his true wishes with his obligations, his subjectivity with his objectivity,—he is free. The whole nature of man is *freedom*. It is superfluous to mention, [162] that lawlessness, the indulgence of momentary caprice, is not freedom, but *slavery*,—because it is the subservience of the real nature of man, his reason, to his self-estrangement, his particularities and passions. There is, in a word, slavery only where there is subordination of mind to matter.

The inevitable and natural consequences of a government which is not the incorporation of the nation's will, and whose laws are not its expressed consciousness and reason,—of a government, therefore, which does not keep pace with the development of society,—are sudden, violent, and calamitous revolutions. Man is the eternally active spirit; his nature is reason, and therefore development. So long as society lives, it will be impossible to hem it in by everlasting forms, however perfect they seem.

It has been often enough insisted upon now, that, wherever there is mind, there can be question no longer of subservience of any kind. I repeat, whatever is mind is absolutely egotistical. The person is not a tool of the family or the state; he subordinates himself to both, because in so doing he fulfills his own being,—because, in losing his particular self in society he recovers his true self. The whole, society, is not something antagonistic to the individual, by which the latter is to be crushed; the individual attains to his full pride and happiness through society. Just as much, then as the end of the individual is the welfare of organized society, of the state, the end of the latter is the welfare of the individual. The state is consequently bound to provide for the intellectual and physical subsistence of the individuals. I could have saved myself this verbiage by simply repeating the axiom, that the purpose of all social organization is the identification of the individuals, so that the same blood circulates in all, because the same life animates them all. [163] The practical means—the legal foreclosure of encroaching wealth in the hands of individuals, the measures to be taken for preventing the separation of labor from its products, the establishment of institutions for the relief of physical and mental destitution, &c.—do not belong here.

A purposed opposition of the will of an individual to the universal will expressed in law constitutes *crime*. The active assertion of the supremacy of the law in such a case is *punishment*. Its object is obviously no other than to break this individual will, and to reduce it to conformity with its own truth, with the universal will,—correction therefore, not revenge. In this sense, the recent theory, that punishment is the self-defense of society, though true, when properly understood, is liable to misinterpretation. All punishment ought to be educational. Only when the hostile will is perfectly identified with the criminal's being, when there is no possibility of correction, capital punishment is justifiable.*

To regard the state, or any phase in the organization of [164] society (and of nature generally), as a mechanical contrivance for certain particular purposes, to make it therefore a thing dependent upon man's making, a mere question of expediency, is an atrocity. Man is as necessarily a member of organized society as he lives. The state is an incorporation of the Spiritual; in it the Spiritual realizes its eternal intentions, which indeed present themselves to the understanding as finite purposes, and which

* I may be indulged in a remark respecting the recent system of solitary imprisonment, which to me seems to be directly at war with the object of all punishment. The individual is to be brought back to a conformity with society, by perfectly estranging him from it! You want to re-instil into him good-will to man, to a cheerful intercourse with his human kindred, and you make him the prey of despair! You mean to prepare him again for healthy life in the social communion, and you do all in your power to deaden that life; you deprive him of every thing that can awaken a sympathy with mankind, of the means for expressing his feelings, and for listening to the kind response of his fellow. Is not the converse of man with man the principal condition for ennobling, and in this case correcting, the individual? What the consequences are we already know from experience: all mental, moral, and physical diseases, which result from a repression of the manifestations of life,—idiocy, insanity, or at least irretrievable despondency, deadly misanthropy, masturbation, &c. I state this on the authority of an excellent medical friend, whose numerous observations in this sphere are trustworthy.

will, in the true state, be *ipso facto* fulfilled; but it does not follow, that the meaning, the sense and validity, of the state consist in these purposes. All the socialistic schemes, on that account, are materialistic and false,—because they are schemes. Again and again it is to be said, the forms which bind society can be nothing else than the expression of the life of society,—they must proceed from that life; and this, as is amply clear now, can take place only in a democracy. The socialists relapse into the old contrast between *form* and *material.* Whoever attempts to formalize the life of mankind externally, instead of removing the artificial obstacles which impede the life of society in formalizing itself, is—a despot. The more intelligent socialists admit that society is an organism; "But on that account," say they, "the members are but parts of the whole, and therefore entirely subordinate to it. The absolute power is society; therefore all individuality (expressed in property, &c.) disappears. The person, the family, &c., have no validity against the state." True, not against the state, nor without it, but in and with it. In every organism all the inferior stages are preserved in their full validity, though with absolute reference to higher stages. Thus the person and family are an essential existence in society, though they absolutely relate to, and derive their higher authority from, the state. The members of society—persons and families—are not only *parts,* they are also the *whole.* If [165] person and family are ministrative to the maintenance of the state, the state is equally ministrative to the maintenance of the person and family. —Socialism is based upon so many absurdities, that it would be vain to attempt a complete refutation of them; one or two only I will endeavour to point out. The person, as every socialist will admit, is at first, immediately, an egotist of physical desire. He is to renounce this egotism in favor of society. Now over this immense chasm from physical individuality to mental universality the socialist wishes to bound at one leap. There is to be no cultivation of the feelings in the quiet home of the family, no development of fraternal and filial affection, no attachment to country; one salto mortale is to carry the individual from egotistical instinct to the abstraction of universality and reason. There is to be an all-embracing brotherhood in abstract reflection, but the natural feeling, the immediate reality of the relations of brother and sister are to be annulled! There is to be absolute love of humanity, but the eternal love which man bears to man is to become the mockery of—a moment's duration! The fire is to burn but—the hearth is to be destroyed! In short, there are everywhere ends without means. I trust that the statement of this is its own refutation.

Socialism is a lie in the face of nature and history; but it is eventually harmless, and will die from the disease of its birth. There is this truth, however, in the appearance of socialism, that society is to be indeed a community, and that all are responsible for the sustenance of each one. Moreover, there are numerous artificial obstacles to the free evolution of society, which are to be removed; but not by removing also the means, or rather stages, of that evolution. I, for one, despise the man who thinks life with all its wealth and ease and enjoyment worth the having, after you have robbed him of the proud [166] consciousness of being the guide of his own bark and the creator of his own fortune,—of the infinitude and eternity of love,—of the sacred affections of brotherly and sisterly, of parental and filial attachment,—of patriotism,—in short, of every thing that sheds its first hallowing light over the private feelings of the heart.

Mankind.—History

The comprehensive mental realization of the universal Spiritual is mankind, and its history, to which states and nations are again related as individuals. The one principle, that the Spiritual is infinite, eternal, intensive activity, has led us to the inevitable consequence, that it exposes itself without rest or limit on a multitude of stages, and therefore under a variety of forms. We thus meet with the one divine idea in a host of nations, and in a countless succession of epochs. It is present, and present as *mind,* in each and all of them, engaged in the work of its self-production and its self-recognition: for it is eternal activity. And here again, in the immense organism of historical mankind, we find the verification of the law,—that the Spiritual preserves all the phases of its existence, from the lowest to the highest, during every period of its evolution. The spiritual is, as it were, its own biography, headed by its full portrait in the panorama of nations. The epochs, that are past in the life of one nation, are present in that of another. The aspects succeeding each other in time spread themselves out before the eye in the extension of space. The historical cadences, which strike the ear of the thinker as the melody of the Spiritual, are simultaneously heard by him as recollectively present in concertant harmony.

The source of all dependency in life is necessary co-[167]existence and necessary succession; thus in the life of mankind one epoch depends upon another and one nation upon another. The life of the Spiritual is inevitably succession and coexistence,—a revelation in time and space; and yet it is its eternal intention and purpose to reproduce itself as an absolute intensive unity. How is this reconciled? Very simply in this, that the Spiritual is a unital activity, and therefore essentially a revelation,—an unceasing reproduction of itself. The absolute endeavour of the Spiritual to evolve itself as an intensive but universal unity appears, then, externally in the progress of its life as the free play of these dependencies. Free reciprocation of man with nature and with all mankind is therefore the law of our spiritual vitality. Nations and states have for this reason as little right to isolate themselves as individual persons. Liberty of material and mental commerce is the true inscription on every nation's flag. It is the duty of nations, as well as of persons, to diffuse the light of mind and freedom.

It is a very common view, to regard the life of mankind as a web of chance and adventure,—its history as an incoherent tale,—the whole as a confusion of efforts and failures, of hopes and disappointments, whose final boon is despondency, and whose product misery and woe. The scene of history is considered as a gloomy ocean, lit up by no star but the flitting meteors of ambition and deceit, enlivened by no breeze but the storm of passion, strewn therefore with nothing but wrecks, no other hope being left to the individual mariner, than regardless of the general fate, to grasp the first plank that presents itself.

Views such as the above admit of no other refutation here than the simple statement, that the events of history are the events of one connected life,—the life of the Spiritual. Usually this is not altogether denied (except by some materialists); a providence is admitted; but this [168] providence is regarded as something accruing to the world and history, not resident in it. In a word, the world and its history are looked upon as a sphere of finitudes, altogether distinct from the Infinite, which latter only deigns to support the former. It is properly unnecessary here to rebut this assumption, as I have amply proved (in the "Grounds and Positions") that neither the Finite nor the Infinite is any thing by itself, but that they respectively exist in and through the other; that the Infinite, the Spiritual, must, from its nature, distinguish itself in itself, whence all the material differences in time and space arise, and that the Finite must resolve itself and revert to the absolute Spiritual. But I will dwell a moment still upon the palpable and irremovable contradictions of this separation of the Infinite from the Finite, of providence from history, of the Deity from the Universe. If the Finite exist as extraneous, accidental to the Infinite,—if the latter be complete and insular in itself,—then the Finite and Infinite are in every respect two; the one begins where the other ends. One, therefore, is then the absolute limit of the other; instead of an Infinite and Finite, you have consequently two finitudes; and on the other hand, taking it for granted, that the Finite *is* any thing but what it is *in* the Infinite, that it has any existence, however chaotic and lawless, but that in virtue of the Infinite,—but that belonging to and being the Infinite,—that it exists otherwise than *as* the Infinite, you have two existences in themselves, you make the Finite infinite, you have two infinitudes!! You therefore have, not one absolute principle, but *two*,—not one Deity, but two Deities,—you have absolute war, irreconcilable contradiction; the only unital Absolute you have is an absolute—absurdity.

It is evident from this, that the Deity is not a personage who now and then stretches his hand towards the car [169] of history, and shifts it in another direction; nor an artisan, who amuses himself by carving a curious toy, which we afterwards call nature, and whose droll gyrations we term history; nor a quaint alchemist, who occasionally walks into his rusty laboratory, the Universe, and mumbles a formula, and conjures up a bubble; nor a despot, who condescends to say, "Car tel est notre plaisir";—the life, the being, the essence, the existence of the eternal Spiritual is its activity. No act, which is not essential to the Spiritual,—which the Spiritual is not. And you can conceive no existence which is not *in* the Spiritual, which is not a phase of its universal vitality.

History is therefore the life of the absolute Spiritual, and its events are the manifestations in which the Spiritual comes to the knowledge, the identification, the absolute possession of itself, in its eternal self-evolution or origination. And all those who deny this—who assert that nature or history has any other existence, and that their minutest events have any other reality, than that of the Spiritual—deny the Spiritual itself, and are guilty of atheism and blasphemy, however pious their mien, and however religious their garb.

From this the guiding principles in history readily flow. All life is a progress; the absolute life in history, then, is absolute progress. All life is a change of form, and origination and evanescence of phases, in which, nevertheless, there is an ideal constant; the Spiritual therefore bodies itself forth in varying phases, and destroys them again;—but it, the Spiritual, remains, and in it the phase, not merely as a relict adumbration, but as an ideality, with which the Spiritual, as it were, enriches itself. All the phases of life are prefigured in the origin, and every succeeding phase is immediately contained in and produced by the preceding one;—so in universal life.

It is not my object, and it is altogether above my [170] ability, to furnish even a faint sketch of the progress of history in accordance with the foregoing principles. I shall attempt only to make a few general suggestions. —The evolutions of the Spiritual in history are in every respect those of the mind. The first immediate union of the mind with its natural organism presents itself in history as an immediate union of man with nature, where the Spiritual is yet, so to speak, the flower of nature; as such we behold it on its acme (I point out only the heights in each epoch) in Greece. Mental life was there as yet sensual,–the powers of life were objects of direct perception, the serene gods dwelling on Olympus. The Highest, the object of all aspiration, the fulfilment of all truth, was immediately present to the Grecians in the form of the Beautiful, in the forms of classic art, which represented the perfect identity of the Divine with natural being,–the beau-ideal of the human form. The Grecian knew no despondency, no longing, no sentimentality, no opposition between the Individual and Universal; the same life lived in all. Hence, since the Grecian epoch, we nowhere meet with individualities so well balanced on their own centre of gravity, so perfect (perfect as they could be in that inferior phase), so full of equable enjoyment and happiness. But the *depths* of the Infinite, of the Spiritual, were not there in actuality; they only hovered over them in their dark bodings, as the sinister form of fate, which became the ruling power of their tragedies. These depths mastered their consciousness in philosophy, and reduced the Olympic divinities to a shadow. The destiny was consummated; the Grecians struggled, but they perished, and the beauty of Grecian life with them. Rome is nothing but the epoch of transition,–the ferment of the elements that had been scattered by the fall of Olympus. Beautiful, classic individuality is no longer the principle; the Grecian gods in Rome are only recollec-[171]tions and formulae. The vitality of Rome is an abstraction,–*national power,* in which all individualities are lost. Christianity appeared, and the internal life of the Spiritual, the "Beyond" of immediate nature, became the soul of life. Happiness became an aspiration, enjoyment a longing, the delight of existence an infinite grief; for the truth of nature was beyond nature, not its present being. True existence became a mortification, unwearied asceticism. Nature was a stranger to divinity,–nothing but a fabric, ministering to the base wants of man.* For the Grecians nature (and all existences) had been an

* I speak only of that which lies in the fundamental idea of the epoch; in every epoch the following one prepares itself, so that here we gradually find also the recognition of nature. But Christianity, as such, is the principle of perfect secession from material nature.

unconscious growth,—for the Christian it was a structure designed by consciousness for particular purposes; the truth is, of course, the unity of both views,—the self-organization depending upon the laws of mind and consciousness. Christianity evolved the whole significance of life; it revealed the immeasurable expanse of feeling, the boundless exaltation of thought, the infinite power of love, the eternal craving of spiritual redemption, —all the potentialities of the heart and mind; but it detached them from nature and life,—it cast them like shadows in the distance. It separated the activity from its reward, the struggle from its peace (which, from the nature of the Spiritual, is but in the struggle), the labor from the product. History presents nothing nobler, nothing greater, nothing truer, than Christianity. In the Christian epoch, Classic art, the actual presence of divinity in nature, become romantic art, the painful longing for divinity. Grecian beauty was there, but with the expression of inadequacy to its internal consciousness, with the grief of [172] its natural existence, with an infinite craving, on its countenance.

During the epochs when Christianity culminated,—during the Middle Ages,—the Spiritual was present only in and for faith,—not for reason; and it could not be present for this, for reason was then nothing more than the understanding, to which the Infinite is inaccessible. —The Middle Ages were free,—perfect equality reigned at the beautiful time when the church was the state. The true being of man lay beyond this life, and there all differences were equalized. The serf, who saw his lord kneeling with him at the same altar and at the same confessional, who beheld him voluntarily doffing the knightly armor, and humbling himself to the lowest level in the monastery, felt that there was no *real* distinction. The greater the suffering here, the greater the enjoyment hereafter.

I have said, that Christianity in the ages of faith was a truth, and the sublimest truth, which history offers; I say so again. Every earnest man is essentially a Christian,—the epoch of the mind lives within him. But as an actual epoch, the noble days of the Middle Ages, with their benevolence, their chivalry, their romance, are gone by, and cannot and will not again be summoned up. The Spiritual never retraces its steps. We may try to stem the torrent of advance,—it carries us onward. The boundless spiritual resources of the Middle Ages continue in the life of the Spiritual, but this formalizes itself anew. The Christian epoch was that of division, we have seen: creation and the Creator, the Spiritual and the Material, faith and the understanding, labor and thought, were utterly distinct. We see this in the contrast between the classes doomed to toil and those devoting themselves to silent contemplation and religious thought in perfect seclusion from the world. That in our times the reconciliation is [173] preparing, if not effecting itself, cannot be doubted. Science and life, thought and action, are no longer distant from each other. The man of learning is not a recluse now, nor the man of labor a mere machine. —May in our times the infinite meaning of Christianity infuse itself into actuality, and verify and exhibit all its powers in life, revoking the serene individualitics of Greece with all their ancient classic perfection, but with superior, because significant, beauty! May the coming age bring us a mental, humanitarian eudaemonism, and a universal liberty rivaling the sensual, national eudaemonism of the Grecians with their limited freedom! The epoch of Oriental life, with its vague pantheism, bears the same relation to the Grecian epoch as Christianity to the era which is beginning to dawn upon us. Hence the affinity of symbolic art in the East to art in the Middle Ages, and the romantic elements on Oriental poetry, which have recently been so much explored by the German poets of the romantic school. —Protestantism is to Catholicity what Rome was to Greece. [174]

HEGEL

Nature had now been recognized, by Schelling and his followers, in history, and history in nature; the eternal mind, the innermost spiritual being of man, in the material world, and the activities of the material world in the mind. If Locke had annihilated the mind, in beholding there nothing but the shadowy projections of external realities upon a primitive blank, and, as if to avenge it, Fichte had again made these external forms mere evanescent projections from the depths of the mind, it was now understood, that the mind only expanded itself, evolved its faculties, in concentrating outward existences, that its exterioration was simultaneously an introversion, a descent into the depths of its being. This then led to the expiration of absolute idealism, with its independent, innate spiritualities, on the one hand, and of absolute materialism, with its gross actualities, on the other. For the energies of the mind are called into existence by material objectivity, and the external world attains to its true reality in the intelligence of the mind. The world exists not in its truth, unless it be thought by its organized intelligence, man, who is, as it were, the eye with which it surveys itself.

This higher unity of mind and nature was the grand "*appercu*" of the Schellingian philosophy, but it was from its nature intuitive, and its only authentication depended upon the genial intelligence of the philosopher and [331] the poet. The question arose,—What is it that prompts the incessant evolution of the Eternal, the Deity, the Absolute? Why is the Spiritual a history, and nature a generation? Why is the infinite intensity of *mind* brought to light in the infinite extension of *matter*? What forces the idea to become a form, the "word to turn flesh," and the form again to resolve itself into an idea? —The answer to this question is the philosophy of Hegel. Hegel demonstrated, that the great motive principle in the Absolute is its inherent self-opposition. The Absolute, in which all things live, is not, as with Schelling, the abstract identity of two spheres; it is the eternal *spirit, thinking itself* in nature and history. Its being is a process; but, since it is the absolute substance, a process which has itself both for its material and for its object or result. In dualizing itself, it yet remains in its eternal identity. Figuratively speaking, the fundamental ether of the Deity is not repose, but activity,—moreover, activity within itself, which must therefore distinguish itself as the acting subject and the passive object,—and, finally, activity for itself, which produces, evolves, but the intensity of its own inner nature. *Activity in and for itself is thought.* The unit discedes, enters into self-opposition, but only for the purpose of self-recognition,—in order, therefore, to reestablish its unity, not after, but in, the discession. If we reflect upon the expression, "a living unit," we [332] shall perhaps be less disposed to smile at the idea of a unity in the opposition, a unity that requires and contains the antithesis.

Nature is thus a product of thought, and in this all the objections of the philosophy of Kant are met at once. Hegel made it evident, that the difficulty in the results of the Kantian "Critique," the inevitable opposition between the objective reality and the subjective idea, depended upon a misconception rooting in the old philosophical dualism. The reality, the truth of things, is, in the admission of every one, that which bodies itself forth in the series of phenomenal variations; and Hegel proved that this "constant" is the result of the dialectic process of thought. The uncertainty of our cognition of external objects obviously arose from the assumption, that those objects had a real existence independently of thought; that they might be different from what they were thought. The proof, then, *that their being lay in thought*, which is given in the "Phenomenology of the Mind," bridged over the chasm. [333]

In the current philosophical systems, a quiescent substance, absolute quantity, is the material from which all qualitative differences are elaborated; in Hegel's philosophy, absolute difference, absolute quality, forms the beginning, from which quantity proceeds. Hegel does not attempt to evolve concrete forms from an abstraction; his "Absolute" is essentially concrete. —The reason for so many anomalies (as they are termed) in the philosophy of Hegel will now be apparent. Since truth is apprehended, not as something reposing in the bosom of its own being, but as the "Whole in its development," as the Absolute, not abstractly taken, but also in its phenomenal existence, in its individual exterioration, the system of metaphysics, which formerly consisted of nothing but formalities, must encroach upon the domain of all science. Instead of an establishment of certain forms, merely for construing the various material, form and material now stand in necessary relation; the material—nature, &c.,—enter as essentially into metaphysical reasoning as the old formulas. It cannot, therefore, be startling, to see that the natural sciences, history, &c., are an integral part of metaphysics. "The true form in which truth exists," says Hegel, "is its scientific system alone." Formerly, all the realities of life were excluded from philosophical speculation; they were beneath the level of thought; in the Logic, &c., of Hegel, the idealities are exhibited as producing themselves in and through these realities. [337]

It will be borne in mind, that, in the philosophy of Kant, an original duality of principles was presumed,–the principle of mind, of intelligence, on the one hand, and that of the material, on the other. The former only was hitherto (I speak, of course, of the systems whose influence is now felt, and which yet give to our text-books of logic, &c., their tone) the subject of logic and metaphysics; and we have seen how fatal this proved to philosophical certainty. With Hegel, on the contrary, the absolute intelligence or mind, the Absolute, is in itself both the infinite substance (material) of all natural and spiritual life, and the infinite form, the active exterioration of this substance. It is not a bare formality, which would fain subject matter, but, on account of its impotence, remains a mere Ideal; it is at once an unlimited form, a ceaseless activity, and the material upon which it operates. [338]

HEGEL'S PHENOMENOLOGY OF THE MIND

Consciousness

I. *The Certainty of the Senses.* In the "Phenomenology," Hegel begins by showing, that truth does not lie in the immediate data furnished by perception, but that universally the truth of any object involves mediation. –An object is before me, and for the certainty of this I have the vouching of the senses. Now this immediate certainty arises not from the circumstance that my consciousness has unfolded itself in the perception, and that my thoughts have been set into flow,–nor from the multiplicity of relations in the object itself, and of the object to other objects; I simply pos-[351]sess the assurance: the object *is*. I, *this* particular consciousness, become sensible of *this* individual object.

This perception, then, presents the difference between the conscious "I" and the present object. Neither of them is absolutely immediate; I have the certainty of myself in and through the object, and the object is certain for and through the "I." Yet the truth seems to rest with the object; as to its existence, it appears to be a matter of indifference whether or not it be known by the "I." It remains therefore to be seen whether the "being" of that object is really such as the perception of sense exhibits it. What is the "this" before me? It is the "now" and the "here"; upon these two data my certainty of it depends.* Is this "now" any thing directly given? The "now" is night, for instance; but the truth of this vanishes;–if I write it down, it no longer holds good, as every truth should, for truth is permanent. I find, in looking at it again, that the "now" is morning. Nevertheless it is still "now"; it is neither night nor morning, and still it is nothing without them; it is therefore at once night, morning, &c. It is the particular "this" of perception, and likewise not "this." The truth arising from this negation of the Particular, which Particular is, in spite of its necessary negation, indispensable for its existence, is the universal "now."–Similarly, the "here" of the senses is, e. g., a tree. I simply turn around, and the "here" is now, according to the same senses, a house. The simple "here," which remains, is evidently the result of mediation. Mere abstract, general being, but being depending upon negation and mediation, therefore remains as the foundation for the certainty of the senses; and the truth beyond this gener-[352]ality of being attaches itself only to *my* opinion, to *my* knowing of the object. The relation between the object and my knowledge of it has now been inverted. The object, which was originally asserted to be the only thing essential to the certainty, has at present resolved itself into a bare generality; its truth as this object now lies in my knowing of it. I behold, hear, &c., this object; the "now" is day, because I see it; the "here" is a tree for the same reason. "I, this particular 'I,' assert the tree to be the 'here'; another 'I,' however, sees the

* There is question here merely of a certainty of the object as *being,* which is, in fact, all the senses pretend to furnish; not of the certainty respecting the qualitative *nature* of the object.

house, and asserts *that* to be the 'here.' Both are attested by the same immediateness of sight, and yet the one vanishes in the other."* The only thing which does not vanish is the generality of the "I," whose seeing is neither a sight of the house, nor of the tree, but simply seeing, which, notwithstanding all this, again depends upon the mediating negation of *this* house, &c.,—in short, of the Particular. The seeing "I" is therefore as general as the "now," "here," or "this," and it is as impossible to say what is meant by the "I" as what is understood by "here" and "this." We are thus forced to place the nature of the certainty of the senses neither in the object nor in the "I," but in the totality of the two, such as it is immediately given. It is to be seen, then, what is immediately given.

The "now" is pointed out; this "now." In being pointed out it has already ceased to be; the actual "now" is no longer that pointed out,—it has been. Its truth therefore is, that it has been; but what has been, is not. The immediate presentation of an object is essentially a *movement.* First the "now" is pointed out and asserted as the truth; but next it is pointed out only as having been,—the first truth, its *being,* is revoked; thirdly, what has been, is not,—the revocation is revoked, [353] the negation denied, and I return to the original truth as general: the "now" is. This movement exhibits the truth of the "now," namely, a "now" reflected into itself, a *general* "now," a multiplicity of "nows" comprised in a unity.

In an analogous manner the "here" pointed out is first an "above"; but next it is not an "above," but a "below," and so on. The one "here" vanishes in the other; what remains is nothing more than a negative "here," a simple complex of many "heres."

The dialectics of the certainty of sense thus consist simply in the history of its own movement, in its own experience, and are nothing forcibly superadded; nay, the certainty of the senses is nothing but this movement.

II. *Observation.* There is consequently no truth in the so-called individualities of sense; the truth is the Universal, which is not *perceived* (by the senses), but *observed* (*wahrgenommen*). Uni-

* Compare the "*Phänomenologie des Geistes,*" pp. 75, 76.

versality (generality) is the principle of observation; its immediate constituents, the "I" and the object, are both general. Simultaneously with the principle of generality these constituents have originated; the subjective observation is simply the movement in which the object is exhibited, and the object the same movement as a *unity*. The object is essentially the same as the subjective movement; the latter the development and separation of the items, the former their unital comprehension. For us, then, *generality as a principle* is the essence of observation; the subject observing and the object observed are not essential. But each of these separately is a generality; since they are opposed to each other, we are forced again to inquire to which of the two [354] the essentiality belongs. Now the subjective movement of observation, being inconstant, is unessential, and the essence must lie in the comprehensive unity, in the object. The principle of this object, generality, is a *mediated,* not an immediate unity; it is simple only from the comprehensiveness of the movement of which it is the result. This, then, must appear as a feature in its nature; the object is one of many qualities. But quality is determination; determination depends upon negation; the "this" is consequently stated at the same time as "*not-this.*"

The different qualities are independent of each other, and only meet, interpenetrate without interference, in the simple generality of the object, in the "here" and "now,"—the abstract medium of the many qualities. But these qualities themselves are simple generalities; this salt, for example, is a simple "here," but it is at the same time white, and acrid, and cubical, and of definite specific gravity, &c. These different qualities interpenetrate in the simple "here" without affecting each other. They are, however, *definite* qualities; they refer, therefore, not to themselves alone, but also to other qualities opposed to them. This negation of the opposite qualities does not take place in the simple medium, in the mere "and"; this medium is, consequently, likewise exclusive in its nature; it is a *unit.*

The object as the truth of observation, when complete, is therefore (a.) indifferent, passive generality, the "and" of the many qualities, or rather, materials; (b.) the simple negation, the exclusion of other qualities; and (c.) the many qualities themselves, and the two preceding momenta referred to each other: the negation relating to the indifferent medium. In so far as the differences belong to the indifferent medium, they are general, relate to themselves alone, and do not affect each [355] other; but in so far as they belong to the negative unit, they are exclusive. The generality of observation becomes a quality only by developing out of itself, distinguishing and uniting, exclusive unity and pure generality.

By this object, then, as it now stands, consciousness is determined as an observing subject. It is sensible of the possibility of an illusion: for, though it immediately faces the "without," this is annulled as immediate, since generality has become the principle. The criterion for the truth of the object, then, is self-equality. We are therefore to inquire what is the experience of consciousness in its observation.

The observed object presents itself as absolutely *one, individual;* but it is observed also as a *quality,* which is general, and thus goes beyond individuality. My first observation, in which I took the object as individual, was therefore incorrect; the generality of the quality forces me to take the object likewise as a generality. Again: the quality is definite,—opposed to another quality and excluding it. I am consequently again compelled to abandon the generality, and to state the object as an exclusive *one.* There being, however, many qualities in the exclusive unity which do not mutually affect each other, the object is to be apprehended as a general medium, in which different qualities separately exist as generalities of sense, and yet as exclusive, since they are definite. The simple object is therefore observed as an individual quality, which again is not a quality, since it does not belong to an individual unity, nor definite, since it does not refer to other qualities. It is therefore the mere being of sense, and we have thus returned to the point whence we started. Consciousness in its observation of truth is reflected into itself, just as before in the certainty of sense; with this difference, however, that in the latter instance it appeared to contain the truth of the [356] object, whereas now it contains the untruth. Of this, however, it is aware, and in this manner the object is maintained in its purity. —The object is first observed as a unit; then it ceases to be such, and presents the difference of qualities only to *my consciousness.* "This object is indeed white to *my* eye, acid to *my* tongue, cubic to *my* touch; I am therefore the general medium in which this separation of qualities takes place."

But the object, though a unit, is a determinate one, and determination depends upon contrast, upon exclusion. Thereby the qualities as different again become attributes of the object; the object is white, and acid, and cubical, &c.,—the simultaneous and independent existence of the different qualities. Their compenetration occurs in my consciousness. This gives me again a reversal of the relation; formerly consciousness attributed to itself the *multiplicity* of qualities in the object; now it makes itself responsible for their *unity.* The result of its experience, then, is, that the duplicity is inherent in the object. The object by itself is a unity, equal to itself; but it is likewise for others, depending upon a difference from them. *Immediately* the objects do not differ from themselves, but simply from each other; this relation, however, is mutual, and each object is necessarily affected with the difference. Properly, then, it contains a twofold difference: first, the difference of its various qualities (the salt, e.c., being white inasmuch as it is not cubical, and *vice versa,* &c.), and, secondly, the difference from its counter object. Nevertheless, the latter only of these differences is essential to the object, conferring upon it a distinct individuality. But this latter difference is a relation to other objects; in virtue of this, the independent existence of the object is annulled; as determined, the individual object is nothing more than the relation to other objects. The very relation, then, which was said to be [357] essential to the existence of the object, proves to be the *negation* of its self-existence; the object perishes through its essential quality.

III. *Force and Understanding. —Phenomenal and Supersensual World.* We thus become the sport of a series of contradictions: of an individuality, which is at the same time a generality,—of an essence, which is unessential,—of an unessentiality, which is yet necessary; and we see that these contradictions are incident to the object. Our consciousness is in this manner forced to abandon its particular ideas, and to take the object as the unconditionally General, since that alone is lasting, invariable: having been informed, moreover, that *being for itself* and *being for other objects* are identical. —This absolute generality, moreover, precludes the difference between form and substance; for, were the substance something distinct from the form, it must be a particular mode of being for itself and being for other objects; but being for itself and being for other objects *abstractly* constitute the true nature of the object, the unconditionally General. Yet, in considering the object as one of our consciousness, or in its existence independent of our consciousness, we distinguish between form and substance. In the latter view we behold the object, first, as the general medium of several independent qualities, and again, as a unit reflected into itself, in which that independence is annihilated. In the one case, the object is taken in its being for other objects, in its passivity, where self-existence is destroyed; in the other case, it is assumed in its being for itself. As to the former, each of the independent qualities is a medium; the generality of the object is essentially a multiplicity of generalities. These generalities, however, com-[358]penetrate, and thereby again annul their separation, thus returning to the unital medium. This movement, by which the unity effuses itself into multiplicity, and the multiplicity resumes itself in unity, is called *force,* which appears as twofold: first in its exterioration, as the independent qualities in their being, and again as reintroversion, or as force properly so termed.

Some readers will find this transition to force odd and perchance unintelligible. Hegel has shown that the intimate nature of the object is unity and multiplicity. If I take the object as one, this very unity forces itself into multiplicity, and conversely.

The understanding only makes this distinction and induces the duplicity, which does not subsist in the absolute being; exterioration and self-introversion are utterly inseparable. For the understanding, this duality of the force is not only necessary, but even substantial; it is, on the one hand, the mere introverted unital intensity, being for itself, and, on the other, the unfolded multiplicity of the different qualities; both of them, however, in necessary mutual transition. The unity of the force excludes the existence of the multiple qualities; yet it is the nature of that unity to be these qualities; it therefore unfolds itself into them, gives itself form. It seems, then, as if the form had been solicited from without; but this "without" is the object's own exterioration, the form itself, and the object now exists as the medium of the unfolded qualities; this unity in its turn becomes the "without" of its present existence, soliciting it to self-introversion.

We have now an insight into this virtual duplication of the force; we have two forces, whose existence, however, is such a movement, that the being of each is a mere statement, a mere position in and by means of its coun-[359]terpart. The one exists only by dint of its transition into the other; the two are not independent extremes connected by an intervening medium, but they exist solely in and through this medium.

"Through the medium of this play of the forces, then, we look into the background of things."* This medium, the being and simultaneous evanescence of the force, which co-includes the two extremes of its inner unity, and the outer multiplicity of the understanding, is the *phenomenon.* Our object has thus become a syllogistic trinity, whose extremes, the inner unital nature of things, on the one hand, and the multiplicity of the understanding, on the other, coalesce in their phenomenal medium. We look into the interior of things only through the phenomenon; the interior itself is transcendental, a "beyond," for our consciousness. This transcendental interior, however, reveals nothing whatever to consciousness; no more, to use Hegel's own simile, than pure darkness or pure light reveals any thing to the gaze. But the supersensual "beyond" results from mediation; it proceeds from the phenomenon, and the phenomenon is its reality. The Supersensual is but the Sensual† taken in its truth, taken as a phenomenon, and not as a permanent reality, which it has amply proved

* *Phänomenologie des Geistes,* p. 105.

† I use the word "Sensual" in preference to the word "sensuous" introduced by Coleridge and others, because the former is more idiomatic, and not here liable to become ambiguous.

itself not to be. We behold the play of the forces, a continual shifting of determinate appearances, whose truth consists merely in the *law* which manifests itself there. The law is the permanent image of the fleeting phenomenon. The supersensual world is a quiet realm of laws, indeed beyond the world of observation, since this exhibits the law only in con-[360]tinuous change; but it is nevertheless *present* in the world of observation, and its immediate type.

Yet the law thus present in the phenomenon realizes itself differently under different circumstances; it is a *determinate* law. This leads at once again to a multiplicity of laws, which multiplicity in turn contradicts our consciousness of a unital interior. The various laws must consequently reduce to *one* law, in which the determination is simply omitted, without an actual identification of the individual, determinate laws. These in their determination are then phenomenal, and the determination disappears in the reduction. But even in this general law we meet with a duplicity, since in it the internal difference (between its intense, introverted unity, and the exterior, unfolded multiplicity) is immediately apprehended, whereby the two momenta are at once stated as absolutely subsisting. Now, according to the above, these differences must return into the simple unity of the interior; and thus we have the law, first, as the expression of the subsisting integrants or momenta, and, next, as their return into unity, which may again be termed *force*. To use the instance adduced by Hegel: electricity as simple is force; as dually existing, as positive and negative, it is law. In the capacity of a simple principle, electricity is indifferent as to its duality; yet when it exteriorates, manifests itself, it is necessarily as positive and negative. —The force, as such, then, is indifferent to its discession in the law, in its exterioration. Moreover, the integrants in that exterioration are indifferent with respect to each other. E. g., motion, as a law, divides itself into time and space,—into distance and velocity, which, in themselves, do not express their origin in this motion; they are conceived without it and without each other. Now the definition of motion cannot be that of a simple principle of simple [361] being; division, duality, is necessary to it, and yet there is no necessity of the resultant parts (time and space) for each other. The necessity is, then, simply an illusory one, belonging to the understanding only. The understanding, therefore, is drawn into the same movement as that exhibited in the play of forces; a difference is stated, which is at the same time no difference, and hence revoked. It thus experiences, that this absolute movement is the law of the interior; that the force decomposes itself into two factors, and again, that these factors recompose themselves into a unity; in other words, that, in the nature of objects, "there is necessary self-repulsion of the Homonymous, and necessary attraction of the Heteronymous. The force, the Homonymous, places itself in a self-opposition, which appears as an absolute difference; but this difference is really none, since the Homonymous repels itself, and, being identical with itself, necessarily re-attracts itself."*

By this principle the quiet domain of the laws, the immediate image of the observed world, becomes its own counterpart. We have therein a second supersensual world, "an inverted world," in the words of Hegel, in which the difference or internal discession of the interior becomes an immanent one. This supersensual world is an absolute self-antithesis, pure contradiction. As Hegel himself expresses it,—"This internal difference is to be apprehended as the self-repulsion of the Homonymous, and its reversal, the equality of the Unequal *as* the unequal,—re-attraction of the Heteronymous. In aspiring to the truth of objects, we must apprehend *abstract change*, pure contradiction. The contradictory is not one of two,—for then it would be independent being,—but the contradictory of a contradictory. Though I place the [362] one contradictory (one term) here and the other there, still, as I have the contradictory *as such*, each is its own antithesis, the '*alterum*' of itself."†

In short, we are inevitably driven to a unity *in* the opposition, to an identity *in* the difference,—in other words, to an infinitude *in* the Finite. Through this infinitude we see the law completed to a necessity in itself, i.e., we understand the transition of its unity

* *Phänomenologie des Geistes*, p. 107.
† *Phänomenologie des Geistes*, p. 121.

into external variety, and conversely; and all the momenta, the phases of the phenomenon, are received in, reconciled with, the unity of the Interior. The simple unity of the law is infinitude, i.e., according to what has been said, 1st, it is self-equality, and nevertheless absolute internal difference,—the Homogeneous repelling itself, the simple force becoming a duality; 2d, the factors of this duality appear as self-existing, independent, truly different; 3d, since they exist only as essentially different, as the contradictory of a contradictory, vitalized mutually as + and −, their nature is again unity and their duality annuls itself.

"This simple infinitude is the simple being of life, the soul of the world, the universal blood, which in its omnipresence is not disturbed by any contradiction, which comprises in its being all contradictions and their solution, which pulsates in itself without movement, and vibrates without disturbance."

We have now arrived at the point where the system of Hegel takes its root,—at this simple being, which is internally differential. The reader has a sufficient idea of Hegel's objective dialectics, which force every phase, meeting us at the first blush as permanent, into its very reverse, a palpable verification that it is but a phase, and affected with its own negation, with its counterpart. In the ensuing portions of the Phenomenology, Hegel, with [363] the most trenchant acumen, dissolves the whole sphere of objectivity in this manner, so that the Phenomenology is, as it were, his Philosophy inverted. These investigations are of no immediate interest to us, because the same categories emerge in the body of the system itself. [364]

HEGEL'S SOCIAL MORALITY (POLITICS)

Social morality is the truth of the subjective and objective mind,—the universal rational will, in which self-conscious freedom has become the nature of the individual. —The substance which knows itself as free has its reality in the spirit of a nation. The abstract dimension of this spirit is its particularization in *persons*, of whose independence it is the internal power and necessity. But the person knows itself as essentially this substance, and looks upon the latter as its absolute end and object, as prompt-[515]ing its activity, thus attaining to its freedom. The dependencies of the individual, in the relations into which the substance particularizes itself, constitute the moral duties of the individual. The moral substance is

1. The immediate or natural mind,—*the family;*
2. The relative totality of the relations of individuals as independent persons to a formal universality,—*civil society;*
3. The self-conscious substance as the mind developed to an organic reality,—*the state.*

I. *The Family.* As immediate, the individual has its substantial existence in a natural universality, founded upon the sexual relation, in the family,—the unity of love and mutual confidence.

II. *Civil Society.* The substance which as mind particularizes itself into many *persons* (families or individuals) becomes a system of atomism, in which it (the substance) remains merely the general mediating connection between independent extremes and isolated, personal interests; and as such it is *civil society.* It is founded upon mutual wants, the necessary division of labor, the consequent distinctions of rank, &c. The morality appears here as confidential honesty and honor. —Hegel distinguishes three ranks in society, which he considers as permanently necessary; I shall be sufficiently understood if I forego his phraseology and designate them as *proletarians, ordinary citizens* holding property, and the *higher classes* of society, including the intellectual laborers. [516]

III. *The State.* The state is the self-conscious substance of morality, the union of the principles of the family and of civil society.

The state is (a.) its internal organization,—the *constitution,* the *internal law;* (b.) a particular individual in its relation to other states,—*external* (international) *law;* (c.) these two as momenta in the development of the universal idea of the mind,—*history.*

a.) Constitutional Law. The nature and essence of the state is the universality of the rational will, by which, on the one hand, the persons are maintained and promoted in their individuality, and, on the other, reduced to the life of the universal substance and thus to annul their individuality. The laws are, first, limits, bounds for the individuals; secondly, they are purposes for the labor of the different classes; and, thirdly, the substance of the free will and morality of all. The constitution is the organization of the state power,—existing *justice* as the reality of *freedom* in the development of all its rational determinations.

The guaranties of a constitution are contained in the spirit and consciousness of the nation, and the conformity of the state organization to this. —The living totality of the state and its constitution is the government. In the government as the organic totality, *subjectivity, the power of the prince,* is the pervading unity.* "In the perfect form of the state, in which all the momenta of the idea have their free existence, this subjectivity is not a so-called moral person, or a resolution of the majority,—forms, in [517] which the unity of the resolving will has no real existence,—but a real individuality, the will of one resolving individual,—*monarchy.*" (!!!) The monarchical constitution is therefore the constitution of developed reason; all other constitutions belong to inferior stages of development.

It is without interest to expose the remainder of Hegel's disquisitions on this particular subject; they all hinge on the scheme of a very equivocal constitutional monarchy.

b.) International Law. A state of war endangers the independence of states, while, on the other hand, it leads to the mutual recognition of the different nations, which is established in *treaties of peace.*

c.) History. The spirit of a nation is determined by geographic and climatic particularities; it exists in time and necessarily precurs the development of a particular principle, and therewith the development of a particular consciousness and reality,—it has an internal history. As a limited spirit it is subordinate to *universal history,* whose events exhibit the dialectics of nations,—the world's *judgment.* This movement is that in which the spiritual substance liberates itself, in which the absolute purpose of the world is realized, and becomes the *spirit of the world.* This

* As if the true subjectivity of a state, or of any thing organic, could be something extraneous,—which the power of the prince always is,—something else than a *reflex objectivity!* But Hegel wrote in Prussia.

liberation and its labor is the supreme and absolute right. The self-consciousness of a particular nation is the bearer of a stage in the development of the universal spirit and the objective reality in which this states its will. Against this will that of the other nations is without right; but even this will is annulled and transcended. The individuals active in this appear as instruments, whose boon is renown. [518]

From *The Temple of Truth*[2]

BY PETER KAUFMANN

FOUNDATION OF KNOWLEDGE

Man, casting his eye into the vast expanse of nature—though he by a single glance over the whole perceives its parts to exist contemporaneously, one along-side of another, that is, in space —he yet can not accurately see or contemplate its countless objects all at once and at the same moment but can do so only by looking at one after another, that is, in succession or time.

The process of impression of the qualities or phenomena of things upon the nerves of the senses or by thoughts upon the intellect is dependent upon the same laws governing the action of light in the Daguerrian and photographic operations. Where there is no perfect calmness of sense or mind, the picture impressed on either by the action becomes slurred, thus an untrue copy of the original and hence elementally an error.

Thought being inherently volatile by intrinsic nature, requires, therefore, in order to hold still, to impress its true shape and image upon the intellect, to be chained to a fixing medium. And as knowledge has been shown to be an accumulation of thought which became possible only by discovering a process to gather the thoughts of many men together; as the thoughts of man are sensually inaccessible to his neighbor and his neighbor's to him; as, further, the thoughts that pass through a man's mind and the objects impressing his senses during a series of years are so numberless that he could not at any time he needs or chooses control his recollecting them at pleasure, be his memory ever so good; and as, finally, if there was no enduring sign by which man could securely mark, to properly distinguish the various things and thoughts from one another, as they pass seriatim and analytically before his mind and hence could have no knowledge of their various qualities (which alone enables him to make use thereof in reasoning): the [47] absolute necessity, from these and other considerations, of such a fixing medium as we have already discovered in language and its words to exist, becomes self-evident beyond the possibility of a doubt.

Without this ability of interchanging thoughts with his fellowman and fixing them to signs for mutual permanent use, there can be no possibility of progress for man. For the savage, though possessed of some limited form of oral speech but destitute of and lacking the machinery to permanently fix the floating thought, barely contrives to secure a stagnant mode of life. Were he deprived even of this imperfect mode of mental interchange, no rational conception can well be framed how he could continue to exist at all.

Language, then,—the divine, first-born immortal child of mankind's Reason—is thus a gift to man of value beyond price. As figures, as will be seen hereafter, form but one of the specific word-classes inherent in the nature of language, of whose peculiar office one part is to denote to man the infinity of things existing in mind within or nature around him, so the words of language and its plastic flexibility in description denote these things themselves and their inherent nature as far as ascertained. For, each word in language, duly understood in its inherent sense, may be said to represent the conjoint incorporated judgment of men living from the beginning of time up to this day upon the thought contained in the word. Hence, words are signs for thoughts and objects as fixed, definite and unerring for him who understands their import, as the figures 1, 2, 3, 4, etc. or of a triangle, square, circle, or any other, as these are nothing else than words belonging to particular classes of the language.

As the object of language is the fixation, interchange, and consequent accumulation of thought, that object is defeated the very moment when the process is consummated defectively. Hence, as thought can not be seen or touched, it becomes not only interesting to examine the mode by which men originally assured themselves that they combined the same thought with the same word and object; but the perception of that process may also become of the utmost value to us for learning how we may arrive at understanding each other's thoughts and words unerringly. [48]

When thus, for instance, the name of sun was first given to the glorious luminary of day, men soon became aware that that name represented a threefold-different modification of one and the same thing before their mind: 1.) it denoted *the word* as the term in language by which the luminary was designated by man; 2.) it denoted the *luminary itself* as it stood, brilliant and glorious above every thing else in nature, in the azure sky; and, 3.) it denoted the *idea, thought,* or *mental image* of the sun, present in man's intellect as a distinct entity from either the word sun or the real sun itself. The same process led to a like equal understanding of the meaning and sense attached to all other words, which possess a homestead pre-emption in the domain of language amongst minds capable of grasping the thought in its disembodied form. As we design to recur to this subject in another place and form, the above may suffice for the present.

It must now begin to become clear to mature reflection that the elements of all thought, sufficing for all possible combinations of reasoning and knowledge, are actually deposited in language, in the unpretending form in which simple, honest custom and general usage of those that understand it has brought it through its long passage of many centuries up to our time and day. All that is needed on our side is a correct understanding and use of the sense, as thought, as it is firmly affixed to every word. So long as we attend to this simple rule, we are understood by and can understand all others observing it in as far as the elements of the matters treated of are known and familiar to the understanding of both the parties.

As such is the unmistakable character of language and its words. It imposes upon us the peremptory rule: a.) To master and discipline our thoughts until we become able to give them an expression in words as definite, unequivocal and concise as if they denoted a geometrical proposition. b.) Next, to understand the words used by others first in their true and exact meaning, and if that denotes more, less, or something different from what they design expressing, then to ascertain by interchange of thought what they really aim at until their real sentiments are understood precisely.

Thoughts thus fixed to their proper words, become clear [49] and explicit to the intellect, are easily retained in the memory without confounding them with others and may be recalled for actual use whenever opportunity arises to need them. Thoughts not thus fixed to words as signs can not be easily secured in the memory nor be mastered sufficiently for ever-ready practical use and, least of all, correctly communicated from one mind to another.

Men have been more or less careless in their proper attention to the laws of language from a want of insight and appreciation of its true nature and real character. Language, from its fewest simple words to its combination into a passage, conversation, speech, or the most ponderous volume, is nothing else than a series of expressed judgments, repeated and accumulated by their author like the links of a chain, all designed by him to show that the truth laid down in the first link of his proposition, in traveling in modified shapes through all the rest of the links till it reaches the last which is his main object or aim, is and remains essentially and equally true at each stage of its progress or in every separate link. If the reasoner is able to show that he has done so, he has performed what logic would call a demonstration, which simply means that he has exhibited to the intellect of his neighbor a string of conclusions upon undeniable premises from which said neighbor has no power to withhold his assent, just as if he had told him $2 \times 2 = 4$, $2 \times 4 = 8$, $2 \times 8 = 16$, $2 \times 16 = 32$, $2 \times 32 = 64$, and so on to any other number. [50]

LOGIC

The mind knows its being in upper or interior and its existence in nether or exterior consciousness* in so absolute a manner [165] that nothing of the sort which is termed in the schools "a demonstration" can either increase or decrease the amount of conviction which man feels of the reality and truth of both. For if the whole world around him would cry: "You imagine me merely to be and see a universe with glittering stars, a glorious sun and a grand beautiful nature all around, but it is all a sham, a deception like yourself, and neither of you has as much existence and reality as a momentary dream," the man thus addressed, even if "solitary and alone" on his side and the whole balance of his race opposing him on the other, would, as we imagine him, neither lose his good humor nor be anywise disconcerted. But would, with a smiling countenance and "calm as a summer's morning," look into the face of the vast host and simply reply to them somewhat in the following manner: "My friends, when you speak to me of that which transpires within yourselves and relates to your own state and mode of being, I will respectfully listen to you, but on attempting to speak to me of myself and that which is within me I would beg leave kindly to remind you that inasmuch as not you are but myself only am within myself, you seem to have entirely forgotten what Paul says, I Cor., ii, 11, 'For what man knoweth the things of man, save the spirit of man which is in him?' as likewise your own knowledge that this is a matter of which you have no knowledge whatever and never will have any until I shall myself see fit to let you know something about it."

This answer, being unanswerable, has the good effect to bring the parties to a rational discussion of and search after the law

* Although we have assumed upon what we consider amply convincing reasons that consciousness in its two poles is identical with fancy and imagination, we still continue using the term consciousness as more definitely expressing the mental actions here concerned than any other term.

governing the differences prevailing in the various views which human intellects form often of one and the same case, resulting in their agreement upon the two following propositions: a.) For that which man's mind knows by consciousness of itself, its forces and thoughts, or of nature from immediate impressions upon its own senses it needs no assistance of exterior logic or foreign dialectics to corroborate or authenticate the grand facts in the case, as they are evidence for themselves of a sort that looks upon all other evidence, volunteered to their aid, as a supernumerary intrusion if not an impertinence. b.) But when the human mind, feeling the necessity of order, method, and system in its pursuit of knowledge [166] enters regularly into the process of accumulating thought, that is, collects the various facts and thoughts of individual consciousness with its various observations of nature, and attempts to collate and harmonize them with its own and among one another for individual as well as the general benefit, then arises the need of having some medium whereby to reconcile or decide differences in conflicting cases. Such medium, acting as an umpire, to be of any true use and value should be of an absolute nature so that all men, willing or not, will have to acknowledge its rule and the validity of its decisions.

From reflections like these, it becomes clear that thinking minds at an early age must come to perceive that the thing they needed and were in search of was a knowledge of the law controlling not only thought, thinking, and the mind's perception of the exterior phenomena of nature, but containing and expressing the very conditions underlying all being, thought, intellectual action and perception whatever, and showing the cause of the permanency of endurance as well in the mode of being and existing as in that of operating and acting, and the last accessible reasons why it was all thus and not otherwise.

That was the thing the mind saw the want of. The gratification of this want to its full extent would have been a consummate system of logic and dialectics, of which the former relates to the form and modes of using and the latter to the nature and essence of fact, knowledge, and truth. That language itself was the twofold medium thus sought was not known at the time and if known would not have helped the case any, for in the same manner in which language is the product not of one individual human intellect but of mankind's conjoint reason, so also will it require a co-operation of truth-loving intellects to fully develop language into that practically all-embracing logic and all-probing dialectics which in theory are fully contained within it.

To help themselves as well as they could and understand how, men of uncommon minds went early to work to frame such systems themselves. Thus Zeno of Elea in ancient Greece, already five hundred years before our era, is termed "The Father of Logic and Dialetics." But Aristotle, about one hundred and sixteen years afterward, was the first who made the successful attempt to form [167] logic by itself into something like a scientific shape.

The system of Aristotle, considerably amended, is still much in use in the higher schools. But systems of that kind, being too abstruse and recondite, are not calculated to be used in every-day practical life. For not only do we find that the vast majority of all men educated at colleges and there hearing lectures upon logic no sooner leave the high school for entering practical life, than they at once abandon all book logic and rely like the great mass of mankind upon the laws innate with reason and judgment; but even gifted men in all nations, eminent as thinkers and authors, openly repudiate logic as a separate science and some like Hegel, under the name of logic, give us a treatise embracing the whole field of so-called metaphysics. This shows not that such men see no need of logic but merely that they consider it present in language in a mode resembling in some degree that in which we consider it. [168]

As a syllogism is an argument presented in a regular logical form, it should be "An argument so expressed, that the conclusiveness of it is manifest from the mere form of expression," without looking at the meaning of the terms. For example: "Every A is Z; B is A, hence it is also Z." Whatever signs or terms are employed in an argument like this, which may serve as the pattern of a shape to which all arguments can be reduced, the consequences are inevitable. By a close examination all arguments will be found to be syllogistic, no matter how irregular the form may be in which they appear.

When generalization has formed a class, be it one of facts, truths, things, or beings, the rule and law thereof is that whatever may by affirmation or denial be predicated of such class, applies to any thing or being therein comprehended. (This is the famous proposition generalized already by Aristotle under the title, "*de omni et nullo*," being valid of all or none.)

The preceding will suffice for what is necessary to be said about logic for the present time, inasmuch as we shall have to recur to the subject at some future day in another place. Before, however, we leave the subject we have, first, to note down one exceedingly curious fact connected with its history which after a while people will hardly be able to believe. This is, namely, the remarkable fact that for a long time the following position was in reality one of the laws or rules in all the systems of logic taught, not partially but generally, at the high schools in the various countries of Christendom and is, perhaps, in some of them retained yet to this very day, to wit: "There are things that are true in the abstract but not in the concrete"; or, in plain language, there are things which are true when beheld as thought by the mind, but [177] proving themselves untrue as soon as tried to be applied in exterior practice. The famous original of this remarkable so-called logical axiom reads: "*quidquid est verum in abstracto, sed non verum in concreto.*" Next, we must show the difference between logic and dialectics, as both have been and still very often are confounded with one another; thus their difference is this: Logic is superintendent and lawgiver over the forms in which truth is to appear, whereas Dialectics perform the same office toward the matter or substance of truth itself, acting, as it were, like a touchstone by which the real gold of truth is unerringly discriminated from all spurious imitations thereof.

DIALECTICS

Hitherto there never yet has existed any thing like a system of reliable dialectics in this world. For such system becomes only a realizable possibility where and after all the main sources of human knowledge have become distinctly known and recognized in number and substance and their relation to one another clearly ascertained and understood, which, as presently will be shown, never heretofore has been the case. For if there had ever been such a criterion on earth, the so-called world of learning and science could not have been led into adopting the monstrous absurdity into their systems of logic as a law of thought which we have just mentioned above—that "certain things could be true in thought, but untrue when attempted to be put into practice."

The condition of human affairs as shown us by history, geography, and daily observation, if calmly surveyed, presents, however, not only the causes of such and the like absurdities but therein also in a considerable measure the apologies for the same. For, whatever is done, thought, perceived or executed by the whole race of man, every single part thereof is, after all, only in reality performed in each case by one single human mind who is charged [178] for the time with the thinking required for its actualization. Such an individual mind, it therefore also was, which from causes which we shall discuss in a coming chapter, found himself induced to introduce the above position into logic, to help himself and those for whom he spoke out of a pinching dilemma from which they perceived no other outlet.

For, when seeing the human world split into innumerable political and religious divisions and perceiving even the men exclusively devoting themselves to science and the ostensible search after truth no less split into a numer of antagonistic schools or philosophical sects all of which combat one another, not seldom with acrimonious vehemence, the mind not deep enough to see to the bottom of the quarrel must come to the sudden and wholesale conclusion that inasmuch as these various parties oppose each other's entire system, they thereby also prove that there is no truth upon which all of them agree. Next, when the young, vigorous, incorrupted youth starts "With a thousand masts of hope into life's unmeasured ocean, returning, silently and alone, with hoary head in the saved skiff into port,"* he discovers that the cause of his blighted ideals and disappointed hopes was not

* Schiller.

alone in his own weakness, ignorance, or inconsistency but that the fickleness, dishonesty, hypocrisy and treachery of many men with whom he came into contact and had to act was fully as much the cause of his painful failures as any neglect or omission on his own side. Hence, the pain under which he smarts induces him to become distrustful of all men although he well enough knows that there are men whose conduct he himself can approve of, laud, praise, and, in a few cases even admire to the degree of worship. The disunion thus discovered in human knowledge and the absence of reliability upon the words, motives, and actions of the larger number of men produce a highly unpleasant and painful impression upon the mind of man whereby he not seldom forgets that although thus often deceived by his fellowman, there is yet all around him an unspeakably grand universe, a beautiful glorious nature, who never deceive and are as reliable or even more so than his well-proved timepiece as long as it is in a working condition to obey nature's laws. [179]

In this condition of mind man is unfit to discover the error in his own reasoning. For if he were able to see what men can and must know and what not and thereby to sift the true convictions of men who by their outward attitude appear almost at sword's point, he would find that the points upon which all those very men, notwithstanding their apparent disagreements, substantially agree are more than ten times as numerous as those upon which they disagree and that these latter are, in fact, not matters of knowledge but of mere opinion, not yet matured into the form of accepted scientific knowledge. But this true state of the case not being known, a ruling opinion more or less general obtains currency among a large number of thinking men akin to that sad state of bottomless doubting which eighteen hundred and some years ago induced Pilate (John xviii, 38) hurriedly to ask Jesus the question, "What is truth?" without expecting or awaiting an answer that in anywise should be capable of curing his mental malady. In a similar manner, many of these men of our day say: "There is no objective Truth, valid for all men, but only individual conviction depending upon the private judgment of every single man."

Well, this assertion is merely that very individual judgment of theirs upon this general case; hence by their own dictum they have no authority to make any such if even it had a foundation in fact. But such not being the case, the assertion is only founded in ignorance and pronounced with inconsiderate rashness and ignorant presumption. For no man who takes the trouble of examining the primary foundations lying at the bottom of all human knowledge of every kind and upon which every child of man is forever alike dependent, as we have done in the preceding pages, can henceforth for a moment again doubt the absolute existence of objective truth all around man, no matter whether properly understood and acknowledged or not.

But separate and apart from the men of the above sort whose bodies, souls, and intellects have all more or less been wounded in life's battle, there always have been almost everywhere a few favored individuals, gifted with profound thought and acute observation, living a sort of retired life in a happy solitude where designedly and exclusively pursuing the study of science [180] and truth, the philosophical equanimity of their temper and the clearness of their judgment's vision could not be disturbed by the surges of life's ocean as these could not penetrate into their well-sheltered cove. Now the wonder is that whenever the assertion above noted respecting objective truth together with the thought of the diversity of human views in general reached the ear or intellect of such profound thinkers, it never struck their minds to enter into a close examination of such questions as the following: What is it that mankind agree upon, differ about, and in common really do and can know? Or, what and which are the sources from which all that men really know and may know has been derived, and on what and why do they differ?

If these, which surely are questions of the highest importance to all men have occurred to reflecting minds, it is at least certain that they never have been satisfactorily answered. For if once thus answered, the consequences of such categorical answer must be unutterably glorious for the bettering of man's destiny on earth; for the correct answer to these queries contains the quintessence of the system of dialectics of which we stand in need as it forms the touchstone for probing the inner nature and truth in all things. We will, therefore, furnish the necessary answer to these important queries and therein lay the foundation and groundwork of the dialectics so urgently needed.

The ineffable Being which ubiquitously fills every point in infinite space, having no beginning and ending and sustaining the existence of the grand order visibly prevailing throughout the universe, has spoken and is speaking to man in and through three distinct cardinal voices, none more nor less, each one of which being actually a revelation or manifestation of God to man and the three constituting conjointly the only exclusive and all-embracing sources of knowledge which man ever had, can, and ever will have—these sources of revelations of God's truth to man, are called: a.) Nature, b.) Reason, and c.) Religion, forming a trinal disclosure of the Being and attributes of the infinite Author of all things and man's relation to God, nature and his neighbor.

a.) Nature, God's throne and footstool, is the revelation of God's boundless power and wealth and a perpetual continuation and exhibition before man's open eyes of his unlimited creative capacity. [181] b.) Reason, compelled by the laws of intellect to think and aspire in all main things, alike in all men from him that first trod the earth to the last, is a revelation of God's wisdom designed to rule, govern and use the vast powers of nature, according to the eternal design creatively impregnated into both nature and intellect. c.) Religion is the revelation of God's aim, object, purpose and design to and for which nature was created and reason given to man to rule and control it.

Now it devolves upon us to define the nature of each one of these threefold revelations so that there is no confounding of each other's domain: a.) To nature belongs the whole of that mighty universe which, surrounding man on all sides, is revealed to him by the action of his six senses as we have seen in their preceding analyzation. Hence, the body of man itself is a portion of this very nature. b.) The revelation of reason is not merely what the reason of one man perceives by thought as present in itself, in nature, in other men, and in the First Cause, but what the assembled reason of the countless human beings from the first to the last man born on earth (if ever there is a last) has thus far discovered in all the past and shall yet therein perceive in all the coming future. c.) The revelation of religion, being a relation of the whole race and all its separate members to that Ineffable Cause which to every one is the tender parent and nearest friend, must find its representing center in a paramount religious truth that is acknowledged at one and the same time as such by all mankind, all nature, and all reason. What, where, and which this particular paramount truth is we shall in the next chapter distinctly point out and specify.

All the knowledge found in the possession of man and all he will ever be able to acquire did, does, and will flow from one or the other or all of this trinal revelation of God to man. That knowledge flows or flowed either from a, or b, or c, separately, from a and b, or a and c, or b and c, combined, or conjointly from a, b, and c, united. As each branch of this threefold revelation emanates equally from the same God, each must necessarily, if divinely understood (that is, interpreted and understood as its Giver wishes it to be), give to man nothing but truth. For, since God found it expedient to give man this revelation in such threefold form, the giving in the form of this precise number must have appeared [182] to God's understanding as indispensably necessary, as the condition of man made it necessary to receive it in this threefold shape and no other. That such a necessity existed, still exists and will forever continue to exist, a single glance at the mutual and permanent relation of these three branches of revelation to and among each other will suffice to show. For remove, for instance, nature as the bottom upon which man stands and exists: how and where could he make use of and apply reason or revealed religion? Or let nature stand and take away reason: of what and for whose use is and remain revealed religion and nature? Or let nature and reason stand and take away revealed religion leaving reason groping in the dark to understand itself and the sphinx of nature; where will nature and reason be? They will be precisely in the horrifying state of chaos and blood-curdling terrors in which, with the shortliving exceptions of brief, locally-confined periods of single bright spots in human history, they always have been and still are in all the main points of practice up to the present day. For, the time is at hand when it will be clearly understood that revealed religion up to this hour has in this world never yet had fair play, that it has been unjustly dealt with by its own pretended friends as well as by its ill-informed, so-called, avowed opponents, that in place of itself its mere shadow was permitted to have some theoretical influence among men. For, paramount as the religious principle is in all men when duly reached, had mankind known the heaven extant in revealed religion, all human suffering and every thing hellish would long have disappeared from the face of the earth and a blooming paradise of universal happiness, virtue and goodness would now with solar brightness fill its dismal place.

The main reason and essential cause why nature, reason, and revealed religion, have been unable to yield man all the great blessings which each of them conceal in their unfathomed bosom is simply because man has, until now, not found out the great secret how duly to use them. Instead of using them at all times and upon all occasions conjointly to obtain their unanimous verdict upon one and the same question as God wants and enjoins him to do, he separates and pits them one against the other so as to place them into actual antagonism. Now, to understand these three eternal voices unerringly, it requires in all cases of any import their conjoint [183] co-operation. Nature can never be understood without the light of reason and religion—of reason, how to comprehend and control it; and of religion, to show the aim and end of such control. To understand and use the wisdom and light of reason it requires the co-operation of nature and religion; nature must furnish reason the ground to stand upon, the field to work in, and the power and tools to work with, while religion must enlighten reason to find what it really needs and never yet has been able to discover by its own unaided light. Religion, finally, needs nature and reason no less than they each need it to duly understand its mystic speech, discover its boundless treasures of infinite value, and enable it to make the whole of them available for us the use and benefit of man.

Now, instead of applying themselves to acquiring a full knowledge of the truth in each one of these equally eternal sources of divine knowledge for the purpose of using them conjointly and harmoniously to mutual interpretation and application, one set of men apply themselves one-sidely and exclusively to a superficial investigation of the surface of nature and without knowing any thing thereof look upon reason as a mere appendage to nature and upon religion as not much more than a dreamed nonentity. Others look upon reason as self-sufficient for its and all of man's purposes, making themselves merely superficially acquainted with the light of their reason as also inspecting but a few small patches of nature's vast domain; and confounding revealed religion with sectarian abuse thereof, imagine themselves to have a sufficiency of truth by reason's light within them and, therefore, maintain that nature gives but little and a dim and religion only an obscure and dubious light. And, finally, come the great host of larger and smaller religious sects and churches, many of whom look upon nature with a shy and squinting eye as if it did not really come from God but from some other undefined, ungodly source while they distrust, yet use, reason but only so far as to confirm themselves in the creed as their ancestors some hundreds of years ago laid it down as their understanding of what religion is or they thought it to be at that time—each sect, however, stopping somewhere midway to copy after some pattern but none going up to the church of the primitive Christians to take its copy from it as the fountain head.

These three main parties with their various subdivisions [184] and varieties are now and have been since many long, long years engaged in open and secret feuds with one another whereby all of them vilify, abuse, slander, and alternately fight against either nature and reason, nature and religion, or religion and reason just as they happen to be blind and unthinking worshipers of eyeless fanaticism, imagining self-deluding reason or the outer shell of crude nature. Now, none of these three parties can know either nature, reason, or religion as they in reality are because each one of these, as above shown, can only be properly understood by the assistance and co-operation of the other two. Hence these men do not know the love and peace of their God, as they harbor hate and ill-will and practice persecution toward one another. And here lies the secret of the world's whole trouble. For the heroic soul of the great Plato, in its divine love of truth without the assistance of that superior religious light which our churches and times possess without duly using it, already from the innate honesty of a true heart declared that "Man should follow truth wherever it leads!"* But the men attached to sectarian views of nature, reason, or religion do not know what real truth is and, taking their error for truth, or what even is worse, some knowing its nature yet for the sake of selfish gain and advantage use it hypocritically, do deceive others, and both endeavor to catch as many new proselytes for their creed as they possibly can. As this same policy is pursued by all alike, the real friends of God's Whole Truth find no place where to attach themselves but must be content to have silent intercourse with God alone and here and there with the honest soul of a God-loving friend. Hence there is neither peace nor progress found in these antagonizing sects but a constant wrangling, combating, and fighting whereby men inflict mutually upon one another all the suffering and misery they can. It is but a poor consolation for the kind heart of the beholder's mind to know that by the laws of God's economy all the mischief thus caused will eventually, with compound interest, fall crushingly upon the devoted heads of the ringleaders and concoctors in all these schemes of evil and wrong. [185]

Nature, reason, and religion each alone and for itself may give man impressions of isolated and detached truths, but these impressions are still subject to the possibility of being also errors. But as there are no other sources from which man can draw any kind of information whatever but only these three embracing all things contained in boundless infinity, it follows with inevitable certainty: 1.) That every proposition in which nature, reason, and religion agree is thereby stamped as an absolute truth. 2.) If all the truths are compiled together in which these three eternal revelations of God thus agree, man therein has the clear and

* ". . . but wherever our Reason, windlike carries us, there must we go." Republic, page 75, Taylor's translation.

unerring revelation of God's own supreme will, intellect, wisdom, and code of law in a form that never will nor can change throughout all coming eternity.

MAN'S END

Nations, peoples, cities, communities and men, in consideration that their leaders have no aims and purposes at heart and in view worthy of man and the age, have of late years by great and nobly aspiring intellects* justly and severely been stigmatized as "Aimless nations, and cities, and men, with purposes so dead as to deserve coffins." As the large majority of men in nations and cities are always more or less in a condition that impels them to follow the same direction which the controlling current of events leads the [186] whole mass to pursue, it must be evident that chaos and confusion must ensue and prevail where there are no great ennobling common aims binding the vast masses together. [187]

Now let us call our three divine witnesses seriatim to the stand and learn their august answers to our all-important, world-adjudging query. First sublime Reason, erst-begotten daughter of uncreated intellect, inborn light of the race of man, please give us thine answer to this the most weighty query of all that are possible for man. "Reason. In accordance with the laws of my being, my action consists in a perpetual series of judgments upon the size, form, contents and value of every thing brought before me, distributing all things into their respective classes, classifying these very classes again into a smaller number, repeating the same process [190] with the latter and their followers until I reach one ultimate unity beyond which my functions do not reach, as unity is oneness with myself.† Here, then, I rest my

* Emerson and Carlyle.

† Let us adduce the following as a sample of the process: If a man would ask me, "Where are you?" My answer would be: "In my room." He then would ask: "Where is your room?" Ans. "In my house." "But where is your house?" Ans. "In the town." So he would continue asking until the last answer would tell him that the town is in the township, it in the county, the county in the State, the State in the Union, the union on the continent, the continent on the globe, the globe in the solar system, and it in the universe, and that in absolute space. Here, then, is the end of the inquiry where reason must stop and forever abide; and similarly in all other cases when reaching the climax in each.

theorizing and step outside into the actual to realize my highest thought by a series of actions corresponding to the series of thoughts preceding and producing it. In conformity with these premises there is among all the countless number of aims which man and men may pursue but one single greatest and supreme one embracing all the rest, and its name is Perfection. All-sided perfection of all the powers and faculties of man, men, nations, and the whole human race harmoniously developed, concordially acting in friendly unison to achieve and realize perfection in all things, is the highest and ultimate ideal aim which my and any thought can reach. At and in it I must thinkingly rest and am constrained practically to strive after its realization. Even now and at all times heretofore before my present definite decision could be known anywhere, I have acted and do act in my function called common sense with all men at all times, on all occasions, and under all circumstances where I act at all upon the grand principle above enunciated; whereby the silent mind of every man as well in its solitary chamber of thought as on the market or highway of noisy life is consciously or unconsciously constrained to adjudge (subject, of course always to the extent and degree of the individual's knowledge) every thing by this great standard and call men and things, words and actions, works and labors, good or bad, useful or hurtful, valuable or worthless, interesting or indifferent, etc., etc., in proportion as the same approximate or recede from the idea of perfection, as they entertain it in the particular case before them. Hence, they patronize the best mechanic, artist, physician, jurist, etc., etc., in preference to the bungler because they know that the works of these men will be the best they can get [191] of the kind or, in other words, come nearer to the standard of perfection than the works of inferior men could ever do. That's mine answer."

AMERICA

Now, of all countries existing upon this globe and of all forms of government that men have ever tried to govern themselves by upon earth, there are none which so evidently have by Providence designedly been prepared, for the purpose of realizing a saviour nation as the land and the institutions of these United

States. The former is large and fertile enough to accommodate and sustain almost, if not fully, one half of the present entire population of the globe; and the latter, having made the people themselves the permanent depository of their own sovereign power, have therein preserved a door widely thrown open for the introduction of all and any improvements, surely not excluding the possibly best, which these sovereigns may possess the wisdom to see and the virtue and patriotism to demand introducing. Hence, even a whole host of various defects, which such people may have inherited from the past and which to remedy neither time nor opportunity have yet been favorable, will, when that proper time eventually arrives, be overcome by conquering even difficulties apparently insurmountable. And as this youngest among the nations is placed upon a new continent lying amidst the great oceans that separate the two extremes of the ancient world, that very geographical position, so easily permitting access to and speedy intercourse with all the countries of the globe, is beyond question a stubborn fact of prophetic significance. For the same nation which, first, by embracing and introducing into its midst Christ's whole love and full purpose, thereby establishing a perfect peace and heavenly friendship among all the members of its body and thus making itself a saving nation of all its own, that very nation will thereby likewise become the model and saviour nation of the rest of mankind by the double action as well of its power as of its transcending example. For a nation which becomes so divinely wise as to aspire through all its citizens and agencies and with the whole immense power at its control after consummate [283] perfection in all its men, things, and institutions thereby makes itself "The city that is set on a hill; hence the light of the world, which can not be hid." Matt. v, 14.

Now, if ever there was country led onward by a "manifest destiny," that country is America, the states of this Union. Hence "Young America" is ambitious, which is right and proper that it should be as it feels itself "beaconed onward" by a grand though as yet not clearly understood destination. If now the young giant at one leap clears all the inferior objects that court his ambition, saying to them all, "I will [have] none of you," but "my, and my country's glory, shall simply consist in this, *that all nations and men, shall look with joy and gratitude upon us,*" then men may prepare for beholding a spectacle upon earth which to enjoy even the immortals in superior mansions will feel eager. For then we shall see a race gifted with great grasp of intellect, endowed with a power of execution of rare elasticity and energy, in possession of means sufficient for all purposes upon which they may resolve, combine these and all their other forces for the accomplishment of the grandest, most glorious purpose that ever expanded the bosom of nation or man. First, like the man (Luke xv, 4) they will wander about among themselves endeavoring to find and reclaim every sheep that in one way or other has become lost. This will enkindle an affection and friendship between man and man as that existing between the members of the most affectionate families. Thereby every man will feel it his duty to be "his brother's keeper," guarding him against harm, poverty, misery, doing all to make him prosperous, happy, joyous, wise, good, and perfect and, in brief, be to him in reality a brother and friend, loving him as his own self. To do this the more effectually will require the mastery over "the science of, or leading to, perfection" which every man as much as he shall need thereof for his case can acquire without any difficulty by simply surrendering himself to be taught by the Comforter, Holy Ghost or Spirit of Truth, for He will lead every man who seeks and desires the truth into all truth. (John xiv, 26) This operation of internal love toward all its own members will cement every private particle of humanity so firmly and closely to the body politic as to make it one unitary mass in sentiment, feeling, and purpose, in aspiration, striving, and action. Next, having now in their [284] dealings with one another firmly habituated themselves to act unswervingly by the principles of unbending honesty, honor, and rectitude, they will carry that habit and in it the external form of their love of truth and man into all their dealings with other nations and the citizens or subjects thereof. They will by this, in the first instance, gain and secure the confidence of them all which will enable them to maintain an increasing commercial intercourse with every one, thereby disposing of the accumulating masses of stock resulting from their steadily increasing productiveness and thus necessarily continue to grow in wealth and the means of power.

Meanwhile the combined flower of the national intellect, supported by the boundless power of the nation's means, will be most assiduously engaged in working out the eternal science of heaven in all its national, humanitary, and cosmical features, embracing with all the known results of definite science the whole ramification of mankind's knowledge, aspiration, aim, and destiny, into one grand all-encircling system which, thus encycling all the truths now in possession of men of whatever sort, will therefore at once be readily and joyously embraced by every thinking and searching intellect inasmuch as it presents all requisite tools, means, and materials to institute and prosecute a regular process of progressing discovery in every direction of the boundless sea of the yet unknown. At the head of that system will stand as a beacon guiding every mariner on life's ocean, rearing its eternal light-flashing cap to the throne of God, that infinite, divine idea which heretofore and until now did dimly and unconsciously but henceforth shall clearly and consciously with ethereal fire inspire, enthuse, and expand the bosom of all America—to-wit: *"the realization of the ultimate perfection and happiness of all mankind,"* by and through America, as the God-appointed savior nation of the whole race. [285]

David Friedrich Strauss[3]

BY MONCURE D. CONWAY

READINGS

Whoso seeketh wisdom shall have no great travail; for he shall find her sitting at his door. She goeth about seeking such as are worthy of her, showeth herself favorably to them in the highways, and meeteth them in every thought. Love is the keeping of her laws. The multitude of the wise is the welfare of the world.

Wisdom is the worker of all things: for in her is an understanding spirit, holy, one only, manifold, subtle, lively, clear, undefiled, simple, not subject to hurt, loving the thing that is good, quick, which cannot be letted, ready to do good; kind to man, steadfast, sure, free from care, having all power, overseeing all things; and going through all understanding, pure and most subtle spirits. Wisdom is more moving than any motion: she passeth through all things by reason of her pureness. For she is the breath of the power of God, and a pure influence flowing from the glory of the Almighty: therefore can no defiled thing fall into her. For she is the brightness of the everlasting light, the unspotted mirror of the power of God, and the image of his goodness. And being but one, she can do all things; and remaining in herself, she maketh all things new: and in all ages entering into holy souls, she maketh them friends of God, and prophets. She is more beautiful than the sun, and above all the order of the stars: being compared with the light, she is found before it; for after day cometh night, but vice shall not prevail against wisdom. —*Wisdom of Solomon.*

The Duke Gae asked about the altars of the gods of the land. Tsae-Wo replied: "The Hea sovereign used the pine-tree, the man of the Yin used the cypress, and the man of the Chow used the chestnut,—to cause the people to be in awe."

Confucius, hearing this, said: "Things that are done, it is needless to speak about; things that have had their course, it is needless to remonstrate with; things that are past, it is needless to blame."

Kee-Loo asked about serving the gods. The Master said: "While you are not able to serve men, how can you serve the gods?"

Kee-Loo said: "I venture to ask about death."

The Master said: "While you do not comprehend life, how can you comprehend death?

"If a man in the morning hear of the right way, he may in the evening die without regret.

"Yew, shall I teach you what knowledge is? When you know a thing, consider that you know it; and when you do not know a thing, understand that you do not know it. This is knowledge.

"For a man to worship a deity not his own is mere flattery.

"To give oneself earnestly to the duties due to men, and, while respecting the gods, to respect also their distance, may be called Wisdom."—*Confucius.*

Mohammed said: Instruct in knowledge! He who instructs, fears God; he who speaks of knowledge, praises the Lord; who disputes about it, engages in holy warfare; who seeks it, adores the Most High; who spreads it, dispenses alms to the ignorant; and who possesses it, attains the veneration and good will of all. Knowledge enables its possessor to distinguish what is forbidden from what is not; it lights the way to heaven; it is our friend in the desert, our society in solitude; our companion when far away from our homes; it guides us to happiness; it sustains us in misery; it raises us in the estimation of friends; it serves as an armor against our enemies. With knowledge, the servant of God rises to the heights of excellence. The ink of the scholar is more sacred than the blood of the martyr. God created Reason, and it was the most beautiful being in his creation; and God said to it: "I have not created anything better or more perfect or more beautiful than thou: blessings will come down on mankind on thy account, and they will be judged according to the use they make of thee." —*Mohammed.*

If morality is the relation of man to the idea of his kind, which in part he endeavors to realize in himself, in part recognizes and seeks to promote in others, religion, on the other hand, is his relation to the idea of the universe, the ultimate source of all life and being. So far, it may be said that religion is above morality; as it springs from a still profounder source, reaches back into a still more primitive ground.

Ever remember that thou are human, not merely a natural production; ever remember that all others are human also, and, with all individual differences, the same as thou, having the same needs and claims as thyself: this is the sum and substance of morality.

Ever remember that thou, and everything thou beholdest within and around thee, all that befalls thee and others, is no disjointed fragment, no wild chaos of atoms or casualties, but that it all springs, according to eternal laws, from the one primal source of all life, all reason, all good: this is the essence of religion. —*Strauss's "The Old Faith and the New."*

DAVID FRIEDRICH STRAUSS

Towards the close of the last century, a young German student was climbing amid the Swiss Alps—alpenstock in hand—gazing with wonder on glaciers, scaling the dizziest peaks. His Alpine wanderings were preliminary to the climbing of nobler summits, commanding vaster prospects. For this was Friedrich Hegel, destined to create an epoch in the history of the human mind. Amid those barren heights and weird chasms of Switzerland there was born in his mind a doubt which has influenced the world. Before those wild desolations he asked himself whether it could be possible that this chaos of rock and glacier had been specially created for man's enjoyment? It was a problem which required for its solution not only his own long, laborious life, but many lives; yet, to the philosophical statement of that one man we owe a new order of religious thought. If I may borrow an expression from geology, it may be said that we are all living in the Hegelian formation; and this whether we understand that philosophy or not, and even if we reject its terms. For Hegel was as a great vitalizing breath wafted from afar, beneath which, as under a tropical glow, latent seeds of thought were developed to most various results. From afar: for really Hegel's philosophy was an Avatar for cultivated Europe of the most ancient faith of our race. Its essence is the conception of an absolute idea which has represented itself in Nature, in order that by a progressive development through Nature it may gain consciousness in man, and return as mind to a deeper union with itself. It is really the ancient Hindu conception of a universal soul of Nature, a vast spiritual sea in which each animal instinct, each human intellect, is a wave. Or, in another similitude, every organic form, however great or small, represents some scattered spark of a central fire in intelligence, on the way back to its source, bearing thither the accumulated knowledge gathered on its pilgrimage through many forms in external Nature.

Briefly, the Hegelian philosophy means a soul in Nature corresponding to the soul of Man. Of course—I have already stated it—it did not originate with Hegel. It may be traced from the Vedic Hymn to the cry of Kepler, when, looking up to the stars, he said, "Great God, I think thy thought after thee!" But with Hegel it gained an adaptation to the thought of Europe, and passed into the various forms of belief and feeling. It inspired all the poetry of Wordsworth. It is reflected in the materialism no less than in the idealism of our age, and may be felt in the philosophy of Huxley no less than in that of its best exponent, Emerson.

Among the many German thinkers who sat at the feet of Hegel there was but one who comprehended its tremendous bearings upon the theology of Europe; but one through whom it was able to grow to logical fruitage; and that one was the great man whose life has just closed—David Friedrich Strauss. Strauss proved himself the truest pupil of Hegel by throwing off the mere form of his forerunner's doctrine, just as that philosopher had thrown off the formulas of his forerunners. The literal Hegelians, of course, regarded Strauss as a renegade; on the surface it would so appear. Hegel called himself a Christian, Strauss renounced Christianity; Hegel was designated an idealist, Strauss a materialist. But we must not be victims of the letter. Fruit is different from blossom; but it is, for all that, blossom in another form.

I need not dwell on the outward biography of Friedrich Strauss. The greatest men live in their intellectual works. The sixty-five years of this man were not marked by many salient or picturesque incidents. As a student of theology at Tübingen, and as a professor, he travelled an old and beaten path,—poverty, hard study, hard work. At the age of twenty-seven he publishes his great work, the *Leben Jesu;* is driven from his professorship; offered another at Zurich University, he is prevented by persecution from holding it, and finally settles himself down to a life of plain living and high thinking. He is elected by his native town Ludwigsburg to the Würtemburg Legislature, but surprises them by his "conservatism," as it was called, and answers their dissatisfaction by resigning. He marries, and, alas! unhappily. Agnes Schebert was an actress, and she was also a clever authoress; but when she was married to Strauss there was shown to be an incompatibility of disposition which led to a quiet separation without recriminations on either side. The lady once wrote a parody on the writing of Hegel, which is amusing, but suggests that she could hardly have been fortunately united with a philosopher who had sat at the feet of Hegel. She left with him a daughter and a son, who were devoted to their father through life, and for whom he wrote a tender and touching account of their mother, that they might think of her with affection.

He lived a busy life, and wrote a large number of admirable works, the absence of most of which from English libraries is a reproach to our literature. His biographies are among the most felicitous that have been written, and have brought before Germans noble figures which are for most English readers mere names,—Ulrich von Hutten, the brilliant radical of the Reformation; the discoverer of lost books of Livy, Quintilian, and other classic authors; the fellow-fugitive of Erasmus before the wrath of the Pope; the lonely scholar who has made classic the islet of Lake Zurich where he died; the Biography of Hermann Reimarus, who one hundred years ago was the leading prophet of Natural Religion;* the Life of Friedrich Daniel Schubart, poet and publicist, who, beginning as an organist in Ludwigsburg, lost his place for writing a parody on the Litany; who in later life was invited by the Duke of Würtemburg to dinner, on his arrival seized and imprisoned in Asberg Castle for ten years, because of an epigram written by the poet,—who, for the rest, has left songs

* His chief works are *The Wolfenbüttel Fragments,* edited by Lessing; *The Principles of Natural Religion,* and *The Instincts of Animals.*

which the Germans still love to sing.* The work of Strauss on Voltaire consists of a series of lectures prepared by request of the Princess of Hesse-Darmstadt (daughter of Queen Victoria), who listened to them; and the work is written in a spirit of high admiration of the great French heretic. If, as I doubt not, the two biographies which he has left—*Lessing* and *Beethoven*—are of equal value to those I have mentioned, Strauss will have left six works at least, apart from his contributions to theology, of a character which must write his name very high among the literary workers of this century.

When the life of Strauss is written, no doubt the details of it will be found of great interest; but nothing relating to his private and personal history will ever be so impressive as the unfolding of his intellectual and religious nature. Fully told, even as traceable in his works, this represents the pilgrimage of a soul from the crumbling shrines of superstition across long deserts of doubt, and the rugged passes of adversity, even to the beautiful Temple of Truth, [158] where his last hymn of joy ended in the gentle sigh of death.

Of this, his mental biography, I can give here but a slight outline. I have already taken up the thread of his life at the point where he was learning the secret of Hegel. That implied a foreground with which many of us are familiar; for he was born to orthodoxy, and had to flee that City of Destruction. So much he had accomplished in his youth, and was ready to set himself to the real task of his life. The philosophy of Hegel left room for mysticism, but none for miracle. Paulus, Schelling, Schleiermacher, and others, each endeavored in their several ways to bridge over the gulf between supernaturalism and reason; they wanted reason, they must have Christianity, and so held on to the miracles without believing them miraculous. But Strauss had already placed before his mind Truth as the one attainable thing worthy of worship; and he set himself to the task of studying the life of Christ, with all its investiture of fable, as a historical

* The principal is one entitled *Caplied* (*Cape Song*), supposed to be sung by soldiers, sold to the Dutch, on their way to the Cape of Good Hope. Another celebrated poem of his is, *Die Fürstengrüft* (*The Tomb of Princes*).

phenomenon. The fables he knew were not true, but he would know how they arose, and he would know what form they would leave were they detached from the New Testament narratives. In reaching his sure result he was aided by the veracity of his mind no less than by his learning. He had but to apply to a miracle found in the Bible the same test which every one applied to a miracle when found in Livy or Ovid. He had but to take the method which Christians used when dealing with the wonders of Buddhism and apply it honestly to the marvels of Christianity. The result was that he tracked all the New Testament marvels back to their Pagan or Judaic origin; he found that they were the some stories that had been told about Moses, Elijah, David, about Isis and Osiris, Apollo and Bacchus. In a word, he proved that they were myths, such as in unscientific ages—when the laws of Nature and the nature of laws were unknown—had arisen and gathered about every teacher who had become an object of popular reverence.

In denying the value of miracles as historical events in the life of a particular man, Strauss was impressed by the perception that these myths which had come from every human race to invest Christ represented something more important than the career of any individual; they represented humanity. They were born out of the human heart in every part of the world, and were types of its aspirations, hopes, and spiritual experiences. That which could not be respected as history could be reverenced as a reflection of the religious sentiment. He would place an idea where the Church set an individual. "Humanity," he wrote, "is the union of the two natures—God become man, the infinite manifesting itself in the finite, and the finite spirit remembering its infinitude; it is the child of the visible Mother and the invisible Father, Nature and Spirit; it is the worker of miracles, in so far as in the course of human history the spirit more and more completely subjugates nature, both within and around man, until it lies before him as the inert matter on which he exercises his active power; it is the sinless existence, for the course of its development is a blameless one, pollution cleaves to the individual only, and does not touch the race and its history. It is humanity that dies, rises, and ascends to heaven, for from the negation of its phenomenal life there ever proceeds a higher spiritual life."

When this lofty faith in humanity as the true Christ, which had unconsciously symbolized itself as the life of one man, shone out upon the mind of Strauss, all interest in the individual Jesus paled under it. Since his great work was published—near forty years ago—we have, by standing on the shoulders of such men as he, been able, no doubt, to see somewhat further. The rational study of the New Testament has disclosed certain fragments of real history, and by piecing these together we can shape out the figure of a great man,—great enough to show why it was that the human heart brought all its finest dreams and marvels to entwine them around that single brow. But the grand generalization of this scientific thinker, who pierced the veil of fable and recognized beyond it the face of humanity transfigured with divine light, is one which can hardly be paralleled by any utterance since the brave words of Paul: "We henceforth know no one according to the flesh; and if we have ever known Christ according to the flesh, yet now we no longer know him." "The Lord is a Spirit!"

Having disposed of the old Christology, Strauss proceeded to apply his method—the method of science—to all the theories of Nature and of human life which were intertwined with it. What the results of his inquiries were are summed up in his last work, *The Old Faith and the New*. And at the outset I must say that the whole purport of that book has been falsely interpreted for English readers by the blundering exposition of it given by Mr. Gladstone in a speech delivered in Liverpool. The late Prime Minister, it will be remembered, held up Dr. Strauss before the school-children as an awful example of what they would come to if they once began exercising their own faculties. He admitted his own incompetence to answer the arguments of Strauss; it would have been well if he had also acknowledged his inability to translate his words correctly. In describing that "Universum" which Strauss had declared to be the highest and divinest conception of human intelligence, the cosmos which man should adore in place of the old deity of dogma, Mr. Gladstone said that the author represented it—the adorable universe—as without reason. The word which Strauss really uses is "Vernünftvoll"—full of reason! This inexcusable error makes all the difference between theism and atheism. "Our highest idea," says Strauss, "is the law-governed cosmos, full of life and reason;" and he censures Schopenhauer, who declares Nature to be hopelessly evil. "We consider it," he says, "arrogant and profane on the part of a single individual to oppose himself with such audacious levity to the cosmos whence he springs, from which, also, he derives that spark of reason which he misuses. We recognize in this a repudiation of the sentiment of dependence which we expect from every man. We demand the same piety for our cosmos that the devout of old demanded for his God."

In this his last work, *The Old Faith and the New*—the translation of which we owe to a woman as we do that of his first work—Strauss embraces with enthusiasm the theory of evolution. Thereby his old Hegelian idealism is transmuted to Darwinian materialism. Of course, many people fancy that materialism is something which is inconsistent with a belief in a deity or even in religion. But really, with regard to divine existence and religion there is no difference between idealism and materialism. Strauss justly pronounces the religious issue between the two a quarrel about words. They both and alike "endeavor to derive the totality of phenomena from a single principle—to construct the universe and life from the same block"; in this equally opposing the Christian dualism which divides man into body and soul, and severs God from Nature. In their common endeavor after unity idealism starts from above, materialism starts from below; "the latter constructs the universe from atoms and atomic forces, the former from ideas and idealistic forces. But if they would fulfil their tasks, the one must lead from its heights down to the very lowest circles of Nature, and to this end place itself under the control of careful observation; while the other must take into account the higher intellectual and ethical problems." In short, all that the idealist says of soul the materialist says of brain; all that any worshipper can say of his God, Strauss says of Nature.

What the creed of this thinker was may be found in this last work, wherein it is expressed with an exaltation which becomes more impressive now that we know that, even while he was so uttering his perfect faith in the fair universe, the terrible cancer was destroying him. These are his words: "We perceive in Nature tremendous contrasts, awful struggles; but we discover that these do not disturb the stability and harmony of the whole,—that they, on the contrary, preserve it. We further perceive a gradation, a development of the higher from the lower, of the refined from the coarse, of the gentle from the rude. And in ourselves we make the experience that we are advanced in our personal as well as our social life the more we succeed in regulating the element of capricious change within and around us, and in developing the higher from the lower, the delicate from the rugged. This, when we meet with it within the circle of human life, we call good and reasonable. What is analogous to it in the world around us, we cannot avoid calling so likewise. The cosmos is simultaneously both cause and effect, the outward and the inward together. We stand here at the limits of our knowledge; we gaze into an abyss we can fathom no farther. But this much at least is certain,—that the personal image which meets our gaze there is but the reflection of the wondering spectator himself. At any rate, that on which we feel ourselves entirely dependent is by no means merely a rude power to which we bow in mute resignation, but is at the same time both order and law, reason and goodness, to which we surrender ourselves in loving trust."

In one very important matter many of the admirers of Strauss have felt distress at his position and influence. Politically, he has the reputation of being a reactionist and conservative. This reputation—obtained when he resigned his seat in the legislature because of disagreement with his radical constituency—has been confirmed by his treatment of political subjects in his latest work. My own belief is that the views of Strauss on these matters are very seriously misunderstood by reason of the fact that they are altogether conceived from the Hegelian standpoint. Those who study Hegel know that his apparent conservatism was the crust outside a fiery radicalism. The political philosophy of Hegel is contained in the following extract from his writings: "Moral liberation and political freedom must advance together. The process must demand some vast space of time for its full realization; but it is the law of the world's progress, and the Teutonic nations are destined to carry it into effect. The Reformation was an indispensable preparation for this great work. The history of the world is a record of the endeavors made to realize the idea of freedom and of a progress surely made, but not without many intervals of apparent failure and retrogression. Among all modern failures the French revolution of the eighteenth century is the most remarkable. It was an endeavor to realize a boundless external liberation without the indispensable condition of moral freedom. Abstract notions based merely on the understanding, and having no power to control wills of men, assumed the functions of morality and religion, and so led to the dissolution of society, and to the social and political difficulties under which we are now laboring. The progress of freedom can never be aided by a revolution which has not been preceded by a religious reformation."*

That a similar conviction was rooted in the mind of Strauss I became aware by personal intercourse with him. Some years ago, as I walked with him on the banks of the Neckar, he declared to me that the motives he had in publishing his *Life of Christ* were hardly less political than religious. "I felt oppressed," he said, "at seeing nearly every nation in Europe chained down by allied despotism of prince and priest. I studied long the nature of this oppression, and came to the conclusion that the chain which fettered mankind was rather inward than outward, and that without the inward thraldom the outward would soon rust away. The inward chain I perceived to be superstition, and the form in which it binds the people of Europe is Christian supernaturalism. So long as men accept religious control not based on reason they will accept political control not based on reason. The man who gives up the whole of his moral nature to an unquestioned authority has suffered a paralysis of his mind, and all the changes of outward circumstances in the world cannot make him a free man. For this reason our European revolutions have been, even

* See Gostwick and Harrison's *Outlines of German Literature,* p. 481.

when successful, merely transfers from one tyranny to another. I believed when I wrote that book that, in striking at supernaturalism, I was striking at the root of the whole evil tree of political and social degradation."

At another time, when speaking of Renan, whose portrait was the most prominent in his study, he said: "Renan has done for France what I had hoped to do for Germany. He has written a book which the common people read; the influence of my *Life of Christ* has been confined to scholars more than I like, and I mean to put it into a more popular shape. Germany must be made to realize that the decay of Christianity means the growth of national life, and the progress of humanity."

After this it was very plain to me what Strauss's conservatism amounted to. It means only that he had no faith in the abolition of an abuse here and there when the conditions which produce every abuse remain unaltered,—no faith in sweeping away a few snow-drifts when winter is still in the air, the whole sky charged with snow. We may wish that he had felt more sympathy with some of the popular movements around him; but we must remember that as a philosophical radical he regarded the ever-recurring enthusiasms of the people,—believing that they would reach the millennium by abolishing capital punishment, or abolishing a throne,—as so much waste energy. He saw hopes born in revolutions only to perish in disaster and reaction. He came to rest his hope for humanity, which he loved, on his faith in the omnipotence of that truth which he sought to enthrone above it.

Such was the faith, such the work, of the great man to whose memory we pay this day our heartfelt homage. In his writings I have met with but one allusion to himself. It is in the last pages that he ever wrote, and is as follows: "It is now close upon forty years that as a man of letters I have labored, that I have fought on and on for that which appeared to me as truth, and still more perhaps against that which has appeared to me as untruth; and in the pursuit of this object I have attained, nay, overstepped, the threshold of old age. Then it is that every earnest-minded man hears the whisper of an inner voice: 'Give an account of thy stewardship, for thou may'st be no longer steward.' Now, I am not conscious of having been an unjust steward. An unskilful one at times, too probably also a negligent one, I may, Heaven knows, have been; but on the whole I have done what the strength and impulse within prompted me to do, and have done it without looking to the right or the left, without seeking the favor or shunning the displeasure of any."

These few words represent the benediction of conscience upon a faithful man, felt by him as life was ebbing away, and the dark portal growing more distinct before him. His bitterest enemy need not impugn that approving smile of his own heart. It was all the wage of his work. Others have toiled in full view of heavenly reward. He labored on with hope of no recompense for devotion and self-sacrifice beyond the consciousness of having made his life an unfaltering testimony to truth. Even those who believe that they see gleams of light irradiating the dark valley may count his honor not less but more that he gave his service uncheered by such visions.

In Heilbronn, where he was residing, he once pointed out to me, near an ancient church, the trace of the old and sacred fountain which gave the town its name, which signifies "healing fountain." He said, with his gentle smile: "The theory of the priests is that the fountain ceased to flow when I came here to reside." When I looked up to his magnificent eyes, and the grand dome of his forehead, I could but marvel at the depth of that superstition which could permit this man to live as a hermit in communities which will one day cherish each place of his dwelling as a shrine. Holy wells may dry up, and the churches beside them crumble, but men will repair to the spots where the lonely scholar sat at his task, and tell their children—Here it was that in the wildernesses of superstition living waters broke out, and streams in the desert. [159]

On Man, History, and Socialism[4]

BY AUGUST WILLICH

WHY DO SO FEW RELIGIOUS WORKERS PARTICIPATE IN LABOR MOVEMENTS?

We cannot completely explain this lack of participation as resulting from tendencies toward persecution and witch-hunting. In these movements there must necessarily be something lacking which represents a deeper need to the religious workingman than the immediate, apparent goals of the movement can satisfy. To ascertain this we should inquire as to what human need lies at the basis of religion. Then we shall come upon the key, that this need persists as essential to human nature even if all that is called religion disappears and that religion, insufficient by itself to enchain the human spirit, loses its power as this need is satisfied in a deeper and more real way. So long as we confuse religion with its external organization in the church we cannot understand it any more than we can understand human rights through law courts or humanity through the police department.

What need of human nature lies at the basis of religion? From what natural law does this need arise? It is the basic law of all life—and in nature everything is alive,—it is the *law of self-preservation.* The self-preservation drive is thus so much at one and inseparable from the life-urge that it can never be repressed and never be rejected—yes, so inseparable that it lies even at the basis of suicide, where we would least seek it. If, however, only this *single* drive of self-preservation lies at the basis of *all* life, why then do we thus have diverse religions and why are we able to dispense with them? The answer is difficult and easy. Difficult for anyone who has not yet learned to realize his most noble capacity, free thought, and easy for thinking men.

The human organism is the result and epitome [*Inbegriff*] of all the organic life of our earth, and in it all the powers of nature are united to a single creative, fundamental power—*Thought.* Whoever has not learned to recognize thought as the epitome and result of all the powers of nature—not only as the most mighty among them, but *as nature's power*—asks himself whether there is something besides *human thought* which, through our machines, masters the forces of nature, blind in themselves. Will he not discover an outcome of human thought in everything that surrounds him? Thus is thought *our* essence, the life-source of our existence. As far as our thought extends, as far as we strive to extend our existence and what we can think, that far do we will to *live,* to exist. Thought is infinite, *i.e.,* it is not limited in space and not limited in time. Hence our life-drive is infinite and our existence should be infinite since the human drive for self-preservation is the drive maintaining life as infinite.

Life as infinite has been given many names but man has never been able to renounce it without at the same time renouncing his true human essence. With his feeling and awareness of the infinity of life man has also lost power over life. He has split himself and become shallow. He has deprived political life of all deep significance and driven beauty from his social life. He has fallen into a wretched and superficial daily existence out of which are born the powder-puff and coiffure, the white collar, clerical robes and livery, the follies of artificial gentlemen and the crudeness of the rowdy, the upturned nose of the gossiping woman and the shamelessness of the streetwalker, the fighting of our legislators in congress, and the filibuster-politics of Buchanan. The form and name with which mankind most readily designates infinite life is *"immortality of the soul."*

We have acknowledged the indwelling life-force in the human organism as the epitome and unity of all the powers of nature. We have seen that thought as the power of infinity in man allows him no peace if he extricates himself from the total life of nature and humanity and wants to content himself with a small, fragmented, circumscribed place in life.

The power of thought drives him forth, but life, out of which thought comes as its substance, its concentrated ideal content, must win thought back again.

This life, however, is the infinite life of nature, of humanity. The fact that a particular man is at once an "individual" and on the other hand, as thinker, the universal nature or *the essence* of the universe—this is the basic cause of the opposition in human nature. World history unrolls before our eyes the battle which is and will become the transcendence and resolution of this contradiction. The general comprehension of world history as the battle to overcome this contradiction is only a result of modern times, though a similar depth may have been achieved by thinkers of the ancient world and expressed in particular aspects. Only in modern times has cultural history been identified with *history itself.*

The self-preservation drive in man appears to us as much in history as in our civic and social life, with every experience and every particular act we commit, corresponding, in double form, to the contradiction in the human organism. At several points of attention we will find man's self-preservation drive as individual (commonly called egoism) opposed to his self-preservation drive as an embodiment of the whole (commonly called reason, humanity) as much in the falling and rising of races and nations at war as in the buying and selling of a 5 cent article, voting, a few hours with a good book or listening to a lecture or with beer and a game of cards.

Where the self-preservation drive on one side of the opposition heavily contends with the self-preservation drive on the other, men exist either as representatives of humanity, as individuals in whom the mass of mankind sees itself personified and in whom it recognizes its own essence (the so-called great men of history) or as individuals who are thrust out of the community of mankind as criminals. There are periods in the history of peoples in which one or the other direction of the self-preservation drive comes to the fore. Where the former side predominates, we see the rich development of national life. All powers become alive. Agriculture, industry, trade, art, science bloom and the nation exerts a dominating and civilizing influence on the life of other nations.

Ancient Greece with its Athens presents the most beautiful picture of such a development.

Where the other side is preponderant national life deteriorates. Crudeness, the drive for oppression, physical and moral degeneration become general and national life sinks into the healthier life-development of another nation. The Roman empire and its destruction by our forefathers shows us the terrible picture of this process. In any case, the more powerful both sides of this opposition are at the same time in the same political community, *as in this our republic,* so much stronger is the development-process and so much *greater* will be the *nation* and the *individual* resulting from it.

We shall next see how religion, art, science, politics, and economics originate in the self-preservation drive as we see how far and in what ways each of these enterprises of the human spirit is reconciled and in some cases absorbed in the self-preservation drive of the individual (called egoism). This will clarify the developmental stages of humanity and the individual for which religion was and is justified and show where the justification of religion yields and must yield to science.

We have seen that the history of mankind, essentially developmental history, is the cultural history of man, that the self-preservation drive of man presents itself as the thinking essence, the personal totality of the whole life of humanity and nature in a necessary opposition to the self-preservation drive as single in man and nature. In the first form, the self-preservation drive is concerned with man's maintenance as species, as universal individual, and thus with the preservation of the whole. In the second, it appears as the single man striving to maintain himself in the struggle for existence against other individuals and nature. This opposition in the nature of man was perceived in the earliest ages of mankind and in one way or another appears in the consciousness of men as the opposition between God and the devil, heaven and hell, good and evil, light and darkness, spirit and nature, truth and falsehood, reason and sensibility, sacrifice and selfishness. There is no experience or thought of mankind which does not contain in itself this opposition.

While both directions of the self-preservation drive appear mutually exclusive, they are inseparable from one another for they are united in one and the same man. One simple drive for self-preservation is the source of both directions. As man seeks to maintain himself as the whole or universal, as he seeks to maintain God and Reason as his essence, he also finds therein the other side as Devil, as sensuality, etc. He has never created for himself a god without a devil, the good without the evil, spirit without nature, or vice-versa. Every effort to realize fully one side of the preservation-drive without the other ends in the self-destruction of life-power. The life of the individual as well as humanity consists only in working through both opposites to full harmony and unity. This struggle of opposites to reach harmony is the life-process of man, of humanity.

Rational man appears as a result of this struggle. Rational man is nature become reason or mind become nature. In this result God and Devil are recognized as creations of one and the same mind and become simple thought-concepts to man, their creator. Man needed these concepts in his development just like other concepts of opposites such as light and darkness, the whole and its parts, which also exist independently as particular thought-concepts but in actuality belong to one and the same thing as the whole is nothing but its parts, only the parts in their unity, etc. Man has necessarily had these thought-concepts, we say, in order to recognize, find, and become harmony and unity in the infinite manifoldness of the universe and of life.

If we have recognized this briefly-developed opposition in man's self-preservation drive and the necessary interpenetration and unity of both of its directions, it will be easy to grasp the various areas of man's spiritual and material activities and the basic views related to them, their origination and necessity, as *developmental stages* of mankind at which they were necessary and beneficial and equally to recognize *where* this necessity and efficacy cease and become detrimental. Thus we will acknowledge all religions in their historical justification and likewise in their insufficiency to satisfy the life preservation-drive of mankind if the human spirit as knower has looked more deeply into its own essence, if the human spirit as immanent power over nature has penetrated more deeply into its secrets, and if the human spirit as nature's creative power self-consciously restores to human nature what seemed to be blind power. It will become apparent how the same life-need out of which religion arose is also the source of the free philosophical work of the mind. We shall see that religion was deserted by the free mind only because the free mind fights for its life with more powerful weapons than religion can provide. We shall also recognize, however, that we can only achieve this life if we are able to struggle against and overcome mind-limiting prejudices and body-restricting political and social abuses with greater seriousness and energy than religion can muster. He who takes no part in this work, takes no part in life.

THE STATE

Yesterday fourteen fathers of families among us were buried under a collapsed church wall—today their wives who were left behind are helpless widows and their children are given the sympathy reserved for orphans. Not many weeks ago hundreds of workers were buried under the debris of a factory whose state of delapidation was well known to the owners; the lives of these hundreds were deliberately bound to the quicker procurement of the dollar. What happened to those left behind? A collection was taken! Such large-scale butcherings on railroads and steamships have become regular, recurrent facts, and through the death of nearly every one sacrificed to the Moloch of profit another family is thrown into misery or into the arms of charity.

At this moment we see many thousands of men whose existence is based on a shoe factory engaged in a violent struggle with those who, through capital and credit, have in their hands control over this area of production. Why? Because in the present state of civilization, a 12–14 hour working day is no longer sufficient to secure a bare existence for their families from day to day, much less to get property with which to secure their old age so as not to be a burden on their families. As it is with these men, so is it with the overwhelming mass of citizens of the republic. They are overcome in a bitter fight being led against them. Through capital and credit, management has in its hands the factories and businesses necessary for the preservation of the whole. In the area of culture it is the same as in material products. The immense treasures of our knowledge are closed to the majority of citizens. They have an education today which they could have had for the last 1000 years. The great spirits of humanity have not lived for them.

Let us consider the area of law! We have only to look around to see the most shocking contradictions. Yesterday a girl stole an umbrella valued at 75 cents—she will be sentenced to 4 months in jail,—and you need not look far to find palaces or palatial houses whose owners have stolen from their fellow citizens many, many thousands of dollars through bankruptcy and other swindles. We do not want to go further into these contradictions. They can't all be enumerated, but the question immediately arises: is such a condition the characteristic of the state?

If we look back into history, we must answer this question "*Yes.*"

If we take in hand the Constitution of our Republic, the Declaration of the Rights of Man, we will indignantly shout "*No.*"

The Declaration of the Rights of Man and the Constitution have done nothing to produce the present situation. This condition appears as criminal when measured against them. If we examine the bases of the historical European states and our own republic, we find absolute opposition between the two. However, if we examine the conditions of the people living in both, this opposition disappears. There are even some aspects of life in the historical states which could be preferred to our own.

Where is the opposition between the basis of the historical state and the basis of the republic to be found?

All institutions of historical states were designed for the domination of individuals, several or one class, to organize and protect the remaining people, *i.e.*, to hold them in servitude. The basic principle of these states is that men, which with them means subjects, exist not for their own sake but only as means for the rulers. The whole tax system is nothing but a system of tribute developed scientifically, as much as possible by the subjects, to secure the domination of those ruling over them. The whole economy is only a science which makes the subjects more capable of paying taxes. The whole science of law has no other purpose than to demonstrate dependence or submission as a citizen's duty on the basis of apparently general principles. The whole religion of historical states is concentrated in the propositions, "The government is from God" (the legitimacy-principle which the *N.Y. Staatszeitung* claims for the republic in a recent article), "Render unto Caesar that which is Caesar's and to God what is God's," "Submit to the authorities," etc. This is the essence of the historical state which is founded on historical right in contrast to rational right.

What is the essence, the basis, of our republic?

No man has a real right of possession either of men or of the control of the state—men are born equal and remain equal in rights. No man is a means to another but is himself his own end. The free community, the republic, has no historical, no supernatural, no legitimacy-basis but is grounded on reason which in turn rests on free will. As the institutions of the historical state seek to safeguard the domination of individuals, the republic, as a state, is no more and no less than a *mutually based insurance association on a large scale.*

All of our institutions have no other meaning and no other purpose than the mutual assurance of life, of freedom, of education, of the free use of our capabilities, of the unrestricted enjoyment of the value of our labor, of the care of widows and orphans—in a word, all of human goods on which everyone in a free community equally depends and which, through the free cooperation of millions of men, must all be protected from accident and loss.

What more the free community, the republic, has than such mutual assurance it has derived from the historical state. What it has less is the robbery perpetrated by the few on the many. The free community is incorrectly called "state." The state is of a political nature, it has "political justice" and, therefore, also "special privileges" since the two are inseparable. In the republic we need no political authority, because we have no opposing political rights to adjust. Insofar as such rights remain, our republic is still not a republic. In a republic we need only an administrative-organization. To make this concept still more meaningful, one could also refer to it as a partnership of the assembled citizens.

But how did our community get into its present circumstances? Simply because while on a republican basis, on the basis of human rights, a constitution was devised which might leave those rights subject to hostile interpretation, the religious, social, and legal institutions of historical states, the monarchies, were grafted onto human rights and eventually submerged them. But these rights alone are rooted in the earth, and if the European grafts can be snipped from their stem, then will their own fruit-bearing twigs branch forth.

In Europe a man is a rebel and a traitor who, on the basis of human rights, fights political and social injustice. In our republic, he is a bad citizen and a traitor if he does not, on the basis of human rights, fight everything opposing them.

KARL MARX'S SYSTEM OF POLITICAL ECONOMY

We urgently call our readers' attention to the work in political economy whose announcement we reprint in its entirety from *Das Volk* in London.

Knowledge of political economy is the essential prerequisite for the self-government and self-management of a free people. Where such knowledge is lacking, the republican form of government becomes in many respects a mere illusion as is the case with our republic, the United States. Where such knowledge is lacking in the masses, a republic differs from a monarchy only in that the political authority over and exploitation of the people, which in the latter is the hereditary property of certain aristocrats, becomes available as easy plunder to all those who are cunning and crafty enough to use the wants and good feelings of the people to achieve popularity so that through their official position they can get their fingers into the public treasury and even private pockets as well. Only where this knowledge of political economy is lacking is it possible that there can be material want, poor education, degradation of the youth—in a word, "misery"—in a republic.

Those of our readers who have the means should get this book for themselves; we will seek to acquaint the others generally with its main features. If, as we suspect and hope, this work marks a transition-period in political economy, the moment of its appearance is the more significant because it coincides with the time of transition from Europe's old political forms to new ones.

"Under the title 'Contribution to a Critique of Political Economy' the first volume of a writing on political economy by Karl Marx has been published by F. Duncker in Berlin, a writing through which the author's social perspective is for the first time brought into German science. The book is the result of such serious, prolonged, and extensive study that it must be studied deeply before we venture to pass judgment on it. For the present we welcome it as gratifying evidence that the men of *our* party at least did not waste their period of exile, and we take this opportunity to save the editors of German newspapers any further effort to find the name of the expert strategist and author of the pamphlet 'Po and Rhine' in the ranks of the Prussian generals. We hereby share it with them. It was Friedrich Engels who—as the papers of Zabel and Dumont, as well as Binke and other parliamentary greats who appealed to the authority of this strategist, will still recall—was formerly co-editor of the *Neue Rheinische Zeitung*."

From Marx's book we present only the preface, in part, since it contains an interesting sketch of the scientific development to which we owe the book before us:

> I investigate the system of bourgeois economy in the following order: *capital, property in land, wage labor, the state, foreign trade, world market.* Under the first three headings I examine the conditions of the economic life of the three large classes which comprise modern bourgeois society; the relationship of the three remaining headings is immediately apparent.

The first part of the book dealing with capital consists of the following chapters: 1) Commodities. 2) Money or simple circulation. 3) Capital in general. The first two chapters form the context of the present book. The entire material lies before me in the form of monographs, written at long intervals and for self-clarification not publication, and their systematic elaboration on the plans above will depend on circumstances.

My specialized study was in jurisprudence which I pursued, however, only as subordinate to philosophy and history. In 1842–43, as editor of the "Rheinische Zeitung," I first found myself in difficulty when I had to take part in discussions concerning so-called material interests. The proceedings of the Rhine Diet in connection with wood-stealing and the division of landed property; the official controversy about the conditions of the Mosel peasants into which Herr v. Shaper, then president of the Rhine Province, entered with the "Rheinische Zeitung"; and finally the debates on free trade and protection, gave me the first impulse to concern myself with economic questions. At the same time a faint, philosophically-colored echo of French socialism and communism made itself heard in the "Rheinische Zeitung" in those days when the good will "to go ahead" greatly outweighed knowledge of the facts. I declared myself against such bungling but had to admit at once in a controversy with the "Allgemeine Augsburger Zeitung" that my previous studies did not permit me to hazard a judgment on the substance of the French tendencies. When, therefore, the supporters of the "Rheinische Zeitung" conceived the illusion that by a less aggressive policy the paper could be saved from the death sentence pronounced on it, I was happy to take the opportunity to retire from the public stage into my study.

The first work undertaken to resolve the doubt that troubled me was a critical revision of Hegel's philosophy of law; the introduction to that work appeared in the "Deutsch-Französchische Jahrbücher" published in Paris in 1844. My investigation brought me to the conclusion that neither legal relations nor forms of the state could be understood by themselves or explained from the so-called general evolution of the human mind, but that they are rooted in the material conditions of life whose totality Hegel, following the English and French of the 18th century, summed up under the term "civil society," and the anatomy of civil society is to be sought in political economy. The study of the latter, which I had begun in Paris, I continued in Brussels whither I emigrated as a result of Herr Guizot's order of expulsion. The general conclusion at which I arrived and which, once achieved, became the leading thread in my studies, can be briefly summarized as follows: In the social production in which men live they enter into definite and necessary relations independent of their will, productive relations which correspond to a definite stage of the development of their material powers of production. The totality of these productive relations constitutes the economic structure of society, the real foundation on which rise legal and political superstructures and to which definite forms of social consciousness correspond. The mode of production in material life determines the general character of the social, political, and mental processes of life. It is not the consciousness of men that determines their existence, but, on the contrary, their social existence determines their consciousness. At a certain stage of their development the material forces of production in society come into conflict with existing relations of production, or—what is only a legal expression for the same thing—with the property relations within which they had previously moved. From forms of development of the forces of production these relations turn into their fetters. Then comes a period of social revolution. With the change of the economic foundation the entire immense superstructure is more or less rapidly altered.

In considering such transformations the distinction should always be made between the material transformation of the economic conditions of production which can be determined with the precision of natural science, and the legal, political, religious, aesthetic, or philosophical—in short, ideological forms in which men become aware of this conflict and fight it out. Just as our opinion of an individual is not based on what he thinks of himself, so can we not judge of such a period of transformation by its own consciousness; on the contrary, this consciousness must rather be explained from the contradictions of material life, from the existing conflict between the social forces of production and the relations of production. No social order ever disappears before all the productive forces, for which there is room in it, have been developed; and new higher relations of production never appear before the material conditions of their existence have matured in the womb of the old society. Therefore, mankind always takes up only such problems as it can solve; since, looking at the matter more closely, we shall always find that the problem itself arises only when the material conditions necessary for its solution already exist or are at least in the process of formation. In broad outlines we can designate the Asiatic, the ancient, the feudal, and the modern bourgeois methods of production as so many epochs in the progress of the economic formation of society. The bourgeois relations of production are the last antagonistic form of the social process of production—antagonistic not in the sense of individual antagonism, but of one arising from conditions surrounding the life of individuals in society. At the same time the productive forces developing in the womb of bourgeois society create the material conditions for the resolution of that antagonism. With this social formation, therefore, the prehistory of human society ends. [. . .]

Of the scattered writings in which Friedrich Engels and I collaborated to present one or another aspect of our views to the public, I mention here only the "Manifesto of the Communist Party" written by Engels and me together and a "Discourse on Free Trade" written by me. The leading points of our theory were first presented scientifically, though in a polemic form, in my "Poverty of Philosophy, etc." directed against Proudhon published in 1847. An essay on "Wage Labor," written by me in German, and in which I put together my lectures on the subject delivered before the German Workmen's Club at Brussels, was prevented from leaving the hands of the printer by the February revolution and my expulsion from Belgium which followed it as a consequence.

The publication of the "Neue Rheinische Zeitung" in 1848

and 1849, and the events which took place later on, interrupted my economic studies which I could not resume before 1850 in London. The enormous material on the history of political economy which is accumulated in the British Museum; the favorable view which London offers for the observation of bourgeois society; finally, the new stage of development upon which the latter seemed to have entered with the discovery of gold in California and Australia, led me to the decision to resume my studies from the very beginning and work up the new material critically. These studies partly led to what might seem side questions, over which I nevertheless had to stop for longer or shorter periods of time. Especially was the time at my disposal reduced by the imperative necessity of working for a living. My work as contributor to the leading Anglo-American newspaper, the "New York Tribune," at which I have now been engaged for eight years, has caused very great interruption in my studies, since I engage in newspaper work proper only occasionally. Yet articles on important economic events in England and on the continent have formed so large a part of my contributions that I have been obliged to make myself familiar with practical details which lie outside the proper sphere of political economy.

This sketch of the course of my studies in political economy is simply to prove that my views, whatever one may think of them, and no matter how little they agree with the interested prejudices of the ruling classes, are the result of many years of conscientious research. At the entrance to science, however, the same requirement must be put as at the entrance to hell:

> Qui si convien lasciare ogni sospetto
> Ogni vilta convien che qui sia morta.
> [Here all misgiving must thy mind reject.
> Here cowardice must die and be no more. Dante]

ORGANIZATION OF LABOR

In a series of brief articles about the "9 hours strike" in England, we find the following position in the *Pionier:* "The workers should, may, and must unite and organize, *i.e.*, they must not unite temporarily, but construct a permanent, ordered organism. They must draw the capitalists themselves into this organism, not through threats but by way of persuasion."

Quite right! Such an organism, however, can come about only through organization by occupations; otherwise it ceases to be *organism* and becomes a mechanism like our present political arrangement. The majority of the other opinions expressed in the above-mentioned articles reveal the incorrectness of the basic view dominating the whole series. This basic view consists in accepting the position of the laborer as permanent and seeking all improvements only in the shortening of working hours and the increase of wages.

What does it mean, then, that our system of production presupposes the position of the laborer? It means nothing less than that the administration of our system of production forever excludes the application of republican principles. The laborer is not a free member of the producing community. He has no voice in the administration or other affairs of the factory. The only connection between him and that community consists in his bartering away his work, or rather himself, as expensively as possible, by day or week. The worker's relation in the area of economics is the same as that of a subject in the political sphere or that of forced conscience in the ecclesiastical. The principle of free citizenship, the principle of the republic, carried over into the area of economics becomes the principle of the free association of labor.

According to this principle, the unity at the basis of the community is no longer a heterogenous mass of interests of subordinate groups but the various employment associations or, as the Americans say, "Trades Unions" or "Unions of callings" of each city or county. They form an organic community whose essential purpose is protection against the disturbances and irregularities of productive life. No man, regardless of his calling—not even a newspaper writer—is excluded from this labor organization, and no man is hindered by it in his free movement, *i.e.*, any change he might want from one occupation to another. Further, the various associations of each particular occupation organize a general association throughout the republic which Americans call a "National Trades Union." Assembled, these link themselves into one great association, a "National Trades Assembly," which takes the place of the present political state. That would probably fulfill the intent of the words just cited from the *Pionier.*

Would the author of the articles in the *Pionier* agree and if not, what does he understand by a "permanent, ordered organism" of workers in which the capitalists should be admitted? Does the author not see that *"to admit capitalists into the organization,"* if it has a meaning at all, means only "to admit capital into the association, or rather, to convert it into the capital of the association?" His acceptance of the present position of the laborer throws a false light on all the rest of his well-intentioned ideas.

However, if the author asks how we would let capital be absorbed by the labor-association, then it appears that he does not know how to judge correctly the nature of the presently dominant, *so-called* capital. Real capital is the means of labor: machines, factories, conditions of employment, means of communication, and means of transportation, which with improvement have achieved greater capacity for production from the soil, more skillful and scientific means of production, etc., etc. The precious metals, whose value has been determined by their relative cost of production, are actual representatives of capital and as such may also be called capital.

If we now had these forms of capital or their actual representatives, then nothing could be complained about the dependence of labor upon capital, because this capital must be earned, created, and is completely sound. But the presently dominant, *so-called* capital is no actual capital. It is only apparent capital. Most paper money actually represents no capital because the capital does not exist. Similarly, credit certificates do not represent capital because the capital does not really exist. Both represent nothing more nor less than the monopoly given by the state to corporations to disrupt the regular exchange of actual values with illusory values, to raise taxes from employees and workers, and finally, as it happens in fact, not only to snatch away the real capital already produced but even the capital newly produced by labor.

These forms of legislation of the monopolists for the monopolists must be brought to an end. Hence is necessary, first and foremost, an organization of working and useful men according to occupation, an organization opposed to the immense swarm of economic, political, and religious plunderers who not only without any productive activity but even through destructive and poisonous activities have ruined a great part of our national wealth and have appropriated another part for themselves.

Or can the writer in the *Pionier* set forth another definite organizational form for labor? In his articles only impractical wishes are set forth, impractical because they contain a contradiction within themselves.

UNIONS

Gentlemen Mechanics! Fellow Workmen! As I am designated to speak in German to those members of the workingmen fraternity who are of German origin, I wish to expose to you the general idea of what I intend to say to them.

Since the beginning of human history the great masses have been oppressed by the few and have struggled for emancipation. This has been the same under despotical as well as under republican governments. In what consisted that oppression and by what means was it exercised? The oppression existed independently if it had the form of slavery; if that of daily hired labor, it consisted therein that the many were forced to work to the advantage of the few, that the many had no part in the administration of the national wealth they produced, that they were excluded as well from the intellectual as the economical capital of society, that they were only boarders on earth and the few were the landlords.

What were the means of oppression since the beginning of History? Were not the many stronger than the few? Those means consisted therein that the many were kept in a state of disunion by the few, and that in this state they oppressed each other to the benefit of the few, they kept each other in servitude under the few.

By what means did the few succeed to keep the many in disunion? By carefully cultivating prejudices amongst the many, which prejudices hindered them to learn that they all had the same interest in life. Those prejudices were of a religious, national, political, and social nature. Those prejudices created hatred amongst the hard working masses. They killed and oppressed each other because they had different notions of the life after death, because they were proud of one kind of occupation or trade and despised the other. By what means can we therefore succeed in the emancipation of the masses, of the workingmen? First to take out of the hand of the oppressors the means to keep us in disunion, we must break down the ruling prejudices. The first step to conquer the prejudices is to defend our own interest, the interest of our families; to defend the value of our labor by forming the unions, the Trades Unions, and then to connect those unions with each other. Then we will be able to form legislatures, in which all the different callings are represented on which men rely for their living; then we will be able to form a Government by and for the producing and useful classes of society. Then we will be able to say to everyone: Make thyself useful, work, and then thou willst have a happy and independent home, thine children will receive as well as the children of any other man the best education society can give—thou does not want to be afraid of thine old age—thou shallt enjoy, when thou canst work no more.

Therefore fellow workingmen, let us first be unionmen before we are Catholics or Methodists or Philosophers. Let us first be unionmen before we are Americans, Irish, Germans, English, French. Let us first be unionmen before we are moulders, physicians, cabinetmakers, mathematicians, farmers, or teachers or anything else. And when we succeed to create as unionmen a happy life and we come to die, and come as unionmen to heaven, God lord will respect us the more for that and give us a fine and comfortable place. And when by chance we should come to Hell, and we come there as unionmen, I am sure the evil Spirit, the

Devil, will be afraid of us. As unionmen we will turn to advantage the Fires of Hell, we will make of Hell a well organized unionfoundry, and furnish heaven with all the ironwork they want there.

As trades unionmen nothing wrong will withstand us. We are strong enough to conquer all evils and to create all that is just, good, and beautiful. Therefore fellow workingmen let the word be amongst us, UNION FOREVER.

This I will explain in German to the workingmen fraternity who accidentally have been born on the other side of the Atlantic. And let us hope that the day will come when the tie of brotherhood of the producing-class will no more be interrupted either by the Atlantic or the Pacific.

REFERENCE NOTES

I. THE INTELLECTUAL AND SOCIAL MILIEU

1. Cf. H. G. Townsend, *Philosophical Ideas in the United States* (New York: American Book Co., 1934), p. 127; W. G. Muelder, L. Sears, A. Schlabach, *The Development of American Philosophy* (Boston: Houghton Mifflin Co., 1960), p. 212.

2. Alvin S. Haag, "Some German Influences in American Philosophical Thought from 1800 to 1850," unpublished Ph.D. dissertation, Boston University, 1939, p. 194 f.

3. J. W. Alexander, A. B. Dod, and C. Hodge, *Two Articles from the Princeton Review Concerning the Transcendental Philosophy of the Germans and of Cousin* (Cambridge: John Owen, 1840), pp. 27–30.

4. *Ibid.*, pp. 73–79, 90, 100.

5. R. W. Emerson, "The Transcendentalist," quoted in O. B. Frothingham, *Transcendentalism in New England* (New York: Harper Bros., 1956), p. 127.

6. Theodore Parker, *Critical and Miscellaneous Writings* (Boston: James Monroe Co., 1843), pp. 295, 297.

7. See G. W. F. Hegel, *The Phenomenology of Mind*, trans. J. B. Baillie (New York: The Macmillan Co., 1931), p. 762 ff.; David Friedrich Strauss, *The Life of Jesus*, trans. George Eliot [Marian Evans] (London: Swan Sonnenschein and Co., 1913), pp. 65, 86.

8. Theodore Parker, "The Transient and Permanent in Christianity" in Perry Miller, ed., *The American Transcendentalist* (New York: Doubleday and Co., 1957), p. 116. Cf. Parker, *A Discourse of Matters Pertaining to Religion* (Boston: Little and Brown, 1842), pp. 357–361.

9. John Weiss, *Life and Correspondence of Theodore Parker* (New York: D. Appleton and Co., 1864), I, 166, 169. Cf. Parker,

op. cit., p. 91; H. A. Pochmann, *German Culture in America* (Madison: University of Wisconsin Press, 1957), p. 219 ff.

10. See Howard J. B. Ziegler, *Frederick Augustus Rauch, American Hegelian* (Lancaster, Pa.: Franklin and Marshall College, 1953), pp. 21–34, 36 f.; F. A. Rauch, *Psychology; or, A View of the Human Soul; Including Anthropology* (New York: M. W. Dodd, 1841), p. vii ff.

11. Rauch, *op. cit.*, p. vi.

12. *Ibid.*, p. 287. Cf. G. W. F. Hegel, "Naturphilosophie," *Encyclopädie der philosophischen Wissenschaften* (Leipzig: Felix Meiner, 1930), Secs. 247–248.

13. Rauch, *op. cit.*, p. 304 f. Cf. G. W. F. Hegel, *Philosophy of Mind*, trans. William Wallace (Oxford: At the Clarendon Press, 1894), Sec. 474.

14. Rauch, *op. cit.*, p. 344. Cf. G. W. F. Hegel, *The Philosophy of History*, trans. J. Sibree (New York: Dover Publications, 1956), p. 9 f., 19, 64.

15. Rauch, *op. cit.*, p. iv.

16. J. W. Nevin, "Eulogium on Dr. Rauch" in Theodore Appel, *The Life and Work of John Williamson Nevin* (Philadelphia: Reformed Church Publication House, 1889), p. 141 f.

17. James Murdock, *Sketches of Modern Philosophy, Especially Among the Germans* (Hartford: John Wells, 1842), p. 120.

18. See *ibid.*, pp. 122–128.

19. Asa Mahan, *A System of Intellectual Philosophy* (New York: Saxton and Miles, 1845), p. 261. Cf. *ibid.*, pp. 262–269, 274–278.

20. See Haag, *op. cit.*, pp. 207–218.

21. F. H. Hedge, *Prose Writers of Germany* (Philadelphia: Carey and Hart, 1847), p. 446. Cf. Pochmann, *op. cit.*, p. 662 f.; Haag, *op. cit.*, p. 211 f.

22. See Pochmann, *op. cit.*, pp. 257–281.

23. See W. T. Harris, "Philosophy in Outline," *Journal of Speculative Philosophy*, 17 (1883), p. 300 f. Cf. W. T. Harris, *Hegel's Logic: A Book on the Genesis of the Categories of the Mind* (Chicago: S. C. Griggs and Co., 1890), pp. xv, 137–140.

24. See Harris, "Philosophy in Outline," p. 310 ff. Cf. Harris, *Hegel's Logic*, pp. 109–114.

25. See "Philosophy in Outline," p. 354 f. Cf. Harris, "The Concrete and the Abstract," *Journal of Speculative Philosophy*, 5 (1871), p. 5; Kurt Leidecker, *Yankee Teacher, The Life of William Torrey Harris* (New York: Philosophical Library, 1946), pp. 283, 540 ff., 286–293.

26. Moncure Conway, *Autobiography, Memories and Experiences*, (New York: Houghton, Mifflin and Co., 1904), I, 255. Cf. Carl Wittke, "The Germans of Cincinnati," *Bulletin of the Historical and*

Philosophical Society of Ohio [now entitled *Bulletin of the Cincinnati Historical Society*], 20 (1962), pp. 3–11.

27. See Charles A. and Mary R. Beard, *A Basic History of the United States* (Philadelphia: Blakiston Co., 1944), pp. 201–208.

28. See Wilbur D. Jones, "Some Cincinnati German Societies A Century Ago," *Bulletin of the Historical and Philosophical Society of Ohio,* 20 (1962), p. 41 ff.; William A. Baughin, "Bullets and Ballots: The Election Day Riots of 1855," *Bulletin of the Historical and Philosophical Society of Ohio,* 21 (1963), p. 269 f.

29. Philip Schaaf, *America* (Cambridge: Harvard University Press, 1961), p. 55. Cf. *ibid.,* pp. xix, 37–41, where Schaaf, who shared Hegel's conception of historical development, sees "true freedom"—rational self-determination through order—as characteristic of America and well illustrated in the Maine prohibition law.

30. Hegel, *Grundlinien der Philosophie des Rechts,* Secs. 243–244. Cf. Hegel, *Philosophy of Right,* trans. K. M. Knox (Oxford: At the Clarendon Press, 1953), p. 149 f.

II. EVOLUTIONARY IDEALISM OF THE YOUNG STALLO

1. Biographical details in this chapter, unless otherwise noted, are from H. A. Rattermann, "Johann Bernhard Stallo, Deutsch-Amerikanischer Philosoph, Jurist und Staatsmann," *Gesammelte Werke* (Cincinnati: Selbstverlag der Verfasser, 1911), Bd. XII, pp. 11–55; W. J. Youmans, "Sketch of J. B. Stallo," *Popular Science Monthly,* 34 (1888–1889), pp. 548–555; G. D. Wilkinson, "John B. Stallo's Criticism of Physical Science," unpublished Ph.D. dissertation, Columbia University, 1941, pp. 5–25.

2. John Bernard Stallo, "Psychologie," (Vechta, ca. 1838), manuscript in Cincinnati Public Library. I am indebted to Dr. Harry Bahrick (Psychology, Ohio Wesleyan University) for aid in deciphering and translating this manuscript.

3. Überall Er, der das Weltall lenket,
In dem jedes Dasein sich versenket;
Überall auch Seine Harmonie!
Wenn Gestirne ihrer Bahnen wallen:
In den zügen ihrer Feuerstrahlen
Schwebt der Gottheit Wesen, hehr wie sie.

4. J. B. Stallo, *The General Principles of the Philosophy of Nature, With an Outline of Some of Its Recent Developments Among the Germans, Embracing the Philosophical Systems of Schelling and Hegel, and Oken's System of Nature* (Boston: William Crosby and H. P. Nichols, 1848), pp. vii–viii.

5. *Ibid.,* p. 13.

6. *Ibid.,* p. 16.

7. *Ibid.*, p. 24.
8. *Ibid.*, p. 46.
9. *Ibid.*, p. 43. Cf. G. W. F. Hegel, *Philosophy of History*, trans. J. Sibree (New York: Dover Publications, 1956), p. 17.
10. Stallo, *General Principles*, p. 44.
11. *Ibid.*, p. 59.
12. *Ibid.*, p. 47.
13. *Ibid.*, p. 131.
14. *Ibid.*, p. 132.
15. *Ibid.*, p. 354.
16. *Ibid.*, p. 134.
17. *Ibid.*, p. 357.
18. *Ibid.*, p. 159.
19. *Ibid.*, p. 166.
20. *Ibid.*, p. 517 f.
21. *Ibid.*, p. 170.
22. *Ibid.*, p. 337.
23. Rattermann, *op. cit.*, p. 34. See Wilkinson, *op. cit.*, p. 15; Stallo, *Concepts and Theories of Modern Physics* (Cambridge: Harvard University Press, 1960), p. 6.
24. See Youmans, *op. cit.*, p. 550 f.; T. S. Hunt, *The Domain of Physiology* (Washington, 1881), p. 23; T. S. Hunt, *A New Basis for Chemistry* (Boston, 1888), p. vii.
25. See Kurt Leidecker, *Yankee Teacher, The Life of William Torrey Harris* (New York: Philosophical Library, 1946), p. 321; J. Lowenberg, ed., *Hegel Selections* (New York: Charles Scribner's Sons, 1929), p. 102, *et passim;* Youmans, *op. cit.*, p. 553; H. A. Pochmann, *German Culture in America* (Madison: University of Wisconsin Press, 1957), p. 646.
26. George Ripley, "*General Principles* . . . by J. B. Stallo," *The Harbinger*, 4 (1848), p. 150 f. quoted in C. L. F. Gohdes, *The Periodicals of American Transcendentalism* (Durham, N.C.: Duke University Press, 1931), p. 120; J. Elliot Cabot, "J. B. Stallo's *General Principles*," *Massachusetts Quarterly Review*, 1 (1848), p. 265; quoted in Pochmann, *op. cit.*, p. 245.
27. Pochmann, *op. cit.*, p. 199.
28. E. W. Emerson and W. E. Emerson, eds., *Journals of Ralph Waldo Emerson* (Boston: Houghton Mifflin Co., 1912), VIII, 77; MS Journal in Pochmann, *op. cit.*, p. 200.
29. R. W. Emerson, *Complete Works*, Centenary Edition, ed. E. W. Emerson (Boston: Houghton Mifflin Co., 1875), VI, 22, 31, 49.
30. *Ibid.*, VII, 4–11.
31. See *Journals of Ralph Waldo Emerson*, X, 460; VIII, 69;

MS Journals in Pochmann, *op. cit.*, p. 200. Cf. Stallo, *General Principles*, pp. 335–344, 400–407 on "The Absolute."

32. *Journals of Ralph Waldo Emerson*, X, 423.

33. Emil Klauprecht, *Deutsche Chronik in der Geschichte des Ohio-Thales* (Cincinnati: G. Hof and M. A. Jacobi, 1864), p. 182.

34. See J. B. Stallo, *Reden, Abhandlungen und Briefe* (New York: E. Steiger and Co., 1893), pp. 3–9.

35. See *ibid.*, pp. 11–15.

36. See *ibid.*, p. 18 ff.

37. See *ibid.*, p. 77 f.

38. See *ibid.*, p. 82 f.

39. *Ibid.*, p. 86.

40. *Ibid.*, p. 100.

41. *Ibid.*, p. 102.

42. See Stallo, *General Principles*, pp. 46, 360 ff.

43. See Stallo, *Reden*, p. 41 f.

III. PRINCIPLES OF FREEDOM AND PHENOMENALISM IN STALLO'S MATURE YEARS

1. Biographical details in this chapter, unless noted otherwise, are from H. A. Rattermann, "Johann Bernhard Stallo, Deutsch-Amerikanischer Philosoph, Jurist und Staatsmann," *Gesammelte Werke* (Cincinnati: Selbstverlag des Verfassers, 1911), Bd. XII, pp. 11–55; W. J. Youmans, "Sketch of J. B. Stallo," *Popular Science Monthly*, 34 (1888–1889), pp. 548–555; G. D. Wilkinson, "John B. Stallo's Criticism of Physical Science," unpublished Ph.D. dissertation, Columbia University, 1951, pp. 5–25.

2. See Carl Wittke, "Ninth Ohio Volunteers," *Ohio Archaeological and Historical Publications*, 35 (1926), pp. 409–413; J. B. Stallo, *Reden, Abhandlungen und Briefe* (New York: E. Steiger and Co., 1893), p. 268.

3. See Stallo, *op. cit.*, pp. 214 ff., 227 ff., 405–418.

4. See Leo Pfeffer, *Church, State, and Freedom* (Boston: Beacon Press, 1953), p. 379 ff. Cf. Nancy R. Hamant, "Religion in the Cincinnati Schools," *Ohio Historical and Philosophical Society Bulletin*, 21 (1963), pp. 239–251.

5. See Gustav Körner, *Das Deutsche Element* (New York: Steiger Co., 1884), p. 222 f.

6. Stallo, *op. cit.*, p. 176 f.

7. *Ibid.*, p. 185; cf. *ibid.*, p. 181 f., 432 f., 184, 435.

8. *Ibid.*, p. 272 f.

9. From "Board of Education of Cincinnati vs. Minor," 23 Ohio St. 211 (1872), quoted in Pfeffer, *op. cit.*, p. 380.

10. Stallo, "Remarks," *Tilden, Hendricks and Reform* (Cincinnati: Democratic Ratification Meeting, 1876), p. 12 f. Cf. Stallo, *Reden, Abhandlungen und Briefe*, pp. 436–464.

11. J. B. Stallo, *State Creeds and Their Modern Apostles* (Cincinnati: Clarke and Co., 1872), p. iii. The copy of this booklet in the Andover-Harvard Theological Library once belonged to Francis Ellingwood Abbot as a gift of the author, indicating that Stallo was in contact with a leading figure among the "free religionists" and those devoted to "the scientific study of theology."

12. *Ibid.*, p. v, 21 f.

13. *Ibid.*, p. 19.

14. *Ibid.*, p. 25.

15. *Ibid.*, p. 23 f.

16. *Ibid.*, p. 34.

17. Stallo, *Reden, Abhandlungen und Briefe*, p. 214 f.

18. Stallo, *State Creeds*, p. 35.

19. *Ibid.*, p. 37.

20. See P. W. Bridgman, "Introduction" to J. B. Stallo, *Concepts and Thories of Modern Physics* (Cambridge: Harvard University Press, 1960), p. viii. Cf. Rattermann, *op. cit.*, p. 32, and Wilkinson, *op. cit.*, p. 73.

21. Stallo, *op. cit.*, pp. 3, 5. Cf. *ibid.*, pp. 10, 41.

22. *Ibid.*, p. 60 f.

23. *Ibid.*, pp. 4, 14.

24. *Ibid.*, p. 114 f.

25. *Ibid.*, p. 116 f.

26. *Ibid.*, pp. 112, 133 f., 141.

27. J. B. Stallo, *The Concepts and Theories of Modern Physics* (London: Kegan Paul, Trench and Co., 1882), p. 133 ff.

28. Cf. Stallo, *The Concepts and Theories of Modern Physics* (Cambridge: Harvard University Press, 1960), p. 29; Stallo, "Speculative Science," *Popular Science Monthly*, 21 (1882), p. 151 f. Stallo referred particularly to Max Müller in connection with his interest in linguistics. Cf. Müller, *Lectures on The Science of Language* (New York: Charles Scribner, 1862), pp. vii, 97, 111, 135–145, 377 f. on the relation of philosophy to language and particularly p. 381 f. stating, "Language and thought are inseparable. Words without thought are dead sounds; thoughts without words are nothing. To think is to speak low; to speak is to think aloud. The word is the thought incarnate."

29. See Stallo, *The Concepts and Theories of Modern Physics* (Cambridge: Harvard University Press, 1960), p. 159 f.

30. See *ibid.*, pp. 204–214.

31. *Ibid.*, p. 201.

32. *Ibid.*, p. 216.

33. *Ibid.*, p. 257.
34. *Ibid.*, p. 285 f.
35. Stallo, *Concepts and Theories* (London: Kegan Paul, Trench and Co., 1882), p. 295 f. (Cambridge: Harvard University Press, 1960), p. 302.
36. See W. J. Youmans, review of *Concepts and Theories, Popular Science Monthly*, 20 (Feb. 1882), pp. 557–560; W. T. Harris, "Notes and Discussions," *Journal of Speculative Philosophy*, 7 (1873), p. 90; W. J. Youmans, "Sketch of J. B. Stallo," *Popular Science Monthly*, 34 (1888–1889), p. 553.
37. See P. G. Tait, "Modern Physics," *Nature*, 26 (1882), p. 521 f.; Youmans, *op. cit.*, p. 553; Stallo, "Speculative Science," *Popular Science Monthly*, 21 (1882), pp. 145–164.
38. T. J. McCormack, "John Bernhard Stallo: American Citizen, Jurist, Philosopher," *Open Court*, 14 (1900), p. 276.
39. See Joergen Joergensen, *The Development of Logical Empiricism* (Chicago: University of Chicago Press, 1951), pp. 4–11; Philip Frank, *Modern Science and Its Philosophy* (New York: Collier Books, 1961), pp. 13–61, 246, 250.
40. Ernst Mach, "Vorwort" (1901), J. B. Stallo, *Die Begriffe und Theorien der Modernen Physik*, trans. Hans Kleinpeter (Leipzig: Johann Barth, 1911), p. xiii. Cf. *ibid.*, pp. iii, xii f.
41. *The Education of Henry Adams* (New York: Modern Library, 1931), pp. 344, 449, 452.
42. H. Poincaré, *The Foundations of Science* (Lancaster, Pa.: Science Press, 1913, 1946), p. 10.
43. Wilkinson, *op. cit.*, pp. 34, 123, 130–136; McCormack, *op. cit.*, p. 277; Mach, *op. cit.*, p. x.
44. See P. W. Bridgman, *op. cit.*, p. xvi f.; Stillman Drake, "J. B. Stallo and the Critique of Classical Physics," *Men and Movements In the History of Science* (Seattle: University of Washington Press, 1959), pp. 22–37.
45. Stallo, *Concepts and Theories*, p. 6 f.
46. *Ibid.*, p. 178.
47. Ernst Cassirer, *The Problem of Knowledge*, trans. W. Woglom and C. W. Hendel (New Haven: Yale University Press, 1950), p. 101.
48. See Stallo, *General Principles of the Philosophy of Nature*, pp. 131–135, 354–357; Hegel, *Phenomenology of Mind*, trans. J. B. Baillie, pp. 168–178.
49. See Mach, *op. cit.*, pp. v-ix.
50. Bridgman, *op. cit.*, p. xxviii.

51. Stallo, *Concepts and Theories of Modern Physics* (New York: D. Appleton and Co., 1881), p. 8.

52. I am indebted to Drs. Harry Bahrick and Kurt Guddat (Psychology and German, Ohio Wesleyan University) for aid in deciphering and translating the old script of Stallo's letters and to the Ernst-Mach-Institut, Freiburg i. Br., Deutsche Bundesrepublik, for providing me with microfilm copies of these hitherto unpublished letters.

IV. PETER KAUFMANN ON SOCIAL PERFECTION AND DIALECTICS

1. Biographical details are from Ernest Wesson, "The Peter Kaufmann Collection," Typescript (Mansfield, Ohio: Midland Rare Book Co., 1956) and Gustav Körner, *Das Deutsche Element* (New York: Steiger and Co., 1884), pp. 228–229. At a number of points, as noted, these sources have been supplemented and corrected from manuscripts and papers in the Peter Kaufmann Collection, Library of the Ohio Historical Society, Columbus, Ohio.

2. Peter Kaufmann, *Betrachtung über den Menschen* (Philadelphia: Conrad Zentler, 1825), p. 13.

3. *Ibid.*, p. 89; cf. *ibid.*, p. 92.

4. See *ibid.*, p. 168 ff.

5. See *ibid.*, pp. 187, 241.

6. See Everett Webber, *Escape to Utopia* (New York: Hastings House, 1959), pp. 100–113.

7. Peter Kaufmann, Letter to Eda B. Reim, 23 January 1827, Peter Kaufmann Collection, Box 2, with minor editorial emendations.

8. Peter Kaufmann, *et al.*, "Constitution of the Society of United Germans at Teutonia," *Westlicher Beobachter*, 2 (28 Nov. 1827), p. 1, and bilingual handbill, Peter Kaufmann Collection, Box 2.

9. Webber, *op. cit.*, p. 108 ff.

10. Peter Kaufmann, *A Treatise on American Popular Education* (Canton: Kaufmann and Co., 1839), p. 3 ff.

11. *Ibid.*, p. 5.

12. *Ibid.*, p. 9 f.

13. *Ibid.*, p. 12.

14. *Ibid.*, p. 48.

15. *Ibid.*, p. 26.

16. Book orders, May 1, 1840, and September 19, 1840, Peter Kaufmann Collection, Box 6.

17. See H. U. Johnson, "History of the Trumbull Phalanx," *Western Reserve Chronicle*, 81 (May 5, 1897), p. 9; Benjamin Robbins, *et al.*, "Constitution of the Trumbull Phalanx." (From a typed copy in possession of Mr. Almon Rood of Phalanx Mills who lived on the

property belonging to the Phalanx, purchased by his father and cousin in 1866), Arts. III–IV, VI.

18. Letter from Electa Newton, 29 August 1847, Peter Kaufmann Collection, Box 7, with slight editorial emendations.

19. See D. D. Egbert and S. Persons, eds., *Socialism in American Life* (Princeton: Princeton University Press, 1952), I, 193 f.

20. Andrew Smolnikar, Announcement, Peter Kaufmann Collection, Box 7.

21. Letter to the Rev. Wm. R. [sic] Channing, Boston, March 1847, Peter Kaufmann Collection, Box 7, with slight editorial emendations.

22. Peter Kaufmann, *The Temple of Truth or The Science of Ever-Progressing Knowledge; containing the foundation and elements of a system for arriving at absolute certainty in all things; being a message of never-ending joy, and the abiding herald of better times to all men of a good will, or desirous of acquiring it. –Rev., xiv, 6.* (The preface was signed from "Cincinnati, Ohio, July 4, 1858." On the facing flyleaf of the copy in Harvard's Widener Library there appears the inscription: "To Rev. M. Conway By the Author Sept. 14 '59.")

23. Kaufmann, *Temple of Truth,* p. iii with editorial emendations of punctuation, italicization, and capitalization for greater ease in reading here and in all subsequent quotations.

24. *Ibid.,* p. 21 ff.

25. *Ibid.,* p. 48.

26. *Ibid.,* p. 49.

27. See *ibid.,* p. 84 ff.

28. See *ibid.,* p. 88.

29. G. W. F. Hegel, *Logic,* trans. William Wallace (Oxford: At the Clarendon Press, 1892), Sec. 20. See J. Lowenberg, *Hegel Selections* (New York: Charles Scribner's Sons, 1929), p. 99 f.

30. Kaufmann, *Temple of Truth,* p. 174.

31. *Ibid.,* p. 171.

32. *Ibid.,* p. 168.

33. Hegel, *op. cit.,* Sec. 162. Cf. *ibid.,* Sec. 24.

34. Kaufmann, *Temple of Truth,* p. 181.

35. *Ibid.,* p. 183.

36. See *ibid.,* pp. 206, 230 ff.

37. See *ibid.,* p. 197.

38. *Ibid.,* p. 284.

39. Körner, *op. cit.,* p. 228. Cf. Joseph Blau, "Food for Middlewestern Thought" in John J. Murray, ed., *The Heritage of the Middle West* (Norman, Oklahoma: University of Oklahoma Press, 1958), p. 188 asserting that much in *The Temple of Truth* suggests its basic source was Hegel's *Philosophy of History,* though Hegel was mentioned by

name only once. As noted earlier, however, Kaufmann studied Hegel's *Logic,* and his main debt to Hegel centered on the "concrete universal" and "dialectic."

40. Letter from William Mann, Superior, Wisconsin, December 20, 1858, Peter Kaufmann Collection, Box 9.

41. R. L. Rusk, ed., *Letters of Ralph Waldo Emerson* (New York: Columbia University Press, 1939), V, 73.

42. *Ibid.,* 122 f.

43. Clippings of reviews in book of subscribers to *The Temple of Truth,* Peter Kaufmann Collection, Box 9.

44. *Constitution of the Workingmen's Union of Stark County* (Canton, Ohio: Office des "Deutschen in Ohio," 1861), p. 6.

45. *Ibid.,* pp. 10, 17 f., 22.

46. Letter from Col. Robert McCook, 24 July 1862, from Cincinnati before leaving to rejoin his regiment in Kentucky after recovery from wounds, Peter Kaufmann Collection, Box 9.

V. RELIGIOUS NATURALISM AND REFORM IN THE THOUGHT OF MONCURE CONWAY

1. Biographical details in this chapter, unless otherwise noted, are from Moncure Daniel Conway, *Autobiography, Memories and Experiences,* 2 vols. (New York: Houghton Mifflin and Co., 1904), and Mary Elizabeth Burtis, *Moncure Conway* (New Brunswick, N.J.: Rutgers University Press, 1952).

2. See H. A. Pochmann, *German Thought In America* (Madison: University of Wisconsin Press, 1957), pp. 165–168.

3. See Samuel Taylor Coleridge, *The Complete Works* (New York: Harper and Brothers, 1853), pp. 241–253.

4. *Ibid.,* p. 367. Cf. Pochmann, *op. cit.,* pp. 90–95; Harold Höffding, *A History of Modern Philosophy,* trans. B. E. Meyer (New York: The Macmillan Co., 1900), II, 374–377.

5. See M. D. Conway, "Emerson," London, 1873, manuscript in Conway Collection, Dickinson College Library.

6. Conway, "Theodore Parker," Cincinnati, Ohio, 1860, manuscript in Conway Collection, Columbia University Library, printed with some revisions in *The Dial,* 1 (1860), p. 446 f.

7. Conway, "The Old and the New," Washington, D.C., 1855; "What Is Man That Thou Art Mindful of Him?" Washington, D.C., 1856, manuscript in Conway Collection, Columbia University Library.

8. Conway, *Autobiography,* I, 269.

9. David Mead, "Theodore Parker in Ohio," *Northwest Ohio Quarterly,* 21 (1949), p. 19.

10. Conway, "Art Thou He that Should Come or Do We Look for

Another," Cincinnati, n.d. and London (omitting quoted passage), 1865, manuscript in Conway Collection, Columbia University Library.

11. See O. B. Frothingham, *Transcendentalism in New England,* Intro. Sydney E. Ahlstrom (New York: Harper and Brothers, 1959), pp. 43–46, 356, xviii.

12. See Frothingham, "The Christianity of Christ," *The Dial,* 1 (1860), pp. 742, 746, 755 f.

13. Conway, "A Word to our Readers," *The Dial,* 1 (1860), p. 11.

14. Conway, "The Two Premiers, Gladstone and Strauss," London, 1873, manuscript in Conway Collection, Columbia University Library.

15. Conway, "David Friedrich Strauss," *The Index,* 2 (April 1874), p. 158.

16. *Ibid.*

17. *Ibid.*

18. *Ibid.,* p. 159.

19. Hegel, *Phenomenology of the Spirit,* trans. by J. B. Baillie, rev. by C. J. Friedrich in *The Philosophy of Hegel* (New York: Modern Library, 1954), p. 515 f.

20. Strauss, *The Life of Jesus,* trans. George Eliot [Marian Evans] (London: Swan Sonnenschien and Co., 1906), p. 65. Cf. *ibid.,* p. 68.

21. Nast, *A Commentary on the Gospels of Matthew and Mark* (Cincinnati: Poe and Hitchcock, 1864; German edition, 1860), p. 83. Cf. L. D. Easton, "German Philosophy in Nineteenth Century Cincinnati," *Bulletin of the Ohio Historical and Philosophical Society,* 20 (1962), p. 22 ff.

22. Conway, *Autobiography,* I, 280 f. Cf. Conway, "Letter to Charles Eliot Norton," 4 April 1903, manuscript in Conway Collection, Dickinson College Library.

23. Conway, "A Discourse [On Truth]," Cincinnati, 1859, manuscript in Conway Collection, Columbia University Library.

24. Conway, *Autobiography,* I, 281 f.

25. "On the Origin of the Species," *The Dial,* 1 (1860), p. 197.

26. Conway, "David Friedrich Strauss," *The Index* (2 April 1874), p. 159 from D. F. Strauss, *The Old Faith and the New,* trans. Mathilde Blind (New York: Henry Holt and Company, 1874), p. 162 ff.

27. Cf. Gladstone's copy of Conway's address on Strauss in the Conway Collection, Dickinson College Library, with marginal markings bearing on Conway's charge of misrepresentation, Strauss's endorsement of the theory of evolution, and Hegel's "fiery radicalism."

28. Conway, *op. cit.,* p. 159.

29. *Ibid.* Cf. Conway, *Autobiography,* II, 13 f.

30. Conway, "David Friedrich Strauss," *The Index* (2 April 1874), p. 159. Cf. Strauss, *op. cit.*, Secs. 76–82.

31. Conway, "Socinius," Cincinnati, 1857, manuscript in Conway Collection, Columbia University Library.

32. Conway, "The Skeptic," *Tracts for Today* (Cincinnati: Truman and Spofford, 1858), p. 40 f.

33. See Conway, *Tracts for Today*, pp. 268, 301 ff.

34. Conway, "Hold Fast the Form of Sound Words," manuscript in Conway Collection, Columbia University Library, pp. 1–5. "The Word," *The Dial*, 1 (1860), p. 98 f. Cf. Matilda Jones, Letter to Miss Dewey, Washington, D.C., 1855, typescript in Conway Collection, Dickinson College Library.

35. *The Dial*, 1 (1860), p. 99. Cf. Conway, "Hold Fast the Form of Sound Words," pp. 22–25.

36. *Testimonies Concerning Slavery* (London, 1864), p. 76 quoted in Burtis, *op. cit.*, p. 115. Cf. Conway, *Addresses and Reprints* (New York: Houghton Mifflin Co., 1909), pp. 154–159.

37. Mark E. Marsden, "General Minutes, Finsbury Chapel South Place," Jan. 29, 1865, manuscript in South Place Ethical Society, Red Lion Square, London.

38. Marsden, *op. cit.*, Feb. 23, 1869.

39. See Scrapbook of Newspaper Clippings, Conway Collection, Columbia University Library.

40. Conway, "Two Photographs," *The Radical*, 1 (August, 1866), p. 489. Cf. Karl Blind, Letters to Conway, manuscripts in Conway Collection, Columbia University Library; Blind, Marsden, *et al.*, Letter of Invitation to Lectures, Nov. 18, 1865, Conway Papers in South Place Ethical Society, Red Lion Square, London.

41. Conway, "Humboldt," Sept. 12, 1869, manuscript in Conway Collection, Columbia University Library.

42. Conway, "The Lesson of the War," Sept. 4, 1870, manuscript in Conway Collection, Columbia University Library.

43. See Karl Marx and Friedrich Engels, *Letters to Americans* (New York: International Publishers, 1953), p. 83 f; Conway, *Autobiography*, II, 268 ff.

44. See Conway, *Republican Superstitions* (London: King and Co., 1872), pp. 1–8, 10–17, 48–53 and "Sursum Corda," *The Radical*, 1 (April, 1866), pp. 291–294.

45. Conway, *Republican Superstitions*, p. 98.

46. See Conway, "The Theist's Problem and Task," *The Radical*, 10 (1872), p. 427 f. and "Huxley on Berkeley," *The Radical*, 9 (1871), p. 179 f.

47. See Strauss, *op. cit.*, Sec. 39.

48. Ludwig Feuerbach, *Essence of Christianity*, trans. George Eliot

[Marian Evans] (New York: Harper and Bros., 1957), pp. II, 29 f. Cf. *ibid.*, p. 285 f.; Conway, "Feuerbach," Jan. 22, 1882, manuscript in Conway Collection, Columbia University Library.

49. Conway, *op. cit.*, Cf. Feuerbach, *op. cit.*, p. 269.

50. Conway, *Autobiography*, II, 382 f.

51. Conway, "Individual and Species," *Lessons for the Day* (London: E. W. Allen, 1882), I, 63, *et passim*. Cf. *ibid.*, II, 11, 135–143.

52. Conway, *What Is the Religion of Humanity?* (London: Waterlow and Sons, 1880), p. 9, *et passim*.

53. Conway, *Addresses and Reprints* 1850–1907 (New York: Houghton Mifflin Co., 1909), p. 367; *Autobiography*, II, 14.

VI. AUGUST WILLICH'S LEFT-HEGELIAN SOCIALISM

1. Herbert Spruth, *Sammlung Pom. Stammreihen* (Berlin-Dahlem), Familienblatt Willich.

2. Charles Stewart, "Biographical Notes" in typescript, Milwaukee Public Library, Milwaukee, Wisconsin.

3. See Charles Stewart, *op. cit.;* Moncure Conway, *Autobiography* (New York: Houghton Mifflin and Co., 1904), I, 269; *Marx-Engels Gesamtausgabe*, ed. D. Rjazanov (Berlin: Marx-Engels Verlag, 1929), Abt. III, Bd. 1, p. 520, *et passim;* Friedrich Engels, Letter to August Bebel, 17 February 1890, International Institute for Social History (Amsterdam).

4. See Harold Höffding, *History of Modern Philosophy*, trans. B. E. *Meyer* (New York: Macmillan Co., 1900), II, 199.

5. Friedrich von Beust in *Westdeutschen Zeitung* quoted in E. Czobel, "Zur Geschichte des Kommunistenbundes," *Archiv für die Geschichte des Sozialismus und der Arbeiterbewegung*, 11 (1925), p. 316.

6. See B. Nikolajewsky, "August Willich, Ein Soldat der Revolution von 1848," *Der Abend* (Berlin), 4 May 1931.

7. August Willich, *Im preussischen Heere! Ein Disciplinarverfahren gegen Premier-Lieutenant v. Willich . . . mit Vor- und Nachwort* (Mannheim: Verlag von Heinrich Hoff, 1848), p. ix.

8. *Ibid.*, p. 28 f.

9. *Ibid.*, p. 38.

10. *Ibid.*, p. 47.

11. See *ibid.*, p. 50.

12. See Auguste Cornu, "German Utopianism: 'True' Socialism," *Science and Society*, 12 (1948), p. 101 f.; L. D. Easton, "Alienation and History in the Early Marx," *Philosophy and Phenomenological Research*, 22 (1961), pp. 193–199, 203 f.

13. See Czobel, *op. cit.*, pp. 307, 325.

14. See Nikolajewsky, *op. cit.;* F. Rude, *Les réfugiés allemands à Besançon* (Besançon: Millot Frêres, 1939), p. 9 f.; B. Nicolaievsky and O. Maenchen-Helfen, *Karl Marx, Man and Fighter,* trans. G. David and E. Mosbacher (Philadelphia: Lippincott Co., 1936), p. 187 f.

15. *Marx-Engels Gesamtausgabe,* ed. D. Rjazanov, Abt. III, Bd. 1, p. 110. Cf. Marx-Engels, *The Communist Manifesto* with Introduction and Explanatory Notes by D. Ryazanoff, trans. E. and C. Paul (London: Martin Lawrence, 1930), pp. 213–223.

16. Marx and Engels, *Werke* (Berlin: Dietz Verlag, 1960), Bd. 7, pp. 247 f., 249, 252. Cf. Franz Mehring, *Karl Marx,* trans. E. Fitzgerald (New York: Covici Friede, 1939), p. 229 f.

17. From "Supplement" to D. Rjazanov, "Zur Frage des Verhältnisses von Marx zu Blanqui," *Unter dem Banner des Marxismus,* 2 (1938), p. 144 f. Cf. Marx and Engels, *Werke,* Bd. 7, pp. 553 f., 615; H. Draper, "Marx and the dictatorship of the proletariat," *Études de Marxologie,* 6 (1962), p. 35 f.

18. "Sitzung der Central Behörde vom 15 Septbr 1850" in B. Nicolaievsky, "Toward a History of the Communist League, 1847–1852," *International Review of Social History,* 2 (1956), p. 249. Cf. Karl Marx, *Enthüllungen über den Kommunistenprozess zu Köln* (Berlin: Dietz Verlag, 1952), p. 39.

19. Wilhelm Liebknecht, "Reminiscences of Marx" in *Reminiscences of Marx and Engels* (Moscow: Foreign Languages Publishing House), p. 113, with minor omissions. Cf. Willich, "Doctor Karl Marx und seine Enthüllungen," *Belletristisches Journal und New-Yorker Criminal-Zeitung,* Oct. 28, 1853, p. 329 f.

20. See Ernst Drahn, *Karl Marx und Friedrich Engels Über Die Diktatur des Proletariats* (Berlin: Die Aktion, 1920), pp. 27–29, 30–34. Cf. Nicolaievsky and Maenchen-Helfen, *op. cit.*, pp. 216, 218; copies of Willich's Letters to Becker, Dec. 6, 24, 1850, and Jan. (?), 1851, in possession of Mr. Boris Nicolaievsky (Hoover Institution, Stanford, California).

21. Johanna Mockel Kinkel, *Hans Ibelas in London; ein Familienbild aus dem Fluchtingsleben* (Stuttgart: Cotta, 1860), 2 vols. Cf. E. H. Carr, *The Romantic Exiles* (Boston: Beacon Press, 1961), pp. 146–148.

22. Marx, *op. cit.*, pp. 94 ff., 99 f.

23. See A. E. Zucker, ed., *The Forty-Eighters* (New York: Columbia University Press, 1950), p. 355; C. Wittke, *Refugees of Revolution* (Philadelphia: University of Pennsylvania Press, 1952), pp. 95, 152.

24. See Willich, *op cit.*, Oct. 28, 1853, p. 330.

25. See Willich, *op. cit.*, Nov. 4, 1853, p. 339 f.

26. J. Weydemeyer, A. Cluss, Dr. A. Jacobi, "An der Redaktion," *Belletristisches Journal und New-Yorker Criminal Zeitung*, Nov. 25, 1853, p. 369 f.

27. Marx, "Der Ritter vom edelmütigen Bewusstsein" in Marx and Engels, *Werke*, Bd. 9, p. 514. Cf. "Der grossen Männer des Exils" in *ibid.*, Bd. 8, pp. 235–335, 627—a long attack by Marx and Engels on leading revolutionary emigrants, including Willich who is sarcastically characterized, pp. 320–323, as a partisan leader of "magnanimous spirit," a "man of principle" and fixed ideas, whose front-line "sermons" aimed to bring each of his soldiers to faith in a mystical, Hegelian "higher Idea."

28. Marx and Engels, *op. cit.*, Bd. 8, p. 575; cf. Mehring, *op. cit.*, p. 250.

29. "Karl Marx, Zur Kritik der Politischen Oekonomie (Dem 'Volk' entnommen)," *Cincinnati Republikaner, Organ der Arbeiter*, [hereafter *Republikaner*, and unless otherwise noted, references are to p. 2 of issue indicated by date], Sept. 15, 1859. Cf. *Republikaner*, Sept. 1, 1859, March 23, 1861. Willich did not name Engels as the reviewer of Marx's book, but cf. Engels, *Ludwig Feuerbach* (New York: International Publishers, 1941), pp. 40–81 and Marx-Engels, *Kleine Ökonomische Schriften* (Berlin: Dietz Verlag, 1955), pp. 250–261, 593. On Marx's collaboration with *Das Volk*, a German-language newspaper which appeared in London from May to August 1859, see Mehring, *op. cit.*, p. 306 f.

30. *Republikaner*, Feb. 10, 1859.

31. Ludwig Feuerbach, *The Essence of Christianity*, trans. George Eliot [Marian Evans] (New York: Harpers, 1957), pp. 285, 287.

32. *Republikaner*, June 20, 1859; May 19, 1859; August 5, 19, 1859.

33. *Ibid.*, Nov. 7, 1859; Jan. 29, 1861; March 1, 1860; August 29, 1859.

34. *Ibid.*, June 27, 1859.

35. *Ibid.*, Sept. 1, 1859. Cf. *ibid.*, July 13, 1859 where Willich sharply condemns Karl Heinzen's "wishful thinking" about *The Critique of Political Economy* and his "slander" about Marx as heading a "secret police."

36. See *ibid.*, Dec. 24, 1858; Feb. 4, 1859. Cf. Easton, *op. cit.*, p. 194.

37. See *Republikaner*, Feb. 13, 17, 1860.

38. *Ibid.*, "Der Staat! Was ist die Bestimmung des Staates?" March 2, 1860.

39. *Ibid.*, Sept. 22, 1860. Cf. *ibid.*, Jan. 25, 1859; June 27, 1860; Jan. 19, 1861. Cf. F. A. Sorge, "Die Arbeiterbewegung in den Vereinigten Staaten," *Die Neue Zeit*, XCII (1891), p. 240 noting Wil-

lich's criticism of the *Social Republic* (*Republikaner,* Mar. 16, 1859) for failing to see that the struggle for "human rights" requires a political party of the working class and new fundamental laws to end the "swindle" of capitalism.

40. *Republikaner,* Jan. 3, 1861. Cf. *ibid.,* April 26, 1860; July 30, 1860; March 23, 1861.

41. See Marx, *The Civil War in France* (New York: International Publishers, 1940), pp. 57 f., 15–22. Cf. Martin Buber, *Paths in Utopia,* trans. R. Hull (Boston: Beacon Press, 1950), pp. 13, 82–96.

42. *Republikaner,* Oct. 19, 27, 1860. Cf. *ibid.,* May 19, 1860; Feb. 9, 11, 1861.

43. See *ibid.,* Jan. 5, 1860, and Dec. 3, 5, 1859, obituaries for John Brown.

44. Details on Willich's Civil War record are from James Barnett, "August Willich, Soldier Extraordinary," *Bulletin of the Historical and Philosophical Society of Ohio,* 20 (1962), pp. 60–74. Cf. Charles D. Stewart, "A Bachelor General," *Wisconsin Magazine of History,* 17 (1933), pp. 131–154; Carl Wittke, "Ninth Ohio Volunteers," *Ohio Archaeological and Historical Publications,* 35 (1926), pp. 402–417.

45. Stewart, *op. cit.,* p. 139. Cf. Wilhelm Kaufmann, *Die Deutschen in Amerikanischen Bürgerkrieg* (München und Berlin; R. Oldenbourg, 1911), p. 474; Wilhelm Blos, *Badische Revolutionsgeschichte aus dem Jahren 1848 und 1849* (Mannheim: Verlag der Partei-Buchhandlung, 1910), p. 156.

46. Maj. Gen'l. August Willich, *The Army, Standing Army or National Army?* (Cincinnati: A. Frey, 350 Main St., 1866), p. 21 f.

47. Cf. *ibid.,* pp. 16–21.

48. *Ibid.,* p. 7.

49. *Ibid.,* p. 23.

50. For details on Willich's career as auditor I am particularly indebted to Mr. James Barnett of Cincinnati. Cf. *Cincinnati Commercial,* April 16, 1869, p. 8; June 8, 1871, p. 2; April 13, 1868, p. 1; April 13, 1869, p. 1; *Cincinnati Gazette,* March 3, 1869, p. 2.

51. Stewart, *op. cit.,* p. 134; cf. H. A. Rattermann, "General August Willich," *Der Deutsche Pionier,* 10 (1878), p. 144.

52. *Acta Königl. Friedrich Wilhelms Universität zu Berlin* (Universitäts-Registratur: Littr. A. No. 6, Vol. 411, 1871).

53. *Columbus Westbote,* March 8, 1873, p. 3; March 1, 1873, p. 3.

54. *Cincinnati Commercial,* October 3, 1873, p. 3. For this reference I am indebted to Mr. James Barnett of Cincinnati.

55. Thomas Vickers, *August Willich* (Cincinnati: J. R. Mills and Co., 1878), p. 6 f. Cf. *Cincinnati Commercial,* Jan. 26, 1878, p. 5; Kaufmann, *op. cit.,* p. 475.

VII. HEGEL IN THE LIGHT OF HIS FIRST AMERICAN FOLLOWERS

1. J. B. Stallo, *General Principles of the Philosophy of Nature. With an Outline of Some of Its Recent Developments Among the Germans, Embracing the Philosophical Systems of Schelling and Hegel and Oken's System of Nature* (Boston: William Crosby and H. P. Nichols, 1858).

2. Stallo's note: "I use the word 'Sensual' in preference to the word 'sensuous' introduced by Coleridge and others, because the former is more idiomatic, and not here liable to become ambiguous."

3. Stallo, *op. cit.*, p. 360 f.

4. *Ibid.*, p. vii.

5. *Ibid.*, p. 133 f.

6. J. B. Stallo, *The Concepts and Theories of Modern Physics*, ed. Percy W. Bridgman (Cambridge, Mass.: Harvard University Press, 1960), pp. 6, 178.

7. *Ibid.*, p. 156; cf. G. W. F. Hegel, *The Phenomenology of Mind*, trans. J. B. Baillie (New York: The Macmillan Co., 1931), p. 168 ff.

8. Stallo, *General Principles*, p. 351; *Concepts and Theories*, p. 200.

9. Stallo, *Concepts and Theories*, p. 216 ff.; *General Principles*, p. 337.

10. T. J. McCormack, "John Bernhard Stallo: American Citizen, Jurist, Philosopher," *Open Court*, 14 (1900), p. 277; G. D. Wilkinson, "John B. Stallo's Criticism of Physical Science," unpublished Ph.D. dissertation, Columbia University, 1951, pp. 123, 151.

11. M. D. Conway, *David Friedrich Strauss* (London: South Place, Finsbury, 1874), p. 19. This address also appeared April 2, 1874, in *The Index*, a weekly of the Free Religion Association edited by Francis Ellingwood Abbot and first published in Toledo, Ohio, 1870–1873.

12. *Cincinnati Republikaner*, September 9, 1859, p. 2.

13. Hegel, *Logic*, trans. William Wallace from the *Encyclopaedia of the Philosophical Sciences* (Oxford: At the Clarendon Press, 1892), Sec. 88.

14. Hegel, *The Phenomenology of Mind*, p. 80, *et passim*.

15. Stallo, *General Principles*, pp. 30, 44, 49.

16. *Ibid.*, pp. 15, 59.

17. Cf. H. A. Pochmann, *German Culture in America* (Madison: The University of Wisconsin Press, 1957), pp. 199–202.

18. Stallo, *General Principles*, Sec. 107.

19. M. D. Conway, "Individual and Species" in *Lessons for the Day* (London: E. W. Allen, 1882), I, 65, 71.
20. *Cincinnati Republikaner*, September 5, 1859, p. 2.
21. Peter Kaufmann, *The Temple of Truth or the Science of Ever-Progressing Knowledge* (Cincinnati: Truman and Spofford, and Eggers and Wilde, 1858), pp. iii–iv, 186 ff., 283 ff.
22. J. N. Findlay, *Hegel: A Re-examination* (New York: The Macmillan Co., 1958), p. 25.
23. Hegel, *Logic*, Sec. 459; cf. Findlay, *op. cit.*, p. 304.
24. *Ibid.*, Sec. 552.
25. Hegel, *The Phenomenology of Mind*, p. 530; cf. *ibid.*, pp. 3–48.
26. J. N. Findlay, "Some Merits of Hegelianism," *Proceedings of the Aristotelian Society*, 55 (1956), p. 3.
27. Stallo, *General Principles*, p. x.
28. Stallo, *Concepts and Theories*, p. 178. Cf. *ibid.*, p. 10 ff.; Stallo, "Speculative Science," *Popular Science Monthly*, XXI (1882), 151 ff.
29. Kaufmann, *op. cit.*, p. 48 ff.
30. Conway, "The Word," *The Dial*, 1 (1860), p. 98 ff.
31. Hegel, *The Philosophy of History*, trans. J. Sibree (New York: Dover Publications, 1956), p. 59; Hegel, *Philosophy of Right*, trans. K. M. Knox (Oxford: At the Clarendon Press, 1953), Sec. 145.
32. Cf. Karl Popper, *The Open Society and Its Enemies* (Princeton, N.J.: Princeton University Press, 1950), p. 258; M. R. Cohen, "Hegel," *Encyclopedia of the Social Sciences*, IV, 313; W. H. Walsh, *Philosophy of History* (New York: Harper and Brothers, 1960), p. 146.
33. Hegel, *Philosophy of Right*, Sec. 261.
34. *Ibid.*, Secs. 66, 206, 209, 270. Cf. George Sabine, "Hegel's Political Theory," *Philosophical Review*, XLI (1932), 280.
35. Stallo, *General Principles*, p. 517 n.
36. *Ibid.*, p. 159.
37. Stallo, *State Creeds and Their Modern Apostles* (Cincinnati: Clarke and Son, 1872), p. 34.
38. Conway, *David Friedrich Strauss*, pp. 9, 24 f.
39. Cf. L. D. Easton, "Alienation and History in the Early Marx," *Philosophy and Phenomenological Research*, 22 (1961), p. 197 ff.
40. *Cincinnati Republikaner*, March 2, 1860, p. 2.
41. Emilio Castellar, "The Republican Movement in Europe," *Harpers' New Atlantic Monthly Magazine*, 47 (1873), pp. 578 f., 585.
42. Cf. W. T. Harris, "The Concrete and the Abstract," *Journal of Speculative Philosophy*, 5 (1871), p. 5; Kurt Leidecker, *Yankee Teacher* (New York: Philosophical Library, 1946), pp. 283, 540 ff., 286–293.
43. Karl Rosenkranz, "Hegel, Prussia, and the Philosophy of Right,"

trans. G. S. Hall, *Journal of Speculative Philosophy,* 6 (1872), p. 276.

APPENDIX: KEY WRITINGS

1. J. B. Stallo, *General Principles of the Philosophy of Nature, With an Outline of Some of Its Recent Developments Among the Germans, Embracing the Philosophical Systems of Schelling and Hegel, and Oken's System of Nature.* (Boston: Wm. Crosby and H. P. Nichols, 1848). Numbers in square brackets within the following text indicate original page numbers for the preceding material. Headings and subheads are Stallo's. Italicization and, in some cases, punctuation have been emended to facilitate reading.

2. Peter Kaufmann, *The Temple of Truth, or The Science of Ever-Progressing Knowledge.* (Cincinnati: in English and German by Truman and Spofford, and Eggers and Wilde; Canton, Ohio: By the Author, 1858). Numbers in square brackets within the following text indicate original page numbers for the preceding material. Most subheads have been supplied. Punctuation, italicization, and capitalization have been extensively emended to conform to current usage and facilitate reading.

3. Moncure D. Conway, *David Friedrich Strauss. Commemorative Services at South Place Chapel, Finsbury, London, February 22, 1874. With a Discourse.* (London: 11 South Place, Finsbury, 1874). Also in *The Index,* 5 (Apr. 2, 1874), pp. 158–160. In the text printed here four "commemorative" poems, including one by Goethe, have been omitted from the "Readings."

4. Translated from the *Cincinnati Republikaner, Organ der Arbeiter,* August Willich, *verantwortlicher Redacteur,* in the following order: "Beantwortung der an den Republikaner gestellten Frage: Warum betheiligen sich die religiösen Arbeiter so wenig an den Bewegungen der Arbeiter? II, III, IV," February 5, 8, 10, 1859, p. 2, with minor deletions; "Der Staat! Was ist die Bestimmung des Staates?" March 2, 1860, p. 2; "Volkswirthschaftslehre von Karl Marx," June 27, 1859, p. 2; "Der Pionier über Arbeiterorganisation," April 25, 1860, p. 2; "Arbeiterfest," a speech delivered at an "Arbeiter-Pic-Nic" but "not in the best English," July 30, 1860, p. 2, with formal emendations.

INDEX*

* Arabic numerals indicate pages; Roman numerals indicate chapters.